APPLIED BOTANY

APPLIED BOTANY

By

Dr. Pooja

Deptt. of Botany
R.C.C. College
Ghaziabad (U.P.)
(India)

DISCOVERY PUBLISHING HOUSE PVT. LTD.
NEW DELHI-110 002

Published by:
Tilak Wasan
DISCOVERY PUBLISHING HOUSE PVT. LTD.
4383/4B, Ansari Road, Darya Ganj
New Delhi-110 002 (India)
Phone : +91-11-23279245, 43596064-65
Fax : +91-11-23253475
E-mail : discoverypublishinghouse@gmail.com
sales@discoverypublishinggroup.com
parul.wasan@gmail.com
web : www.discoverypublishinggroup.com

First Edition: **2014**

ISBN: 978-93-5056-405-9

Applied Botany

Printed at:
Dynamic Printers
Delhi

Preface

As with other life forms in biology, plant life can be studied from different perspectives, from the molecular, genetic and biochemical level through organelles, cells, tissues, organs, individuals, plant populations, and communities of plants. At each of these levels a botanist might be concerned with the classification (taxonomy), structure (anatomy and morphology), or function (physiology) of plant life. Historically, botany covers all organisms that were not considered to be animals. Some of these "plant-like" organisms include fungi (studied in mycology), bacteria and viruses (studied in microbiology), and algae (studied in phycology). Most algae, fungi, and microbes are no longer considered to be in the plant kingdom. However, attention is still given to them by botanists, and bacteria, fungi, and algae are usually covered in introductory botany courses.

The study of plants has importance for a number of reasons. Plants are a fundamental part of life on Earth. They generate the oxygen, food, fibres, fuel and medicine that allow higher life forms to exist. Plants also absorb carbon dioxide through photosynthesis, a minor greenhouse gas that in large amounts can effect global climate. It is believed that the evolution of plants has changed the global atmosphere of the earth early in the earth's history and paleobotanists study ancient plants in the fossil record.

Plant cell culture is viewed as a potential means of producing useful plant products such that conventional agriculture, with all its attendant problems and variables, can be circumvented. These problems include: environmental factors (drought, floods, etc.), disease, political and labour instabilities in the producing countries (often Third World countries), uncontrollable variations in the crop quality, inability of authorities to prevent crop adulteration, losses in storage and handling.

A considerable amount of new knowledge today is being generated from studying model plants like *Arabidopsis thaliana*. This weedy species in the mustard family (Brassicaceae) was one of the first plants to have its genome sequenced. The sequencing of the rice (*Oryza sativa*) genome, its relatively small genome, and a large international research community have made rice an important cereal/grass/monocot model. Another grass species, *Brachypodium distachyon* is also an experimental model for understanding genetic, cellular and molecular biology. Other commercially important staple foods like wheat, maize, barley, rye, pearl millet and soybean are also having their genomes sequenced. Some of these are challenging to sequence because they have more than two haploid (n) sets of chromosomes, a condition known as polyploidy, common in the plant kingdom. A green alga, *Chlamydomonas reinhardtii*, is a model organism that has proven important in advancing knowledge of cell biology.

This book will provide an brilliant suggestion matter but also as a sensible point for teachers, research scholars, students and workers in the field of plant and agriculture.

—Author

Contents

1

Introduction

Branch of biology that deals with plants, including the study of the structure, properties, and biochemical processes of all forms of plant life, as well as plant classification, plant diseases, and the interactions of plants with their physical environment. The science of botany traces back to the ancient Greco-Roman world but received its modern impetus in Europe in the 16th century, mainly through the work of physicians and herbalists, who began to observe plants seriously to identify those useful in medicine. Today the principal branches of botanical study are morphology, physiology, ecology, and systematics (the identification and ranking of all plants). Subdisciplines include bryology (the study of mosses and liverworts), pteridology (the study of ferns and their relatives), paleobotany (the study of fossil plants), and palynology (the study of modern and fossil pollen and spores). Botany is the scientific study of plant life. As a branch of biology, it is also called plant science(s), phytology, or plant biology. Botany covers a wide range of scientific disciplines that study plants, algae, and fungi including: structure, growth, reproduction, metabolism, development, diseases, and chemical properties and evolutionary relationships between the different groups.

The study of plants and botany began with tribal lore, used to identify edible, medicinal and poisonous plants, making botany one of the oldest sciences. From this ancient interest in plants, the scope of botany has increased to include the study of over 550,000 kinds or species of living organisms.

HISTORY OF BOTANY

EARLY BOTANY

The history of botany includes many ancient writings and classifications of plants found in several early cultures. Examples of early botanical works have been found in ancient sacred texts from India, ancient Zoroas-trian writings, and ancient Chinese works.

Modern botany traces it's roots back more than twenty three centuries, to the Father of Botany, Theophrastus (c. 371–287 BC), a student of Aristotle. He invented and described many of the principles of modern botany. His two major works, *Enquiry into Plants* and *On the Causes of Plants* constitute the most important contribution to botanical science during antiquity and the Middle Ages, and held that position for some seventeen centuries after they were written. Also from Greece, Pedanius Dioscorides, in the middle of the first century, wrote *De Materia Medica,* a five-volume encyclopedia about herbal medicine that was widely read for more than 1,500 years.

EARLY MODERN BOTANY

German physician Leonhart Fuchs (1501–1566) was one of "the three German fathers of botany", along with Otto Brunfels (1489–1534) and Hieronymus Bock (1498–1554) (also called Hieronymus Tragus).

Valerius Cordus (1515–1544) authored a pharmacopoeia of lasting importance, the *Dispensatorium* in 1546. Conrad von Gesner (1516–1565) and Nicholas Culpeper (1616–1654) also published herbals covering the medicinal uses of plants. Ulisse Aldrovandi (1522–1605) was considered the "father of natural history", which included the study of plants. In 1665, using an early microscope, Robert Hooke discovered cells, a term he coined, in cork, and a short time later in living plant tissue.

During the 18th century, systems of classification were developed that are comparable to diagnostic keys, where taxa are artificially grouped in pairs. The sequence of the taxa in keys is often unrelated to their natural or phyletic groupings.

By the 18th century an increasing number of new plants had arrived in Europe from newly discovered countries and the European colonies worldwide and a larger number of plants became available for study.

Botanical guides from this time were sparsely illustrated. In 1754 Carl von Linné (Carl Linnaeus) divided the plant Kingdom into 25 classes in a taxonomy with a standardized binomial naming system for animal and plant species. He used a two-part naming scheme where the first name represented the genus and the second the species. One of Linnaeus' classifications, the *Cryptogamia,* included all plants with concealed reproductive parts (mosses, liverworts and ferns), and algae and fungi.

The increased knowledge of anatomy, morphology and life cycles, led to the realization that there were more natural affinities between plants than the sexual system of Linnaeus indicated. Adanson (1763), de Jussieu (1789), and Candolle (1819) all proposed various alternative natural systems that were widely followed. The ideas of natural selection as a mechanism for evolution required adaptations to the Candollean system, which started the studies on evolutionary relationships and phylogenetic classifications of plants.

Botany was greatly stimulated by the appearance of the first "modern" text book, Matthias Schleiden's *Grundzuge der Wissenschaftlichen,* published in English in 1849 as *Principles of Scientific Botany*. Carl Willdenow examined the connection between seed dispersal and distribution, the nature of plant associations, and the impact of geological history. The cell nucleus was discovered by Robert Brown in 1831.

MODERN BOTANY

A considerable amount of new knowledge today is being generated from studying model plants like *Arabidopsis thaliana*. This weedy species in the mustard family (Brassicaceae) was one of the first plants to have its genome sequenced. The sequencing of the rice (*Oryza sativa*) genome, its relatively small genome, and a large international research community have made rice an important cereal/grass/monocot model. Another grass species, *Brachypodium distachyon* is also an experimental model for understanding genetic, cellular and molecular biology. Other commercially important staple foods like wheat, maize, barley, rye, pearl millet and soybean are also having their genomes sequenced. Some of these are challenging to sequence because they have more than two haploid (n) sets of chromosomes, a condition known as polyploidy, common in the plant kingdom. A green alga, *Chlamydomonas reinhardtii*, is a model organism that has proven important in advancing knowledge of cell biology.

In 1998 the Angiosperm Phylogeny Group published a phylogeny of flowering plants based on an analysis of DNA sequences from most families of flowering plants. As a result of this work, many of the questions such as which families represent the earliest branches of angiosperms have now been answered. Investigating how plant species are related to each other allows botanists to better understand the process of evolution in plants. Despite the study of model plants and increasing use of DNA evidence, there is ongoing work and discussion among taxonomists about how best to classify plants.

SCOPE AND IMPORTANCE OF BOTANY

As with other life forms in biology, plant life can be studied from different perspectives, from the molecular, genetic and biochemical level through organelles, cells, tissues, organs, individuals, plant populations, and communities of plants. At each of these levels a botanist might be concerned with the classification (taxonomy), structure (anatomy and morphology), or function (physiology) of plant life. Historically, botany covers all organisms that were not considered to be animals. Some of these "plant-like" organisms include fungi (studied in mycology), bacteria and viruses (studied in microbiology), and algae (studied in phycology). Most algae, fungi, and microbes are no longer considered to be in the plant kingdom. However, attention is still given to them by botanists, and bacteria, fungi, and algae are usually covered in introductory botany courses.

The study of plants has importance for a number of reasons. Plants are a fundamental part of life on Earth. They generate the oxygen, food, fibres, fuel and medicine that allow higher life forms to exist. Plants also absorb carbon dioxide through photosynthesis, a minor greenhouse gas that in large amounts can effect global climate. It is believed that the evolution of plants has changed the global atmosphere of the earth early in the earth's history and paleobotanists study ancient plants in the fossil record. A good understanding of plants is crucial to the future of human societies as it allows us to:

- Produce food to feed an expanding population
- Understand fundamental life processes
- Produce medicine and materials to treat diseases and other ailments
- Understand environmental changes more clearly.

HUMAN NUTRITION

Virtually all foods eaten come from plants, either directly from staple foods and other fruit and vegetables, or indirectly through livestock or other animals, which rely on plants for their nutrition. Plants are the fundamental base of nearly all food chains because they use the energy from the sun and nutrients from the soil and atmosphere and convert them into a form that can be consumed and utilized by animals; this is what ecologists call the first trophic level.

Botanists also study how plants produce food we can eat and how to increase yields and therefore their work is important in mankind's ability to feed the world and provide food security for future generations, for example through plant breeding. Botanists also study weeds, plants which are considered to be a nuisance in a particular location. Weeds are a considerable problem in agriculture, and botany provides some of the basic science used to understand how to minimize 'weed' impact in agriculture and native ecosystems. Ethnobotany is the study of the relationships between plants and people.

FUNDAMENTAL LIFE PROCESSES

Plants are convenient organisms in which fundamental life processes (like cell division and protein synthesis for example) can be studied, without the ethical dilemmas of studying animals or humans. The genetic laws of inheritance were discovered in this way by Gregor Mendel, who was studying the way pea shape is inherited.

What Mendel learned from studying plants has had far reaching benefits outside of botany. Additionally, Barbara McClintock discovered 'jumping genes' by studying maize. These are a few examples that demonstrate how botanical research has an ongoing relevance to the understanding of fundamental biological processes.

Medicine and Materials

Many medicinal and recreational drugs, like tetrahydrocannabinol, caffeine, and nicotine come directly from the plant kingdom. Others are simple derivatives of botanical natural products; for example aspirin is based on the pain killer salicylic acid which originally came from the bark of willow trees. There may be many novel cures for diseases provided by plants, waiting to be discovered. Popular stimulants like coffee, chocolate, tobacco, and tea also come from plants. Most alcoholic beverages come from fermenting plants such as barley malt and grapes.

Plants also provide us with many natural materials, such as cotton, wood, paper, linen, vegetable oils, some types of rope, and rubber. The production of silk would not be possible without the cultivation of the mulberry plant. Sugarcane, rapeseed, soy and other plants with a highly-fermentable sugar or oil content have recently been put to use as sources of biofuels, which are important alternatives to fossil fuels, see biodiesel.

Environmental Changes

Plants can also help us understand changes in on our environment in many ways.

- Understanding habitat destruction and species extinction is dependent on an accurate and complete catalogue of plant systematics and taxonomy.
- Plant responses to ultraviolet radiation can help us monitor problems like the ozone depletion.
- Analysing pollen deposited by plants thousands or millions of years ago can help scientists to reconstruct past climates and predict future ones, an essential part of climate change research.
- Recording and analysing the timing of plant life cycles are important parts of phenology used in climate-change research.
- Lichens, which are sensitive to atmospheric conditions, have been extensively used as pollution indicators.

In many different ways, plants can act a little like the 'miners canary', an early warning system alerting us to important changes in our environment. In addition to these practical and scientific reasons, plants are extremely valuable as recreation for millions of people who enjoy gardening, horticultural and culinary uses of plants every day.

History

Early examples of plant taxonomy occur in the *Rigveda,* that divides plants into *Vrska* (tree), *Osadhi* (herbs useful to humans) and *Virudha* (creepers). which are further subdivided. The *Atharvaveda* divides plants into eight classes, *Visakha* (spreading branches), *Manjari* (leaves with long clusters), *Sthambini* (bushy plants), *Prastanavati* (which expands); *Ekasrnga* (those with monopodial growth), *Pratanavati* (creeping plants), *Amsumati* (with many stalks), and *Kandini* (plants with knotty joints). The *Taittiriya Samhita* and classifies the plant kingdom into *vrksa, vana* and *druma* (trees), *visakha* (shrubs with spreading branches), *sasa* (herbs), *amsumali* (a spreading or deliquescent plant), *vratati* (climber), *stambini* (bushy plant), *pratanavati* (creeper), and *alasala* (those spreading on the ground).

Manusmriti proposed a classification of plants in eight major categories. *Charaka Samhita* and *Sushruta Samhita* and the

Vaisesikas also present an elaborate taxonomy. *Parashara,* the author of *Vrksayurveda* (the science of life of trees), classifies plants into *Dvimatrka* (Dicotyledons) and *Ekamatrka* (Monocotyledons). These are further classified into *Samiganiya* (Fabaceae), *Puplikagalniya* (Rutaceae), *Svastikaganiya* (Cruciferae), *Tripuspaganiya* (Cucurbitaceae), *Mallikaganiya* (Apocynaceae), and *Kurcapuspaganiya* (Asteraceae).

Among the earliest of botanical works in Europe, written around 300 B.C., are two large treatises by Theophrastus: *On the History of Plants* (Historia Plantarum) and *On the Causes of Plants.* Together these books constitute the most important contribution to botanical science during antiquity and on into the Middle Ages. The Roman medical writer Dioscorides provides important evidence on Greek and Roman knowledge of medicinal plants.

In ancient China, the recorded listing of different plants and herb concoctions for pharmaceutical purposes spans back to at least the Warring States (481 BC-221 BC). Many Chinese writers over the centuries contributed to the written knowledge of herbal pharmaceutics. There was the Han Dynasty (202 BC-AD 220) written work of the Huangdi Neijing and the famous pharmacologist Zhang Zhongjing of the 2nd century. There was also the 11th century scientists and statesmen Su Song and Shen Kuo, who compiled treatises on herbal medicine and included the use of mineralogy.

Important medieval works of plant physiology include the *Prthviniraparyam* of Udayana, *Nyayavindutika* of Dharmottara, *Saddarsana-samuccaya* of Gunaratna, and *Upaskara* of Sankaramisra. In 1665, using an early microscope, Robert Hooke discovered cells in cork, and a short time later in living plant tissue. The German Leonhart Fuchs, the Swiss Conrad von Gesner, and the British authors Nicholas Culpeper and John Gerard published herbals that gave information on the medicinal uses of plants. In 1754 Carl von Linné (Carl Linnaeus) devided the plant Kingdom into 25 classes. One, the Cryptogamia, included all the plants with concealed reproductive parts (algae, fungi, mosses and liverworts and ferns).

SUB-DISCIPLINES OF BOTANY

- Agronomy—Application of plant science to crop production
- Bryology—Mosses, liverworts, and hornwarts
- Cry to botany—Study of Plants large by considered non-existent
- Dentrology—Study of woody pants, shrubs, trees and lianas
- Economic botany—The place of plants in economics
- Ethnobotany—Relationship between humans and plants
- Forestry—Forest management and related studies
- Horticulture—Cultivated plants
- Lichenology—Lichens
- Mycology—Fungi
- Paleobotany—Fossil plants
- Palynology—Pollen and spores
- Phycology - Algae
- Phytochemistry—Plant secondary chemistry and chemical processes
- Phytopathology—Plant diseases
- Plant anatomy—Cell and tissue structure
- Plant ecology—Role of plants in the environment
- Plant genetics—Genetic inheritance in plants
- Plant morphology—Structure and life cycles
- Plant neuodriology—Behavioural-like aspects
- Plant physiology—Life functions of plants
- Plant systematics—Classification and naming of plants.

We will give you a brief summary about all the sub-disciplines:

AGRONOMY

Agronomy is the science of utilizing plants for food, fuel, feed, and fibre. To do this effectively and in a sustainable manner, agronomy encompasses work in the areas of plant genetics, plant physiology, meteorology, and soil science.

Agronomy is the application of a combination of sciences like biology, chemistry, ecology, earth science, and genetics. Agronomists today are involved with many issues including producing food, creating healthier food, managing environmental impacts, and creating energy from plants.

Agronomists often specialize in areas such as crop rotation, irrigation and drainage, plant breeding, soil classification, soil fertility, weed control, insect and pest control and other areas.

Biotechnology

Agronomists use biotechnology to extend and expedite the development of desired characteristics listed in the Plant Breeding section. Biotechnology is often a lab activity requiring field testing of the new crop varieties that are developed.

In addition to increasing crop yields, reducing crop vulnerability to environmental stresses, improving health and taste of foods, and reducing the need for field applied chemicals, agronomic biotechnology is increasingly being applied for novel uses other than food. For example, oilseed is at present used mainly for margarine and other food oils, but it can be modified to produce fatty acids for detergents, substitute fuels and petrochemicals.

Soil Science

Agronomists study sustainable ways to make soils more productive. They classify soils and reproduce them to determine whether they contain substances vital to plant growth. Such nutritional substances include compounds of nitrogen, phosphorus, and potassium. If a certain soil is deficient in these substances, fertilizers may provide them. Agronomists investigate the movement of nutrients through the soil, and the amount of nutrients absorbed by a plant's roots. Agronomists also examine the development of the roots and their relation to the soil.

Soil Conservation

In addition, agronomists develop methods to preserve the soil and to decrease the effects of erosion by wind and water. For example, a technique called contour plowing may be used to prevent soil erosion and conserve rainfall. Researchers in agronomy also seek ways to use the soil more effectively in solving other problems. Such problems include the disposal of human and animal wastes; water pollution; and the build-up in the soil of chemicals called pesticides, which are used to kill insects and other pests. No-tilling crops is a technique now used to help prevent erosion. Planting of soil binding grasses along contours can be tried in steep slopes. For better effect, contour drains of depths up to 1 metre may help retain the soil and prevent permanent wash off.

Agroecology

Agroecology is the management of agricultural systems with a strong emphasis on ecological and environmental perspectives. This area is closely associated with work in the areas of Sustainable Agriculture, Organic Agriculture, and the development of alternative cropping systems.

BRYOLOGY

Bryology is the branch of botany concerned with the scientific study of bryophytes (mosses, liverworts, and hornworts).

Bryophytes were first studied in detail in the 18th century. The German botanist Johann Jacob Dillenius (1687-1747) was a professor at Oxford and in 1717 produced the work "Reproduction of the ferns and mosses." The beginning of bryology really belongs to the work of Johannes Hedwig, who clarified the reproductive system of mosses (1792, Fundamentum historiae naturalist muscorum) and arranged a taxonomy.

Areas of research include bryophyte taxonomy, bryophytes as bioindicators, DNA sequencing, and the interdependency of bryophytes and other plant and animal species. Among other things, scientists have learned that certain species of mosses are carnivorous.

CRYPTOBOTANY

Cryptobotany is the study of various exotic plants which are not believed to exist by the scientific community, but which exist in myth, literature or unsubstantiated reports. Folk legend and ethnic usage of plants, often as interdisciplinary research, is presented and developed for an unknown species, in the hope of allowing those species to be collected or adequately identified. Any researcher or writer can identify himself or herself as a cryptobotanist; the field is surveyed within cryptozoological or other journals, or with varying degrees of skepticism as a protoscience.

Many plants remain undiscovered or are yet to be classified, however cryptobotany usually focuses on fantastical plants believed to have harmful or therapeutic interactions with people. Sources of data may be secondary or scant; reports may be plausible or outlandish.

Man eating plants, most frequently inhabiting the jungles of Africa in popular fiction, may have been based on initial reports of plants that could trap and kill mammals, such as *Nepenthes rajah*. However, there are unconfirmed reports, primarily from Latin America, that allege the existence of still-undiscovered species of large carnivorous plants, according to British cryptozoologist Karl Shuker's 2003 book *The Beasts That Hide From Man.*

DENDROLOGY

Dendrology (Ancient Greek: *dendron*, "tree"; and Ancient Greek:, *-logia, science of* or *study of*) or xylology (Ancient Greek: *ksulon*, "wood") is the science and study of wooded plants (trees, shrubs, and lianas). There is no sharp boundary between plant taxonomy and dendrology. However, woody plants not only belong to many different plant families, but these families may be made up of both woody and non-woody members. Some families include only a few woody species. This severely limits the usefulness of a strictly dendrological approach. Dendrology tends to focus on economically useful woody plants, their identification and horticultural or silvicultural properties.

Relationship with Botany

Dendrology is often confused with botany. However, botany is the study of all types of general plants, while dendrology studies only wooded plants. Dendrology may be considered a subcategory of botany that specializes in wooded plants.

ECONOMIC BOTANY

Economic botany is the commercial exploitation of plants by people. Economic botany contributes significantly to anthropology, biology, conservation, botany, and other fields of science. This link between botany and anthropology explores the ways humans use plants for food, shelter, medicines, textiles, and much more.

Botany itself came about through medicine and the development of herbal remedies. Thus at its advent, botany was economic as well as systematic. As plants became useful for herbals and curatives, their economic value increased. An early set of instructions drawn up by a cosmographer of Charles the fifth instructed explorers to "determine what are the items of sustenance of the land and which ones are generally used, whether fruits or seeds, and all manner of spices, drugs, or whatever other scents, and find out the time in which one can reproduce the trees, plants, herbs, and fruits that these parts offer, and if the natives use them for medicines, as we do."

Teosinte and rice are two examples of plants modified so that their economic values would increase.

Teosinte

The teosintes are grasses of the genus *Zea*. Native Americans bred and selected teosinte for the traits we see in corn today (large ears, multiple rows of kernels). The first ears of maize were very short, with only 8 rows of kernels. Modern corn is the result of several hundred generations of selective breeding. Modern corn is incapable of reproducing without human help; the kernels will stay firmly attached to the cob and rot. This doesn't represent a useful adaptation for the species, but is excellent for harvesting and transporting corn.

Rice

Rice was first domesticated approximately 5,000 years ago, in Southeast Asia. Rice and American wild rice are believed to have been domesticated separately.[6] Rice variants have been adapted to the tropics where they provide a grain staple, but rice can be grown almost anywhere. The introduction of dwarf rice variants made several rice-producing countries self-sufficient. Rice is suited to countries with high rainfall.

Economically Important Food Plants

Plants that humans use for food are of high economic importance. Research into food plants generally involves increasing the size of the edible plant organ in question, or increasing the areas where the plant can be grown, and less frequently, finding new crop species. Results of such research are often published in the journal *Economic Botany*. The New Zealand-based Plant & Food Research publishes its own journal on cultivar development and sustainable production systems for high quality produce, and the design and development of new and novel functional foods.

ETHNOBOTANY

Ethnobotany is the study of the relationship between plants and people: From"ethno" - study of people and "botany" - study of plants. Ethnobotany is considered a branch of ethnobiology. Ethnobotany studies the complex relationships between (uses of) plants and cultures. The focus of ethnobotany is on how plants have been or are used, managed and perceived in human societies and includes plants used in food, medicine, divination, cosmetics, dyeing, textiles, constuction, tools, currency, clothing, literature, rituals, and social life.

Modern Ethnobotany

Beginning in the 20th century, the field of ethnobotany experienced a shift from the raw compilation of data to a greater methodological and conceptual reorientation. This is also the beginning of academic ethnobotany. The founding father of this discpline is Richard Evans Schultes.

Today the field of ethnobotany requires a variety of skills: botanical training for the identification and preservation of plant specimens; anthropological training to understand the cultural concepts around the perception of plants; linguistic training, at least enough to transcribe local terms and understand native morphology, syntax, and semantics.

Native healers are often reluctant to accurately share their knowledge to outsiders. Schultes actually apprenticed himself to an Amazonian shaman, which involves a long term commitment and genuine relationship.

FORESTRY

Forestry is the art, science, and practice of studying and managing forests and plantations, and related natural resources. Silviculture, a related science, involves the growing and tending of trees and forests.

Modern forestry generally concerns itself with: assisting forests to provide timber as raw material for wood products; wildlife habitat; natural water quality regulation; recreation; landscape and community protection; employment; aesthetically appealing landscapes; biodiversity management; watershed management; and a 'sink' for atmospheric carbon dioxide. A practitioner of forestry is known as a forester.

Forest ecosystems have come to be seen as one of the most important components of the biosphere, and forestry has emerged as a vital field of science, applied art, and technology.

HORTICULTURE

Horticulture is the art and science of the cultivation of plants. Horticulturists work and conduct research in the fields of plant propagation and cultivation, crop production, plant breeding and genetic engineering, plant biochemistry, and plant physiology. The work particularly involves fruits, berries, nuts, vegetables, flowers, trees, shrubs, and turf. Horticulturalists work to improve crop yield, quality, nutritional value, and resistance to insects, diseases, and environmental stresses.

LICHENOLOGY

Lichenology is the branch of mycology that studies the lichens, symbiotic organisms made up of an intimate symbiotic association of a microscopic alga (or a cyanbacterium) with a filamentous fungus.

The taxonomy of lichens was first intensively investigated by the Swedish botanist Erik Acharius (1757-1819), who is therefore sometimes named the "father of lichenology". Acharius was a student of Carolus Linnaeus. Some of his more important works on the subject, which marked the beginning of lichenology as a discipline, are:

- *Lichenographiae Suecia prodromus* (1798)
- *Methodus lichenum* (1803)
- *Lichenographia universalis* (1810)
- *Synopsis methodica lichenum* (1814)

Later lichenologists include the American scientists Vernon Ahmadjian and Edward Tuckerman and the Russian evolutionary biologist Konstantin Merezhkovsky.

MYCOLOGY

Mycology (from the Greek mukçs, meaning "fungus") is the branch of biology concerned with the study of fungi, including their genetic and biochemical properties, their taxonomy and their use to humans as a source for tinder, medicinals (e.g., penicillin), food (e.g., beer, wine, cheese, edible mushrooms) and entheogens, as well as their dangers, such as poisoning or infection.

From mycology arose the field of phytopathology, the study of plant diseases, and the two disciplines remain closely related because the vast majority of "plant" pathogens are fungi. A biologist who studies mycology is called a mycologist.

Historically, mycology was a branch of botany because, although fungi are evolutionarily more closely related to animals than to plants, this was not recognized until a few decades ago. Pioneer *mycologists* included Elias Magnus Fries, Christian Hendrik Persoon, Anton de Bary and Lewis David von Schweinitz.

Many fungi produce toxins, antibiotics and other secondary metabolites. For example the cosmopolitan (worldwide) genus *Fusarium* and their toxins associated with fatal outbreaks of alimentary toxic aleukia in humans were extensively studied by Abraham Joffe.

Fungi are fundamental for life on earth in their roles as symbionts, e.g. in the form of mycorrhizae, insect symbionts and lichens. Many fungi are able to break down complex organic biomolecules such as lignin, the more durable component of wood, and pollutants such as xenobiotics, petroleum, and polycyclic aromatic hydrocarbons. By decomposing these molecules, fungi play a critical role in the global carbon cycle.

Fungi and other organisms traditionally recognized as fungi, such as oomycetes and myxomycetes (slime molds), often are economically and socially important as some cause diseases of animals (such as histoplasmosis) as well as plants (such as Dutch elm disease and Rice blast).

Field meetings to find interesting species of fungi are known as 'forays', after the first such meeting organized by the Woolhope Naturalists' Field Club in 1868 and entitled "a foray among the fungi."

Some fungi can cause disease in humans or other organisms. The study of pathogenic fungi is referred to as medical mycology.[1

PALEOBOTANY

Paleobotany, also spelled as palaeobotany (from the Greek words paleon = old and "botany", study of plants), is the branch of paleontology or paleobiology dealing with the recovery and identification of plant remains from geological contexts, and their use for the biological reconstruction of past environments, and the evolution of both the plant kingdom and life in general. A synonym is paleophytology. Paleobotany includes the study of terrestrial plant fossils, as well as the study of prehistoric marine photoautotrophs, such as photosynthetic algae, seaweeds or kelp. A closely-related field is palynology, which is the study of fossilized and extant spores and pollen.

Paleobotany is important in the reconstruction of ancient ecological systems and climate, known as paleoecology and paleoclimatology respectively; and is fundamental to the study of green plant development and evolution. Paleobotany has also become important to the field of archaeology, primarily for the use of phytoliths in relative dating and in paleoethnobotany.

PALYNOLOGY

Palynology is the science that studies contemporary and fossil palynomorphs, including pollen, spores, dinoflagellate cysts, acritarchs, chitinozoans and scolecodonts, together with particulate organic matter (POM) and kerogen found in sedimentary rocks and sediments. Palynology does not include diatoms, foraminiferans or other organisms with silicaceous or calcareous exoskeletons. Palynology is an interdisciplinary science and is a branch of earth science (geology or geological science) and biological science (biology), particularly plant science (botany). Stratigraphical palynology is a branch of micropalaeontology and paleobotany which studies fossil palynomorphs from the Precambrian to the Holocene.

Chemical Preparation

Chemical digestion follows a number of steps. Initially the only chemical treatment used by researchers was treatment with KOH to remove humic substances; defloculation was accomplished through surface treatment or ultra-sonic treatment, although sonification may cause the pollen exine to rupture. The use of hydrofluoric acid (HF) to digest silicate minerals was introduced by Assarson and Granlund in 1924, greatly reducing the amount of time required to scan slides for palynomorphs.

Palynological studies using peats presented a particular challenge because of the presence of well preserved organic material including fine rootlets, moss leaflets and organic litter. This was the last major challenge in the chemical preparation of materials for palynological study. Acetolysis was developed by Gunnar Erdtman and his brother to remove these fine cellulose materials by dissolving them. In acetolysis the material is treated with acetic anhydride and sulfuric acid, dissolving cellulistic materials and providing better visibility for palynomorphs.

Some steps of the chemical treatments require special care for safety reason, in particular the use of HF which diffuses very fast through the skin and could cause severe chemical burns. Other treatment include kerosene flotation for chitinous materials.

PHYCOLOGY

Phycology (or algology) a subdiscipline of botany, is the scientific study of algae. Algae are important as primary producers in aquatic ecosystems. Most algae are eukaryotic, photosynthetic organisms that live in a wet environment. They are distinguished from the higher plants by a lack of true roots, stems or leaves. Many species are single-celled and microscopic (including phytoplankton and other microalgae); many others are multicellular to one degree or another, some of these growing to large size (for example, seaweeds such as kelp and Sargassum).

Phycology also includes the study of prokaryotic forms known as blue-green algae or cyanobacteria. A number of microscopic algae also occur as symbionts in Lichens. A phycologist is a person who studies algae. In a similar manner, a mycologist is a person who has been professionally trained in mycology, the study of fungi.

PHYTOCHEMISTRY

Phytochemistry is in the strict sense of the word the study of phytochemicals. These are chemicals derived from plants. In a narrower sense the terms are often used to describe the large number of secondary metabolic compounds found in plants. Many of these are known to provide protection against insect attacks and plant diseases. They also exhibit a number of protective functions for human consumers.

Techniques commonly used in the field of phytochemistry are extraction, isolation and structural elucidation (MS,1D and 2D NMR) of natural products, as well as various chromatography techniques (MPLC, HPLC, LC-MS).

PHYTOPATHOLOGY

Phytopathology (plant pathology) is the scientific study of plant diseases caused by pathogens (infectious diseases) and environmental conditions (physiological factors). Organisms that cause infectious disease include fungi, oomycetes, bacteria, viruses, viroids, virus-like organisms, phytoplasmas, protozoa, nematodes and parasitic plants. Not included are insects, mites, vertebrate or other pests that affect plant health by consumption of plant tissues. Plant Pathology also involves the study of the identification, etiology, disease cycle, economic impact, epidemiology, how plant diseases affect humans and animals, pathosystem genetics and management of plant diseases. The "Disease triangle" is a central concept of plant pathology for infectious diseases. It is based on the principle that disease is the result of an interaction between a host, a pathogen, and environment condition.

Plant Pathogens

Fungi

The majority of phytopathogenic fungi belong to the Ascomycetes and the Basidiomycetes. The fungi reproduce both sexually and asexually via the production of spores. These spores may be spread long distances by air or water, or they may be soil bourne. Many soil bourne spores, normally zoospores and capable of living saprophytically, caring out the first part of their lifecycle in the soil.

Fungal diseases can be controlled through the use of fungicides in agriculture, however new races of fungi often evolve that are resistant to various fungicides.

Significant Fungal Plant Pathogens

Ascomycetes:

- Fusarium spp.
- Thielaviopsis spp. (Causal agents of: canker rot, black root rot, Thielaviopsis root rot)
- Verticillium spp.
- Magnaporthe grisea (T.T. Hebert) M.E. Barr; causes blast of rice and gray leaf spot in turfgrasses.

Basidiomycetes:

- Rhizoctonia spp.

- Phakospora pachyrhizi Sydow; causes Soybean rust
- Puccinia spp.; causal agents of severe rusts of virtually all cereal grains and cultivated grasses.

Oomycetes

The oomycetes are fungal-like organisms that until recently used to be mistaken for fungi. They include some of the most destructive plant pathogens including the genus Phytophthora which includes the casual agents of potato late blight and sudden oak death. Despite not being closely related to the fungi, the oomycetes have developed very similar infection strategies and so many plant pathologists group them with fungal pathogens. Significant oomycete plant pathogens

Bacteria

Most bacteria that are associated with plants are actually saprophytic, and do no harm to the plant itself. However, a small number, around 100 species, are able to cause disease. Bacterial diseases are much more prevalent in sub-tropical and tropical regions of the world. Most plant pathogenic bacteria are rod shaped (bacilli). In order to be able to colonise the plant they have specific pathogenicity factors. There are 4 main bacterial pathogenicity factors:

- Cell wall degrading enzymes - used to break down the plant cell wall in order to release the nutrients inside. Used by pathogens such as Erwinia to cause soft rot.
- Toxins These can be non-host specific, and damage all plants, or host specific and only cause damage on a host plant.
- Phytohormones - for example Agrobacterium changes the level of Auxin to cause tumours.
- Exopolysaccharides - these are produced by bacteria and block xylem vessels, often leading to the death of the plant.

Bacteria control the production of pathogenicity factors via quorum sensing.

Significant Bacterial Plant Pathogens

Proteobacteria:

- *Xanthomonas* spp.
- *Pseudomonas* spp.

Phytoplasmas ('Mycoplasma-like Organisms') and Spiroplasmas

Phytoplasma and Spiroplasma are a genre of bacteria that lack cell walls, and are related to the mycoplasmas which are human pathogens. Together they are referred to as the mollicutes. They also tend to have smaller genomes than true bacteria. They are normally transmitted by sap-sucking insects, being transferred into the plants phloem where it reproduces.

Viruses, Viroids and Virus-like Organisms

There are many types of plant virus, and some are even asymptomatic. Normally plant viruses only cause a loss of yield. Therefore it is not economically viable to try to control them, the exception being when they infect perennial species, such as fruit trees. Most plant viruses have small, single stranded RNA genomes. These genomes may only encode 3 or 4 proteins: a replicase, a coat protein, a movement protein to allow cell to cell movement and sometimes a protein that allows transmission by a vector. Plant viruses must be transmitted from plant to plant by a vector. This is normally an insect, but some fungi, nematodes and protozoa have been shown to be viral vectors.

PLANT ANATOMY

Plant anatomy or phytotomy is the general term for the study of the internal structure of plants. While originally it included plant morphology, which is the description of the physical form and external structure of plants, since the mid Twentieth Century the investigation of plant anatomy is considered a separate, distinct field, and refers to just the internal plant structures.

Plant anatomy is now frequently investigated at the cellular level, and often involves the sectioning of tissues and microscopy.

Structural Divisions

Plant anatomy is sometimes divided into the following categories:

- Flower anatomy :
  - Calyx
  - Corolla
  - Androecium
  - Gynoecium
- Leaf anatomy :
  - Leaf anatomy
- Stem anatomy :
  - Stem structure
- Fruit/Seed anatomy :
  - Ovule
  - Pericarp
  - Accessory fruit
- Wood anatomy :
  - Bark
  - Cork
  - Phloem
  - Vascular cambium
  - Heartwood and sapwood
  - branch collar
- Root anatomy :
  - Root structure.

PLANT ECOLOGY

Ecology is the scientific study of the distribution and abundance of life and the interactions between organisms and their environment. The environment of an organism includes physical properties, which can be described as the sum of local abiotic factors such as insolation (sunlight), climate, and geology, and biotic factors, which are other organisms that share its habitat.

The word "ecology" is often used more loosely in such terms as social ecology and deep ecology and in common parlance as a synonym for the natural environment or environmentalism. Likewise "ecologic" or "ecological" is often taken in the sense of environmentally friendly. The term ecology or oekologie was coined by the German biologist Ernst Haeckel in 1866, when he defined it as "the comprehensive science of the relationship of the organism to the environment." Haeckel did not elaborate on the concept, and the first significant textbook on the subject (together with the first university course) was written by the Danish botanist, Eugenius Warming. For this early work, Warming is often identified as the founder of ecology.

PLANT GENETICS

Genetics, study of the function and behaviour of genes. Genes are bits of biochemical instructions found inside the cells of every organism from bacteria to humans. Offspring receive a mixture of genetic information from both parents. This process contributes to the great variation of traits that we see in nature, such as the colour of a flower's petals, the markings on a butterfly's wings, or such human behavioral traits as personality or musical talent. Geneticists seek to understand how the information encoded in genes is used and controlled by cells and how it is transmitted from one generation to the next. Geneticists also study how tiny variations in genes can disrupt an organism's development or cause disease. Increasingly, modern genetics involves genetic engineering, a technique used by scientists to manipulate genes. Genetic engineering has produced many advances in medicine and industry, but the potential for abuse of this technique has also presented society with many ethical and legal controversies.

Genetic information is encoded and transmitted from generation to generation in deoxyribonucleic acid (DNA). DNA is a coiled molecule organized into structures called chromosomes within cells. Segments along the length of a DNA molecule form genes. Genes direct the synthesis of proteins, the molecular laborers that carry out all life-supporting activities in the cell. Although all humans share the same set of genes, individuals can inherit different forms of a given gene, making each person genetically unique.

Since the earliest days of plant and animal domestication, around 10,000 years ago, humans have understood that characteristic traits of parents could be transmitted to their offspring. The first to speculate about how this process worked were Greek scholars around the 4th century BC, who promoted theories based on conjecture or superstition. Some of these theories remained in favor for several centuries. The scientific study of genetics did not begin until the late 19th century. In experiments with garden peas, Austrian monk Gregor Mendel described the patterns of inheritance, observing that traits were inherited as separate units. These units are now known as genes. Mendel's work formed the foundation for later scientific achievements that heralded the era of modern genetics.

PLANT MORPHOLOGY

Plant morphology (or phytomorphology) is the general term for the study of the morphology (physical form and external structure) of plants. This is usually considered distinct from plant anatomy, which is the study of the internal structure of plants, especially at the microscopic level. Plant morphology is useful in the identification of plants.

PLANT PHYSIOLOGY

Plant physiology is a subdiscipline of botany concerned with the function, or physiology, of plants. Closely related fields include plant morphology (structure of plants), plant ecology (interactions with the environment), phytochemistry (biochemistry of plants), cell biology, and molecular biology. Fundamental processes such as photosynthesis, respiration, plant nutrition, plant hormone functions, tropisms, nastic movements, photoperiodism, photomorphogenesis, circadian rhythms, environmental stress physiology, seed germination, dormancy and stomata function and transpiration, both part of plant water relations, are studied by plant physiologists.

Biochemistry of Plants

The list of simple elements of which plants are primarily constructed—carbon, oxygen, hydrogen, calcium, phosphorus, etc.—is not different from similar lists for animals, fungi, or even bacteria. The fundamental atomic components of plants are the same as for all life; only the details of the way in which they are assembled differs.

Despite this underlying similarity, plants produce a vast array of chemical compounds with unusual properties which they use to cope with their environment. Pigments are used by plants to absorb or detect light, and are extracted by humans for use in dyes. Other plant products may be used for the manufacture of commercially important rubber or biofuel. Perhaps the most celebrated compounds from plants are those with pharmacological activity, such as salicylic acid (aspirin), morphine, and digitalis. Drug companies spend billions of dollars each year researching plant compounds for potential medicinal benefits.

Constituent Elements

Plants require some nutrients, such as carbon and nitrogen, in large quantities to survive.

Such nutrients are termed macronutrients, where the prefix macro- (large) refers to the quantity needed, not the size of the nutrient particles themselves. Other nutrients, called micronutrients, are required only in trace amounts for plants to remain healthy. Such micronutrients are usually absorbed as ions dissolved in water taken from the soil, though carnivorous plants acquire some of their micronutrients from captured prey. The following tables list element nutrients essential to plants. Uses within plants are generalized.

Macronutrients. (Necessary in Large Quantities)

Element	*Form of uptake*	*Notes*
Nitrogen	NO_3^- NH_4^+	Nucleic acids, proteins, hormones, etc.
Oxygen	O_2 H_2O	Various organic compounds
Carbon	CO_2	Various organic compounds

Hydrogen	H_2O	Various organic compounds
Potassium	K^+	Cofactor in protein synthesis, water balance, etc.
Calcium	Ca^{2+}	Membrane synthesis and stabilization
Magnesium	Mg^{2+}	Element essential for chlorophyll
Phosphorus	$H^2PO_4^-$	Nucleic acids, phospholipids, ATP
Sulfur	SO_4^{2-}	Constituent of proteins and coenzymes
Chlorine	Cl^-	–
Boron	$H\ BO_3$	–
> Manganese	Mn^{2+}	Activity of some enzymes
Zinc	Zn^{2+}	Involved in the synthesis of enzymes and chlorophyll
Copper	Cu^+	Enzymes for lignin synthesis
Molybdenum	MoO_4^{2-}	Nitrogen fixation, reduction of nitrates
Nickel	Ni^{2+}	Enzymatic cofactor in the metabolism of nitrogen compunds

Pigments

Among the most important molecules for plant function are the pigments. Plant pigments include a variety of different kinds of molecules, including porphyrins, carotenoids, and anthocyanins. All biological pigments selectively absorb certain wavelengths of light while reflecting others. The light that is absorbed may be used by the plant to power chemical reactions, while the reflected wavelengths of light determine the colour the pigment will appear to the eye.

Chlorophyll is the primary pigment in plants; it is a porphyrin that absorbs red and blue wavelengths of light while reflecting green. It is the presence and relative abundance of chlorophyll that gives plants their green colour. All land plants and green algae possess two forms of this pigment: chlorophyll a and chlorophyll b. Kelps, diatoms, and other photosynthetic heterokonts contain chlorophyll c instead of b, while red algae possess only chlorophyll a. All chlorophylls serve as the primary means plants use to intercept light in order to fuel photosynthesis. Carotenoids are red, orange, or yellow tetraterpenoids. They function as accessory pigments in plants, helping to fuel photosynthesis by gathering wavelengths of light not readily absorbed by chlorophyll. The most familiar carotenoids are carotene (an orange pigment found in carrots), lutein (a yellow pigment found in fruits and vegetables), and lycopene (the red pigment responsible for the colour of tomatoes). Carotenoids have been shown to act as antioxidants and to promote healthy eyesight in humans.

Anthocyanins (literally "flower blue") are water-soluble flavonoid pigments that appear red to blue, according to pH. They occur in all tissues of higher plants, providing colour in leaves, stems, roots, flowers, and fruits, though not always in sufficient quantities to be noticeable. Anthocyanins are most visible in the petals of flowers, where they may make up as much as 30% of the dry weight of the tissue. They are also responsible for the purple colour seen on the underside of tropical shade plants such as Tradescantia zebrina; in these plants, the anthocyanin catches light that has passed through the leaf and reflects it back towards regions bearing chlorophyll, in order to maximize the use of available light.

Betalains are red or yellow pigments. Like anthocyanins they are water-soluble, but unlike anthocyanins they are indole-derived compounds synthesized from tyrosine. This class of pigments is found only in the Caryophyllales (including cactus and amaranth), and never co-occur in plants with anthocyanins. Betalains are responsible for the deep red colour of beets, and are used commercially as food-colouring agents. Plant physiologists are uncertain of the function that betalains have in plants which possess them, but there is some preliminary evidence that they may have fungicidal properties.

Signals and Regulators

Plants produce hormones and other growth regulators which act to signal a physiological response in their tissues. They also produce compounds such as phytochrome that are sensitive to light and which serve to trigger growth or development in response to environmental signals.

PLANT HORMONES

Plant hormones, also known as plant growth regulators (PGRs) or phytohormones, are chemicals that regulate a plant's growth. According to a standard animal definition, hormones are signal molecules produced at specific locations, that occur in very low concentrations, and cause altered processes in target cells at other locations. Unlike animals, plants lack specific hormone-producing tissues or organs. Plant hormones are often not transported to other parts of the plant and production is not limited to specific locations. Plant hormones are chemicals that in small amounts promote and influence the growth, development and differentiation of cells and tissues. Hormones are vital to plant growth; effecting processes in plants from flowering to seed development, dormancy, and germination. They regulate which tissues grow upwards and which grow downwards, leaf formation and stem growth, fruit development and ripening, as well as leaf abscission and even plant death. The most important plant hormones are abscissic acid (ABA), auxins, gibberellins, and cytokinins, though there are many other substances that serve to regulate plant physiology.

Photomorphogenesis

While most people know that light is important for photosynthesis in plants, few realize that plant sensitivity to light plays a role in the control of plant structural development (morphogenesis). The use of light to control structural development is called photomorphogenesis, and is dependent upon the presence of specialized photoreceptors, which are chemical pigments capable of absorbing specific wavelengths of light. Plants use four kinds of photoreceptors: phytochrome, cryptochrome, a UV-B photoreceptor, and protochlorophyllide a. The first two of these, phytochrome and cryptochrome, are photoreceptor proteins, complex molecular structures formed by joining a protein with a light-sensitive pigment. Cryptochrome is also known as the UV-A photoreceptor, because it absorbs ultraviolet light in the long wave "A" region. The UV-B receptor is one or more compounds that have yet to be identified with certainty, though some evidence suggests carotene or riboflavin as candidates. Protochlorophyllide a, as its name suggests, is a chemical precursor of chlorophyll. The most studied of the photoreceptors in plants is phytochrome. It is sensitive to light in the red and far-red region of the visible spectrum. Many flowering plants use it to regulate the time of flowering based on the length of day and night (photoperiodism) and to set circadian rhythms. It also regulates other responses including the germination of seeds, elongation of seedlings, the size, shape and number of leaves, the synthesis of chlorophyll, and the straightening of the epicotyl or hypocotyl hook of dicot seedlings.

Photoperiodism

Use the pigment phytochrome to sense seasonal changes in day length, which they take as signals to flower. This sensitivity to day length is termed photoperiodism. Broadly speaking, flowering plants can be classified as long day plants, short day plants, or day neutral plants, depending on their particular response to changes in day length. Long day plants require a certain minimum length of daylight to initiate flowering, so these plants flower in the spring or summer. Conversely, short day plants will flower when the length of daylight falls below a certain critical level. Day neutral plants do not initiate flowering based on photoperiodism, though some may use temperature sensitivity (vernalization) instead.

Although a short day plant cannot flower during the long days of summer, it is not actually the period of light exposure that limits flowering. Rather, a short day plant requires a minimal length of uninterrupted darkness in each 24 hour period (a short daylength) before floral development can begin. It has been determined experimentally that a short day plant (long night) will not flower if a flash of phytochrome activiting light is used on the plant during the night. Plants make use of the phytochrome system to sense day length or photoperiod. This fact is utilized by florists and greenhouse gardeners to control and even induce flowering out of season, such as the Poinsettia.

Environmental Physiology

Paradoxically, the subdiscipline of environmental physiology is on the one hand a recent field of study in plant ecology and on the other hand one of the oldest. Environmental phyiology is the preferred name of the subdiscipline among plant physiologists, but it goes by a number of other names in the applied sciences. It is roughly synonymous with ecophysiology, crop ecology, horticulture, and agronomy. The particular name applied to the subdiscipline is specific to the viewpoint and goals of research. Whatever name is applied, it deals with the ways in which plants respond to their environment and so overlaps with the field of ecology.

Environmental physiologists examine plant response to physical factors such as radiation (including light and ultraviolet radiation), temperature, fire, and wind. Of particular importance are water relations and the stress of drought or inundation, exchange of gases with the atmosphere, as well as the cycling of nutrients such as nitrogen and carbon. Environmental physiologists also examine plant response to biological factors. This includes not only negative interactions, such as competition, herbivory, disease, and parasitism, but also positive interactions, such as mutualism and pollination.

Tropisms and Nastic Movements

Plants may respond both to directional and nondirectional stimuli. A response to a directional stimulus, such as gravity or sunlight, is called a tropism. A response to a nondirectional stimulus, such as temperature or humidity, is a nastic movement. Tropisms in plants are the result of differential cell growth, in which the cells on one side of the plant elongate more than those on the other side, causing the part to bend toward the side with less growth. Among the common tropisms seen in plants is phototropism, the bending of the plant toward a source of light. Phototropism allows the plant to maximize light exposure in plants which require additional light for photosynthesis, or to minimize it in plants subjected to intense light and heat. Geotropism allows the roots of a plant to determine the direction of gravity and grow downwards. Tropisms generally result from an interaction between the environment and production of one or more plant hormones. In contrast to tropisms, nastic movements result from changes in turgor pressure within plant tissues, and may occur rapidly. A familiar example is thigmonasty (response to touch) in the Venus fly trap, a carnivorous plant. The traps consist of modified leaf blades which bear sensitive trigger hairs. When the hairs are touched by an insect or other animal, the leaf folds shut. This mechanism allows the plant to trap and digest small insects for additional nutrients. Although the trap is rapidly shut by changes in internal cell pressures, the leaf must grow slowly in order to reset for a second opportunity to trap insects.

Plant Disease

Economically, one of the most important areas of research in environmental physiology is that of phytopathology, the study of diseases in plants and the manner in which plants resist or cope with infection. Plant are susceptible to the same kinds of disease organisms as animals, including viruses, bacteria, and fungi, as well as physical invasion by insects and roundworms. Because the biology of plants differs from animals, their symptoms and responses are quite different. In some cases, a plant can simply shed infected leaves or flowers to prevent to spread of disease, in a process called abscission. Most animals do not have this option as a means of controlling disease. Plant diseases organisms themselves also differ from those causing disease in animals because plants cannot usually spread infection through casual physical contact. Plant pathogens tend to spread via spores or are carried by animal vectors.

One of the most important advances in the control of plant disease was the discovery of Bordeaux mixture in the nineteenth century. The mixture is the first known fungicide and is a combination of copper sulfate and lime. Application of the mixture served to inhibit the growth of downy mildew that threatened to seriously damage the French wine industry.

PLANT TAXONOMY

Plant taxonomy is the science that finds, describes, classifies, identifies, and names plants. It thus is one of the main branches of taxonomy. Plant taxonomy is closely allied to plant systematics, and there is no sharp boundary between the two. In practice, "plant systematics" is involved with relationships between plants and their evolution, especially at the higher levels, whereas "plant taxonomy" deals with the actual handling of plant specimens. The precise relationship between taxonomy and systematics, however, has changed along with the goals and methods employed.

Plant taxonomy is well known for being turbulent, and traditionally there is no really close agreement on circumscription and placement of taxa.

Identification and Classification

Two goals of plant taxonomy are the identification and classification of plants. The distinction between these two goals is important and often overlooked. Plant identification is the determination of the identity of an unknown plant by comparison with previously collected specimens or with the aid of books or identification manuals. The process of identification connects the specimen with a published name. Once a plant specimen has been identified, its name and properties are known. Plant classification is the placing of known plants into groups or categories to show some relationship. Scientific classification follows a system of rules that standardizes the results, and groups successive categories into a hierarchy.

2

Plant Tissue Culture

Plant cell culture is viewed as a potential means of producing useful plant products such that conventional agriculture, with all its attendant problems and variables, can be circumvented. These problems include: environmental factors (drought, floods, etc.), disease, political and labour instabilities in the producing countries (often Third World countries), uncontrollable variations in the crop quality, inability of authorities to prevent crop adulteration, losses in storage and handling.

Thus, the production of useful and valuable secondary metabolites in large bioreactors located in the consuming country is an attractive proposal. Additional advantages of such processes include: controlled production according to demand and a reduced and requirement.

However, this technology is still being developed and despite the advantages outlined above, there are a variety of problems to be overcome before it can be adopted on a wide scale for the production of useful plant secondary metabolites. The success of Mitsui Petrochemical Industry Co. Ltd. in Japan in producing shikonin on a commercial scale from *Lithospermum erythrorhizon* cultivations and that of Nitto Denko Co. Ltd. also in Japan in mass production of *Panax ginseng* or ginseng cells using 20 kL tanks have demonstrated that many of the problems can be overcome with perseverance.

The economic feasibility of these processes is another question and this will be dealt with in a separate section. In theory, it is anticipated that such large scale suspension cultures will be suitable for industrial production of useful plant chemicals such as pharmaceuticals and food additives, in a manner similar to that of microbial fermentation.

Nevertheless, there are some significant differences between microbial and plant cell cultures that must be considered when attempting to apply plant cell cultures to the available technology.

The problems that can be encountered with plant cell cultures. The sensitivity to shear is due both to the large size of the cells and to the relatively inflexible cellulose cell wall. Thus, with normal blade impellers the cells may twist which will inhibit mitoses and, for this reason, air-lift fermentors are recommended by some researchers.

The large size of the plant cell contributes to its comparatively high doubling time (12 h - several days), which thus prolongs the time required for a successful fermentation run.

Characteristic of Microbial and Plant Cell Relevant to Fermentation

Characteristics	*Microorganism*	*Plant Cell*
Size	2 u	>10 u
Shear stress	Insensitive	Sensitive
Water content	75%	>90%
Duplication time	<1 hour	days
Aeration	1-2 vvm	0.3 vvm
Fermentation time	Days	Weeks
Product accumulation	Medium	Vacuole
Production phase	Uncoupled	Often growth-linked
Mutation	Possible	Requires haploids
Medium cost ($)(MS medium)	8-9/m	65-70/m

The vacuole is the major site of product accumulation, and since product secretion is uncommon, the high metabolite yields seen in microorganisms that secrete product (thereby removing product inhibition of biosynthesis) cannot be expected. There is some ongoing research on membrane permeabilization of plant cells which may serve to relieve the constraints of product inhibition by facilitation of leakage into the extracellular medium. If this would also permit recycling of the biomass (*e.g.* via immobilization) it would help reduce production costs. The low aeration requirement for plant cells is an advantage over microbial cultures in general. In addition, the high cost of running a fermentation vessel over several weeks should be considered, although media costs are much less than those of animal cell cultures.

In addition to the problems outlined above, concerned with fermentation technology, there are also considerable hurdles to be overcome at the biochemical level. The two major problems concern poor expression of products and instability of cell lines.

Cultured plant cells often produce reduced quantities and different profiles of secondary metabolites when compared with the intact plant and these quantitative and qualitative features may change with time. The poor product expression is often attributed to a lack of differentiation in cultures. On the other hand, there are cases of cultures that over-produce metabolites compared with the whole plant.

There are a number of examples of cultured cells producing metabolites not observed in the plant, e.g. *Lithospermum erythrorhizon* cultures have been observed to synthesize rosmarinic acid. It has become apparent that the choice of original plant material having high yields of the desired phytochemical may be important in establishing high-yielding cultures.

Furthermore, the need to repeatedly screen for high-producing lines (due to inherent instability of cell lines) has been emphasized, although the nutritional composition of the medium is also important. Thus, a variety of approaches are being investigated by many researchers to increase productivity of useful plant metabolites in plant cell cultures.

MASS PROPAGATION OF PLANT TISSUE CULTURE

In 1965, French botanist George Morel was attempting to obtain a virus-free orchid plant when he discovered that a millimetre-long shoot could be developed into complete plantlets by micropropagation. This was the beginning of tissue culture. Thereafter, in the 1970s developed countries began commercial exploitation of this technology. It entered the developing world in the 1980s. It was earlier used to develop ornamental plants and flowering plants for export. With tree species, the technique of tissue culture remained confined for many years to the laboratory stage and had generally invited only academic interest. But in most developing countries, the shortage of biomass and the ever-increasing energy requirements created the need to explore possibilities of mass propagation of trees by tissue culture.

Tissue culture or mass cloning methods of elite tree species is done for increasing land productivity. They are being modified or adapted for large-scale modification.

Species are selected for tissue culture on the following basis. Species that have regeneration problems, specially because of poor seed set or germination (as in Anogeissus and bamboo). In these cases, seeds collected from superior trees are used for initiating cultures.

Species that vary markedly in their desirable traits, *i.e.* Eucalyptus. The selected trees are marked from the variant population for the desirable trait such as disease resistance, straight bole, higher productivity, etc. in consultation with officials from state forest department or growers.

Species where plants of any one particular sex is of commercial importance, for example female plants of papaya and male plants of asparagus

In tissue culture cells, tissues, and organs of a plant are separated. These separated cells are grown especially in containers with a nutrient media under controlled conditions of temperature and light. The cultured plant requires a source of energy from sugar, salts, a few vitamins, amino acids, etc. that are provided in the nutrient media. From these cultured parts, an embryo or a shoot bud may develop, which then grows into a whole new plantlet. Similarly, portions of organs or tissues can be cultured in a culture media. Generally, these give rise to an unorganized mass of cells called callus (soft tissue that forms over a cut surface).

Tissue culture plantlets have poor photosynthesis efficiency and lack the proper mechanism to control water loss. They need to be hardened gradually by moving them along a humidity gradient in the greenhouse. Once these plants are in the research fields, they are evaluated under field conditions and the data is collected every 6 months. A large number of tissue culture plants that have grown into trees are remarkably uniform and show an increase in biomass production over the conventionally raised plants.

APPLICATION OF TISSUE CULTURE

Micropropagation: Rapid vegetative multiplication of valuable plant material for agriculture, horticulture, and forestry.

Production of disease-free plants: When the apex of shoot is used for multiplication by tissue culture, we get disease free plants because the shoot apical meristem, a group of dividing cells at the tip of a stem or root, is free from pathogens.

Plant breeding: Tissue culture has also been successfully used in plant breeding programmes.

Production of disease- and pest-resistant plants: Plants grown from tissue culture usually pass trough callus phase and show many variations. These show some agronomic characteristics like tolerance to pests, diseases, etc.

Cloning

Genetically identical plants derived from an individual are called clones. Processes that produce clones can be put under the term 'cloning'. This includes all the methods of vegetative propagation such as cutting, layering, and grafting. Propagation by tissue culture also helps in producing clones. Using the shoot tip, it is possible to obtain a large number of plantlets. This technique is used extensively in the commercial field for micropropagation of ornamental plants like chrysanthemum, gladiolus, etc. and also crops such as sugar cane, tapioca, and potato. Thus an unlimited number of plants that are genetically similar or are clones can be produced in a short span of time by tissue culture.

Large-scale Propagation

To bridge the gap between research and application, the Department of Biotechnology, Government of India sponsored the setting-up of two pilot-scale facilities for large-scale propagation of elite planting material of forest trees through tissue culture. One of these facilities has been established at TERI's 36-hectare-campus in Gual Pahari, Haryana with an annual capacity of a million plantlets. Research at these facilities focuses exclusively on developing new protocols for mass cloning of elite planting material, mainly of trees.

Till date, over 4 million plants have been dispatched for field plantation from these facilities. The tissue culture raised plants are presently being evaluated under field conditions. This is being done in tandem with the forest departments of Haryana, Uttar Pradesh, Madhya Pradesh, Bihar, Jammu and Kashmir, and Orissa. For initial screening for phenotypically superior trees only a few hundred plantlets of the same are raised and tested under various agroclimatic zones. The best clones are then mass multiplied and monitored regularly for their performance. Field data suggest a survival percentage of more than 90% even in the harsh conditions of Aravalis without the life-saving irrigation. At half the rotation age some of the selected clones of Eucalyptus are showing a significant increase in productivity as compared to the conventional seed raised progenies.

MATERIALS AND METHODS OF PLANT CALLUS TISSUE

MATERIALS

Plant

Plant species can be employed to induce callus tissue, however the successful production of callus depends upon plant species and their qualities. Dicotyledons are rather amenable for callus tissue induction, as compared to monocotyledons; the callus of woody plants generally grow slowly. Stems, leaves, roots, flowers, seeds and any other parts of plants are used, but younger and fresh explants are preferable as explant materials. Explants obtained must be sterilized using ethanol, sodium hypochlorite and/or other chemicals to remove all microorganisms from the materials and a typical sterilization procedure will be described later as an example.

Inorganic Salts

To induce a callus from an explant and to cultivate the callus and cells in suspension, various kinds of media (inorganic salt media) have been designed. Agar or its substitutes is added into the media to prepare solid medium for callus induction.

One of the most commonly used media for plant tissue cultures is that developed by Murashige and Skoog (MS) for tobacco tissue culture. The significant feature of the MS medium is its very high concentration of nitrate, potassium and ammonia. The B5 medium established by Gamborg *et al.* is also being used by many researchers. The levels of inorganic nutrients in the B5 medium are lower than in MS medium. Many other media have been developed and modified and nutrient compositions of some typical media. However, it is not always necessary to test many kinds of basal media when a callus is induced. It would be better to use only one or two kinds of basal media in combination of different kinds and concentrations of phytohormones. The most suitable medium composition should be optimized afterwards in order to obtain higher level of products as well as higher growth rate.

Media for Plant Tissue and Cell Cultures (mg/L)

Components	*Murashige-Skoog (1962)*	*White (1963)*	*Gamborg (1968)*	*Nitsch (1951)*	*Heller (1953)*	*Schenk - Hildebrandt (1972)*	*Nitsch-Nitsch (1967)*	*Kohlenbach-Schmidt (1975)*	*Knop (1865)*
$(NH_4)_2SO_4$	-	-	134	-	-	-	-	-	-
$MgSO_{4\times}\ 7H_2O$	370	720	500	250	250	400	125	185	250
Na_2SO_4	-	200	-	-	-	-	-	-	-
KC1	-	65	-	1,500	750	-	-	-	-
$CaC1_{2\times}\ 2H_2O$	440	-	150	25	75	200	-	166	-
$NaNO_3$	-	-	-	-	600	-	-	-	-
KNO_3	1,900	80	3,000	2,000	-	2,500	125	950	250
$Ca(NO_3)_{2\times}\ 4H_2O$	-	300	-	-	-	-	500	-	1,000
NH_4NO_3	1,650	-	-	-	-	-	-	720	-
$NaH_2PO_{4\times}\ H_2O$	-	16.5	150	250	125	-	-	-	-
$NH_4H_2PO_4$	-	-	-	-	-	300	-	-	-
KH_2PO_4	170	-	-	-	–	-	125	68	250
$FeSO_{4\times}\ 7H_2)$	27.8	-	27.8	-	-	15	27.85	27.85	-
Na_2EDTA	37.3	-	37.3	-	-	20	37.25	37.25	-
$MnSO_{4\times}\ 4H_2O$	22.3	7	10 (1 H_2O)	3	0.1	10	25	25	-
$ZnSO_{4\times}\ 7H_2O$	8.6	3	2	0.5	1	0.1	10	10	-
$CuSO_{4\times}\ 5H_2O$	0.025	-	0.025	0.025	0.03	0.2	0.025	0.025	-

H_2SO_4	-	-	-	0.5	-	-	-	-	-
$Fe_2(SO_4)_3$	-	2.5	-	-	-	-	-	-	-
$NiCl_2 \times 6H_2O$	-	-	-	-	0.03	-	-	-	-
$CoCl_2 \times 6H_2O$	0.025	-	0.025	-	-	0.1	0.025	-	-
$AlCl_3$	-	-	-	-	0.03	-	-	-	-
$FeCl_3 \times 6H_2O$	-	-	-	-	1	-	-	-	-
$FeC_6O_5H_7 \times 5H_2O$	-	-	-	10	-	-	-	-	-
K1	0.83	0.75	0.75	0.5	0.01	1.0	-	-	-
H_3BO_3	6.2	1.5	3	0.5	1	5	10	10	-
$Na_2M_0O_4 \times 2H_2O$	0.25	-	0.25	0.25	-	0.1	0.25	0.25	-
SucroseGlucose	30,000-	20,000-	20,000-50,000	or36,000	20,000-	30,000-	20,000~30,000-	10,000-	—
Myo-Inositol	100	-	100	-	-	1,000	100	100	-
Nicotinic Acid	0.5	0.5	1.0	-	-	0.5	5	5	-
Pyridoxine HC1	0.5	0.1	1.0	-	-	0.5	0.5	0.5	-
Thiamine HC1	0.1-1	0.1	10	1	1	5	0.5	0.5	-
Ca-Pantothenate	-	1	-	-	-	-	-	-	-
Biotin	-	-	-	-	-	-	0.05	0.05	-
Glycine	2	3	-	-	-	-	2	2	-
Cysteine HC1	-	1	-	10	-	-	-	-	-
Folic Acid	-	-	-	-	-	-	0.5	0.5	-
Glutamine	-	-	-	-	-	-	-	14.7	-

Carbon Sources

Sucrose or glucose at 2 to 4% are suitable carbon sources which ai added to the basal medium. Fructose, maltose and other sugars also support the growth of various plant cells. However, the most suitable carbon source and its optimal concentration should be chosen to establish the efficient production process of useful metabolites. These factors depend on plant species and products, therefore it is necessary to optimize the medium compositions including carbon sources in each case. From an economical point of view, the use of more inexpensive carbon sources is appropriate in industry and crude sugars such as molasses have been examined.

Vitamins

Myo-inositol, nicotinic acid, pyridoxine HCl and thiamine HCl. Among these vitamins, thiamine is an essential one for many plant cells and other vitamins stimulate the growth of the cells in some cases. The level of myo-inositol in the medium is 100 mg/L which is very high although it is not clear whether such a high level of the vitamin is required.

Phytohormones

Phytohormones or growth regulators are required to induce callus tissues and to promote the growth of many cell lines. As an auxin, 2,4-dichlorophenoxyacetic acid (2,4-D) or naphthaleneaceic acid (NAA) is frequently used. The concentration of auxins in the medium is generally between 0.1 to 50 μM. Kinetin or benzyladenine as a cytokinin is occasionally required together with auxins for callus induction at concentrations of 0.1 to 10 μM.

Other derivatives of auxin and kinetin are also used in some cases. Since each plant species requires different kinds and levels of phytohormones for callus induction, its growth and metabolites production, it is important to select the most appropriate growth regulators and to determine their optimal concentrations. Gibberellic acid is also added to the medium if necessary.

Organic Supplements

In order to stimulate the growth of the cells, organic supplements are sometimes added to the medium. These supplements include casamino acid, peptone, yeast extracts, malt extracts and coconut milk. Coconut milk is also known as a supplier of growth regulators.

METHODS

Preparation of Media

To prepare the medium, many researchers mix the stock solutions which were made previously since the medium compositions are generally complicated.

For example, MS medium is prepared as follows:

a. MS-Micronutrient stock solution (store in freezer)
   Ingredient mg/100 ml
   H_3BO_3 620
   $MnSO_4$ $4H_2O$ 2230
   $ZnSO_4$ $7H_2O$ 860
   Na_2MoO_4 $2H_2O$ 25
   $CuSO_4$ $5H_2O$ 2.5
   $CoCl_2$ $6H_2O$ 2.5
b. Vitamins (store in freezer)
   Vitamins mg/100 ml
   Nicotinic acid 100
   Thiamine HCl 1,000
   Pyridoxine HCl 100
   Myo-Inositol 10,000
c. Calcium chloride
   $CaCl_2$ $2H_2O$ 15 g/100 ml
d. Potassium iodide (store in amber bottle in refrigerator)
   KI 75 mg/100 ml
e. 2,4-D (2.2 mM)
   Dissolve 50 mg 2,4-D in 2 to 5 ml ethanol, heat slightly and gradually dilute to 100 ml with water. (Store in refrigerator).

f. NAA (2.8 mM)
   Prepare the same as 2,4-D above.

g. Kinetin (1 mM)
   Dissolve 21.5 mg of kinetin in a small volume of 0.5 N HCl by heating slightly and gradually diluting to 100 ml with distilled water. (Store in refrigerator) Similar procedures can be used for other cytokinins.

A certain volume of each stock solution is mixed and an appropriate carbon source is added to the mixture. After pH is adjusted to around 5.5 with 0.2 N K0H or 0.2 N HCl, distilled or deionized water is added to the mixture up to the certain volume required. Agar (0.6 to 1.0% wt/vol) is added for a solid medium.

The medium thus prepared is distributed into vessels such as Erlenmyer flasks (for example, 50 ml of the medium in a 300 ml volume Erlenmyer flask) and sterilized by using an autoclave at 120° C for 15 minutes. The sterilization conditions should be varied based on the volume of the medium and the size of the vessel.

Callus Induction

Explants are sterilized with 2% sodium hypochlorite solution and/or 70% ethanol solution. The period of time for submerging the plant materials in these solutions depends upon plant species, their parts and age. For example, a piece of stem of tobacco plant (approximately 3 cm in length) is submerged in 70% ethanal solution of 2-3 minutes and then in 1.2% sodium hypochlorite solution for 10 minutes. The explants should be rinsed with sterilized water.

The stem or any other part of plants thus sterilized is cut to approximately 1 cm in length using a sterilized scalpel and each piece is transferred with tweezers to a solid medium in a flask or a petri-dish. The plant material is incubated aseptically at around 25° C on the solid medium for several weeks or more and a callus is produced. The callus is subcultured by transferring a small piece to fresh solid medium. After several subsequent transfers, the callus becomes soft and fragile.

Suspension Culture

The growth rate of the suspension cultured cells is generally higher than that of the solid culture. The former is more desirable particularly in production of useful metabolites in a large-scale.

A piece of the callus is transferred to a liquid medium in a vessel such as an Erlenmyer flask and the vessel placed on a rotary or reciprocal shaker.

The culture conditions depend on plant species and other factors, but in general, the cells are cultivated at 100 r.p.m. on a rotary shaker at 25° C; some researchers are fond of much slower, or faster speeds.

By subculturing for several generations, a fine cell suspension culture containing small cell aggregates and single cells is established. The time required to establish the cell suspension culture varies greatly and depends on the tissue of the plant species and the medium composition. The cells in suspension are also used for a large-scale culture with jar-fermentors and tanks.

Scaling-up

For commercialization, it is necessary to progress through several stages increasing the volume at each stage until the requisite bioreactor size is attained.

In theory, it is anticipated that such large scale suspension cultures will be suitable for industrial production of useful plant chemicals such as pharmaceuticals and food additives, in a manner similar to that of microbial fermentation. Generally speaking, the culture period in plant cell cultures is longer than that in microbial cultures, and it is crucial to protect against microbial contamination.

APPROACHES TO INCREASE PRODUCTIVITY

Several products were found to be accumulated in cultured cells at a higher level than those in native plants through optimization of cultural conditions. For example, ginsenosides by *Panax ginseng* (40), rosmarinic acid by *Colleus blumei* (23), shikonin by *Lithospermum erythrorhizon* (41), diosgenin by *Dioscorea* (42), ubiquinone-10 by *Nicotiana tabacum* (43) were accumulated in much higher levels in cultured cells than in the intact plants.

However, many reports have described that yields of desired products were very low or sometimes not detectable in dedifferentiated cells such as callus tissues or suspension cultured cells.

In order to obtain products in concentrations high enough for commercial manufacturing, therefore, many efforts have been made to stimulate or restore biosynthetic activities of cultured cells using various methods. The following are typical approaches that may increase productivity of cultured plant cells.

OPTIMIZATION OF CULTURAL CONDITIONS

Medium

A number of chemical and physical factors affecting cultivation have been tested extensively with various plant cells. These factors include media components, phytohormones (growth regulators), pH, temperature, aeration, agitation, light, etc. This is the most fundamental approach in plant cell culture technology.

Since there are many reports and patents concerning optimization of cultural conditions in order to improve growth rates of cells and/or higher yield of desirable products, it is impossible to give detailed results in this section. Therefore, only a few typical examples will be described.

Researchers tested various well-known basal media for the production of serpentine, an indole alkaloids. The results indicate that the amount of serpentine depends on the composition of the basal medium used.

Among them, Murashige-Skoog's (MS) formulation was recognized to be the most suitable one for the production of this particular alkaloid by Catharanthus roseus suspension. This is of course not always true in other cultures.

Effects of Different Media on Growth and Serpentine Production in Cell Suspension Cultures of *Catharanthus roseus*

*Basal Medium **	*Cell yield g dwt/1*	*Serpentine mg/1*	*Serpentine Content % dwt*
Blaydes	7.6	4.4	0.06
Gamborg - B5; + 2,4-D: 1	4.6	0.5	0.01
mg/1	5.2	0	0
Gamborg + 2,4 D: 2 mg/1	7.6	1.2	0.02
Gamborg + NAA : 1.86 mg/1	5.1	0	0
Gamborg	5.4	6.6	0.12
Heller + IAA:O.175; BA: 1.13	9.3	0	0
mg/1	8.9	10.4	0.12
Linsmaier and Skoog	2.3	2.0	0.09
Murashige and Skoog	5.0	0	0
Nitsch and Nitsch	0.8	0	0
Velicky and Martin			
White			

Sucrose and glucose are the preferred carbon source for plant tissue cultures. The concentration of the carbon source affects cell growth and yield of secondary metabolites in many cases. The maximum yield of rosmarinic acid produced by cell suspension cultures of *Salvia officinalis* was 3.5 g/L when 5% of sucrose was used but it was 0.7 g/L in the medium containing 3% sucrose.

Among a number of other components in the medium phytohormones such as auxins and kinetins have shown the most remarkable effects on growth and productivity of plant metabolites. In general, an increase of auxin levels, such as 2,4-D, in the medium stimulates dedifferentiation of the cells and consequently diminishes the level of secondary metabolites. This is why auxins are commonly added to the medium for callus induction, but they are added at a low concentration or omitted for production of metabolites.

Decendit reported that cytokinins stimulated alkaloid synthesis which was induced by removing auxin from the medium of a cell line of *C. roseus*. However, productions of L-DOPA by *Mucuna pruriens*, ubiquinone-10 by *N. tabacum* and diosgenin by *Diocorea deltoidea* were stimulated by high levels of 2,4-D.

Although kinetin is one of the most popular cytokinins, 4-chloro-2-diphenylurea was reported to stimulate production of an antitumor compound, tripdiolide, by *Triptorygium wilfordii* cell cultures. Gibberellic acid is also effective on plant cell cultures. DiCosmo *et al.* recently reported that the growth of callus of a taxol-producing plant, *Taxus cuspidata,* was significantly promoted by addition of gibberellic acid into the solid medium.

Temperature, pH, Light and Oxygen

The effects of temperature, pH, light and oxygen are all parameters that must be examined in the studies secondary metabolites production. A temperature of 17- 25° C is normally used for induction of callus tissues and growth of cultured cells. But, each plant species may favour a different temperature. Toivonen found that lowering the cultivation temperature increased the total fatty acid content per cell in dry weight.

The medium pH is usually adjusted to between 5 and 6 before autoclaving and extremes of pH are avoided. The optimum pH is determined and controlled using a small scale bioreactor or a jar fermentor with pH control equipment. Present scale-up technology dictates the use of stainless steel tanks for growth of plant cells on an industrial scale, thus in general, eliminating the use of light. However, since there are cases of light-stimulated secondary metabolites production, this factor should be investigated as it could help elucidate regulatory factors. Modification of fermentors with lighting facilities have also been carried out.

The various fermentors have been designed and tested by many researchers. These include modification of impellers or agitators for microbial fermentors, improvement of air-lift fermentors and use of new type reactors such as rotary-drum type fermentors. For hairy root cultures, fermentors equipped with special hangers inside the vessel are being used.

Each plant species has different optimized conditions both for growth of the cells and for production of useful products, so it is necessary to optimize the conditions in each case.

High Cell Density Culture

To increase the productivity of secondary metabolites, high cell density cultures have been investigated. Using a newly designed fermentor and optimized culture medium, *Coptis japonica* cells were grown up to 75 g/L of cell mass. The highest yield of berberine, 3.5 g/L, was produced intracellularly in 55 g/L of the cell mass.

Absorption of Products

Most products are generally accumulated intracellularly by cultured plant cells, but some compounds were reported to be secreted into the media. *Chinchona ledgerina* cells excrete anthraquinones in the liquid medium. Robins *et al.* reported that addition of a resin, XAD-7, into its suspension culture stimulated the production of anthraquinones up to 539 mg/L which was approximately a 15 times increase compared to the medium without resin. The pigments were mostly found to be absorbed by the resin. The yields of ajmalicine and serpentine produced by *C. roseus* were also increased by addition of XAD-7 and the ratio between both alkaloids produced was changed. It is of interest that production of these alkaloids which are known to accumulate inside cells were affected by the presence of resin. A similar approach was conducted by Knoop *et al.* in which addition of active charcoal in the medium stimulated the yield of coniferyl alcohol up to 60-fold in a *Maticaria chamomila* culture.

Becker *et al.* recognized increases of several plant products produced using a continuous extraction process with two-phase organic solvents.

SELECTION OF HIGH-PRODUCING STRAINS

The physiological characteristics of individual plant cells are not always uniform. For example, pigment producing cell aggregates typically consist of producing cells and non-producing cells. In 1976, researchers in Germany obtained cell lines of *Catharanthus roseus* which accumulated higher levels of ajmalicine and serpentine as determined by radioimmunoassay. This is similar to monocolony isolation of bacteria. Following their excellent results, a number of researchers have used cell cloning methods as this is the most promising way of increasing the levels metabolites present. Most of them are related to production of pigments, such as anthocyanins, as visual selection is easy because of the colour.

Typical examples of Cell Cloning Application

Products	*Plants*	*Factors*
Anthocyanins	*Vitis hybrid*	2.3-4
Anthocyanins	*Euphorbia milli*	7
Berberine	*Coptis japonica*	2
Biotin	*Lavendula vera*	9
Ubiquinone-10	*Nicotiana tabacum*	15

Researchers isolated a strain of *Vitis* hybrid using an agar plating feeder method; the culture produced 3.4% (dry wt.) of anthocyanins. A strain of *Euphorbia milli* was also recognized to accumulate about 7 times higher amounts of anthocyanins than that of the parent strain after 24 selections. Statistical and cell-pedigree analysis proved that production of the red pigments was stable.

According to Constabel's investigation with *C. roseus*, anther, leaf, and meristem explants, synthesis and accumulation of alkaloids in cell cultures differ significantly provided the comparison is based on individual alkaloid types. Variation of alkaloid profiles in callus tissue developed from the anther walls and fillaments of *C. roseus* ranged from cell lines with no detectable alkaloids to those with 12 alkaloids representing Corynanthe-, Strychnos-, Aspidosperma-, and Iboga-type alkaloids. Yamada *et al.* repeated cell cloning using cell aggregates of *Coptis japonica,* and obtained a strain which grew faster and produced a higher amount of berberine and cultivated the strain in a 14 L bioreactor. The selected cell line increased growth about 6-fold in 3 weeks and the highest amount of the alkaloid produced was 1.2 g/L of the medium. The strain was very stable, producing a high level of berberine even after 27 generations.

Cultured, green *Lavendula vera* cells grown in the light were found to accumulate a high level of free biotin by Watanabe *et al.*. To select a high-producing cell line, pimelic acid, a precursor of biotin, was used as a selecting agent. The level of biotin accumulated by a selected cell-line was 0.9 μg/L which was 10 times the amount found in the leaves.

Selection of a high ubiquinone-10 producing *Nicotiana tabacum* strain has produced excellent results. A group in the Japan Tobacco Inc. isolated a number of strains producing high levels of ubiquinone-10 from tobacco cell cultures and analysed the contents in the cells by HPLC and by Craven assay. Several strains producing large amounts of ubiquinone-10 in suspension culture were selected and were subjected to further cell cloning. After the 13th recloning, a strain was selected from approximately 4000 cell clones tested giving a ubiquinone-10 level of 5.2 mg per dry weight of cells. When *N. tabacum* BY-2, a parent strain used for the cloning, was isolated as a producer in 1976, the titer for ubiquinone-10 was only 360 μg/g dry weight, therefore the level was increased by more than 14 times by selection. It may be noted that 5.2 mg/g corresponds to 180 times the amount produced by the parent plant.

The selection of high pyrethrin producing tissue cultures derived from *Chrysanthemum cineraliaefolium* and indicated that analytical screening of the tissue lines enabled the selection of a few "high yielding" strains which were derived from high yielding plant selections. A rapid assay method is crucial in the selection of a high yielding cell line. Researchers reported that a procedure using fluorescence assay to select ajmalicine and other major heteroyohimbine alkaloids producing cells of *C. roseus* was of clear advantage even over a radioimmunoassay procedure since almost unlimited numbers of colonies could be screened in this way. However, the cell cloning is especially compatible with selection for high pigment production since selection can be achieved visually, or with the use of simple spectro-photometric analysis.

Cell cloning is undoubtedly a very useful technique to increase the level of secondary metabolites and it should be applied as widely as possible. However, it is not obvious why cultures contain both high- and low-yielding cells. Only a few papers concerned with possible mechanisms have appeared. Bohm indicates that the lack of specific enzyme(s) represents the most important reaction for the inability of plant cell cultures to produce secondary metabolites.

Researchers compared the highest cinnamoyl putrescine producing, p-flurophenylalanine resistant strain TX-4 or *N. tabacum* L. CV Xanthi with a low producing strain for five enzymes of the biosynthetic pathway. As a result, activities of these enzymes, phenylalanine ammonia-lyase, trans-cinnamate-4-hydroxylase, 4-coumarate: CoA ligase, ornithine decarboxylase and arginine decarboxylase were found to be 3 to 10 times higher in TX4 cells.

Protoplasts were also used for the selection of high-shikonin producing cell lines of *L. erythroryzon* and thiophene producing *Tagetes patula* cell lines.

ADDITION OF PRECURSORS AND BIOTRANSFORMATION

Addition of Precursors

Addition to the culture media of appropriate precursors or related compounds sometimes stimulates secondary metabolite production. This approach is advantageous if the precursors are inexpensive. Since Chan and Staba initially examined the production of alkaloids with this approach in the 1960's, many similar experiments have been carried out. For example, amino acids have been added to cell suspension culture media for production of tropane alkaloids, indole alkaloids, and ephedorin and some stimulative effects have been observed.

It is true that some amino acids are precursors of various alkaloids, but generally the biosynthetic steps from amino acids to alkaloids are so complicated that the author doubts whether amino acids added were incorporated into the alkaloids directly in cell culture. Perhaps, they affected not only alkaloid biosynthesis directly as precursors, but also indirectly through other metabolic pathways in the cells.

Phenylalanine is one of the biosynthetic precursors of rosmarinic acid. Addition of this amino acid to *Salvia officialis* suspension cultures stimulated the production of rosmarinic acid and shortened the production time as well. Tabata *et al.* reported that addition of 500 mM tropic acid to the medium of *Scopolia japonica* increased the amount of alkaloids by up to 14 times. The level of an anticancer compound, tripdiolide, produced by *T. wilfordii* cultured cells was increased by addition of 100 μg/L farnesol which is dephosphorylated farnesyl pyrophosphate, and an intermediate in the biosynthesis of terpenoids. Addition of phenylalanine into the agar medium of *Taxus cupsidata* cells to stimulate the biosynthesis of an anticancer compound, taxol.

However, biotransformation using intact cells or immobilized cells is an alternative way of producing a product by adding precursors into the culture media. Scientists reported that *Rauwolfia serpentina* formed a new indole alkaloid, 6-hydroxytaumacline, in significant amounts when the cells were cultivated in the presence of ajmalicine. Arbutin, a skin depigmentation agent, is produced by biotransformation of hydroquinone using *C. roseus* cells. Addition of the precursor into the liquid culture medium of this cell line produced arbutin efficiently.

In order to produce a prodrug, scientists studied the glucosylation of umebelliferone and salicylic acid using *Mallotus japonicus* cells and reported that the latter was converted to its o-glucoside with a yield of 90-95%. The maximum level of the product obtained was 0.9 g/L. The glucoside showed as potent an analgesic activity as salicylic acid, while its effect was more rapid and more long-lived than that of salicylic acid in mice. It is of interest that plant cells are able to form prodrugs having commercial usefulness. Researchers also worked on glucosylation of salicylic acid and its derivatives. They found that cultured *Salix matsudana* cells glucosylated salicylic acid to 2-o-salicylic acid-β-D-glucoside. The cells also converted salicyl alcohol to both salicin (2-o-salicyl alcohol-β-D-glucoside and isosalicylicin

(1-o-salicyl alcohol-β-D-glucoside. However, salicylic aldehyde was converted to β-D-glucosides of salicylic acid and salicyl alcohol instead of helicin.

The conversion of geraniol and nerol to neral and geranial by *Vitis vinifera* cell suspension cultures is also interesting. Using plant cell culture techniques, radioactive labelled compounds can be formed from appropriate substrates as reported by Mangold *et al.*. This is a useful application of the technology because of high value of the product.

Biotransformation

Instead of the addition of a particular compound as a precursor into the culture medium of plant cells, a suitable substrate compound may be biotransformed to a desired product using plant cells. This approach has been extensively applied in the fermentation industry using microorganisms and their enzymes. For example, L-aspartic acid and L-malic acid are being manufactured commercially from fumaric acid, respectively using microorganisms. And various steroids are also produced by microbial biotransformations. Biotransformation of β-methyldigitoxin to β-methyldigoxin using *D. lanata* cells has been extensively investigated by Reinhard and Alfemann in Germany since 1974 because digoxin has a large market as a cardiac glycoside.

About 600-700 mg of β-methyldigoxin per litre was obtained using a 200 L reactor. This process was studied for commercialization by Boehringer Mannheim Co. Allelix Inc. in Canada established processes for production of a very expensive antitumor drug, vinblastine, from catharanthine and vindoline using a biotransformation as well as a simple chemical synthesis. The process is now being developed for commercialization by Mitsui Petrochemical in Japan. Concerning vinblastine-related compounds production, Scientists also reported a biotransformation of catharanthine and vindoline to anhydrovinblastine using horseradish peroxidase and glucose oxidase mediated coupling of vindoline and catharanthine. The author believes that biotransformation processes including addition of substrates into the cultures are one of the most commercially realistic approaches in plant tissue cultures because of economic reasons. However, the availability of inexpensive precursors is a key issue.

MICROBIAL INFECTIONS OF INTACT PLANTS

Microbial infections of intact plants often elicit the synthesis of specific secondary metabolites. The best understood systems are those of fungal pathogens in which case the regulatory molecules have been identified as glucan polymers, glycoproteins and low molecular weight organic acids. Researchers reviewed possible correlations between stress and secondary metabolism in cultured cells. Examples of microbial elicitor induction include psoralen production in parsley diosgenin production in the Mexican yam and many others. A cell line of *Papaver somniferm* that synthesized and accumulated sanguinarine, a quaternary benzophenanthridine alkaloid when exposed to a homogenate of the fungas *Botrytis*. A portion of the sanguinarine was released into the culture medium. Sanguinarine extracted from the intact plants is being used for oral hygienic products. Effects of elicitors on secondary metabolism have been investigated at the enzymatic levels to determine their mode of action.

Researchers added autoclaved culture homogenate of yeast, *Rhodotorula rubra* into the suspension culture of *Ruta graveolens* and found that S-adenosyl-L-methionine:anthranilic acid N-methyltransferase was elicited. A yeast polysaccharide preparation induced L-tyrosine decarboxylase in suspension cultures of *Thalictrum rugosum* and *Eschscholtzia californica*; the enzyme was induced after 5 hours after addition of the elicitor at 30 to 40 μg/g-cell fresh wt.

Researchers also reported a transient increase in rosmarinic acid, a-0-caffeoyl-3,4-dihydroxyphenyllactic acid, content in cultured cells of *L. erythrorhizon* after addition of yeast extract to the suspension cultures: a maximum was reached in 24 hr. When the plant cells were treated with yeast extract on the 6th day of the cultivation, the level of rosmarinic acid increased 2.5 times and the activity of phenylalanine ammonia-lyase in the cells rapidly increased before synthesis of rosmarinic acid. In suspension cultured cells of parsley, *Petroselinum crispum*, Conrath *et al.* found that chitosan elicited a rapid deposition of the 1,3-β-glucan, callose.

Recent developments in phytochemical elicitation have shown that simple inorganic and organic molecules can induce product accumulation. Sodium orthovanadate and vanadyl sulphate induced the accumulation of isoflavone glucosides in *Vigna angularis* cultures and indole alkaloid accumulation in *Catharanthus roseus* cultures, respectively. Other substances found to stimulate alkaloid accumulation in *C. roseus* include sodium chloride, potassium chloride and sorbitol as well as abscisic acid. Processes such as these, employing simple and cheap elicitors have much promise in industrial scale plant cell cultures.

Addition of oxalate to the medium of *Gossypium hirsutum* suspension culture could reduce the amount of *Verticillium dahliae* elicitor to be employed to stimulate metabolite synthesis. Addition of a fungal elicitor often inhibits the growth of plant cells but a combination of the elicitor and oxalate did not reduce the cell mass of the plant, therefore secondary metabolite synthesis was increased up to ten fold.

A combination of phosphate limitation and fungal elicitation synergistically increased production of secondary metabolites. They found that either phosphate limitation or elicitation with a mycelial extract of the fungus, *Rhizoctonia solani* alone results in increased production of the sesquiterpene solavetivone by *Agrobacterium rhizogenes*-transformed hairy root cultures of *Hyoscyamus muticus*. However, when phosphate limitation is coupled with fungal elicitation, the productivity increase is considerably greater than that obtained with either method alone. Although the mechanism by which elicitors increase the productivity of secondary plant metabolites has not been elucidated, their stimulating activity is quite significant if an appropriate elicitor is chosen to stimulate synthesis of a particular product. However, the use of microbial elicitors may not be economical since an elicitor-producing microorganism should be cultivated in a fermentor separately from cultivation of plant cells using another fermentor. The fermentation cost for an elicitor-producing microorganism is not always inexpensive. In this sense, a simple and cheap compound should be employed as an elicitor.

APPLICATION OF IMMOBILIZED PLANT CELLS

Immobilization of plant cells is considered to be of importance in research and development in plant cell cultures, because of the potential benefits that could be provided :

- The extended viability of cells in the stationary (and producing) stage, enabling maintenance of biomass over a prolonged time period;
- Simplified downstream processing (if products are secreted);
- The (putative) promotion of differentiation, linked with enhanced secondary metabolism;
- Higher cell density enabling a reduced bioreactor size, thereby reducing costs and the risk of contamination;
- Reduced shear sensitivity (especially with entrapped cells);
- Promotion of secondary metabolite secretion, in some cases;
- Flow-through reactors can be used enabling greater flow rates;
- Minimization of fluid viscosity increase, which in cell suspension causes mixing and aeration problems.

An immobilization system which could maintain viable cells over an extended period of time and release the bulk of the product into the extracellular medium in a stable form, could dramatically reduce the costs of phytochemicals production in plant cell culture. However, an immobilized system also has the problems described below:

- Immobilization is normally limited to cases where production is decoupled from cell growth;
- The initial biomass must be grown in suspension;
- Secretion of product into the extracellularly medium is imperative;
- Where secretion occurs there may be problems of extracellular degradation of the products;
- When gel entrapment is used, the gel matrix introduces an additional diffusion barrier.

Due to these problems, a system with commercial potential has not yet been developed in plant tissue cultures. However, various immobilization methods have been developed, ie., entrapment, adsorption and covalent coupling.

Some preliminary results have been obtained with immobilized cells. Early work with *C. roseus*, showed that agar, agarose and carageenan were all suitable immobilization matrices suitable for maintenance of cell viability; but alginate was superior in terms of ajmalicine production. The accumulation of serpentine by *C. roseus* and anthraquinones by *Morinda citrifolia* were both enhanced in the immobilized state when compared with freely suspended cells. It should be noted however, that the possibility that alginate acts as an elicitor of secondary metabolism cannot be ruled out. Agar has been shown to stimulate shikonin accumulation in *L. erythrorhizon* cultures. Lambe and Rosevear have successfully immobilized *C. roseus* cells in polyacrylamide with alginate and observed prolonged viability and increased productivity.

Adsorption immobilization has been successfully used with a number of plant species. *Capsicum frutescens* cells immobilized on polyurethane foam produced 50 times as much capsaicin as suspension cells. Similarly, *Solanum nigrum* cells accumulated glycoalkaloids to levels exceeding those found in suspensions. *Datura innoxia* cells accumulated tropane alkaloids with a profile similar to that of the intact plant, whilst in free suspensions productivity was markedly suppressed. In general it appears that mild immobilization either through gel entrapment or surface adsorption enhances productivity and prolongs the viability of cultured cells.

Biotransformation, immobilized cells can also be used as biocatalysts for biotransformations. Such a system compares favourably with the use of freely suspended cells since, in the case of immobilization, the catalyst is theoretically reusable and the product is easily separated from the biomass. The most appropriate example is that of the 12-hydroxylation of β-methyldigitoxin to β-methyldigoxin with alginate-entrapped *Digitalis lanata* cells.

The enzyme activity was maintained by the immobilized cultures for a period of 61 days. Furthermore, the product was located in the extracellular medium. Mild permeabilization of the cells may enable biotransformation rates to be increased. Polyurethane-immobilized *C. frutescens* cells fed capsaicin precursors produced this metabolite at levels of up to 10 times those of non-fed cultures. DiCosmo *et al.* found that glass fibres can be used as a carrier of plant cells to produce useful plant metabolites. *Papaver somniforum* cells were immobilized on fabric of loosely woven polyester fibres arranged in a spiral configuration on stainless steel support frame by Kurz *et al.* to produce sanguinarine, an antibiotic in oral hygiene. The yield was 3.6 mg/g-fw. by immobilized cells and was more than twice as much as by suspension cells.

PLANT PRODUCT SECRETION

Many plant products produced by cell cultures have been reported to be accumulated intracellularly. However, it may be possible to produce much higher level of product if it was secreted into the medium. This is because the product intracellularly accumulated sometimes inhibits its own synthesis by regulation mechanisms such as product inhibition and repression. For many immobilized plant cell systems to work it is essential that a significant amount of product is released into the medium. Two types of immobilization system with *C. roseus i.e.* gel entrapment in polysaccharide beads and in polyacrylamide sheets, have both exhibited alkaloid release by mechanisms that do not appear to be associated with losses in viability. *Capsicum frutescens* cells immobilized on polyurethane released capsaicin entirely into the medium, although other species immobilized by the same method retained the product intracellularly.

To enhance release, permeabilization of cell membranes has been attempted, but with only limited success. Brodelius tested five permeabilizing agents on three different species, and although product release was achieved, cell viability dropped in most cases. The exceptions were DMSO and Triton X-100, applied to *C. roseus* cells. Other attempts to permealize cells have also resulted in non-viable populations and the use of electroporation has also resulted in a viability decrease. The release of betanin by *Beta vulgaris* cells ultrasonicated for 20 to 60 seconds has been reported, with no apparent effect on cell viability. *Chenopodium rubrum* cells, immobilized in alginate beads, secreted the red betacyanin pigment amaranthin into the medium. However, the pigment was subsequently degraded; chitosan and DMSO permitted further product release into the extracellular medium, but this was also accompanied by product degradation. Low concentrations of chitosan (0.01%) and DMSO (5.7%) incubated with the cultures for 96 hr did not appear to affect viability significantly, but a longer incubation period (196 hr) had a deterlerious effect.

The lack of an appropriate means of product release is a serious problem in terms of an industrial approach particularly based on immobilization of plant cells. It is perhaps necessary to examine in vivo physiological mechanisms of release. Thus, some researchers have been investigating the factors involved in vacuolar phytochemical storage. The accumulation of indole alkaloids in *C. roseus* vacuoles has been attributed to an ion-trap mechanism whereby the basic indole alkaloids are trapped in the acidic vacuole due to their positive charge at low pH, preventing diffusion across the tonoplast. This mechanism has also been demonstrated for quinoline alkaloid accumulation in *Cinchona* species.

Active uptake mechanisms have also been reported for indole alkaloids in *C. roseus* vacuoles and isoquinoline alkaloids in *Fumaria capreolata* L. The physiological significance of these two possible mechanisms is not yet clear, since there is obviously strong evidence for both. In terms of product release, it is pertinent to note that in cell cultures, an efflux of alkaloids was observed under certain conditions, indicating an equilibrium between the intracellular and extracellular compartments that could be perturbed by medium acidification with subsequent product release. The release of serpentine by *C. roseus* cells was observed when the cells were filtered and resuspended in fresh or conditioned medium and it was suggested that temporary membrane uncoupling was responsible. Although most plant cell culture products were shown to be accumulated intracellularly, Shuler *et al.* recently reported that almost all of taxol produced by *Taxus brevifolia* cell cultures was detected in the culture filtrate. This is an exceptional case in plant tissue culture research.

MUTAGENESIS IN FERMENTATION INDUSTRY

In the fermentation industry, induction of genetic mutant strains of microorganisms is ubiquitous, and auxotrophic and/or regulatory mutants are used extensively to produce a variety of products including amino acids, nucleotides, antibiotics, etc. However, mutagenesis has limited applicability to plant cell cultures, because of their diploid genetic make-up: the chance of obtaining a double mutation in a target gene is less than 1 in 10^6. Although, in principle, haploid plants can be produced from anther cultures; in practice haploid cell cultures tend to revert to the diploid state. This makes the chance of isolating over-producing cells from mutagen treatment of haploid cells very low. Furthermore, biosynthetic pathways of many secondary metabolites and their regulation mechanisms in higher plants are not always understood precisely, therefore, it is also difficult to know what kind of mutants should be induced in order to increase product synthesis.

However, Berlin induced p-fluorophenylalanine resistant cell lines of tobacco cell cultures and found that five lines of *N. tabacum* and five lines of *N. glauca* out of 31 resistant cell lines accumulated higher levels of phenolics. He and his colleagues also reported that a resistant strain of *N. tabacum* produced 6 to 10 times higher levels of cinnamoyl putrescine than that of the parent strain. The comparison of enzyme activities involved in the biosynthesis of cinnamoyl putrescines in a parent strain, TX1 and a resistant strain, TX4. Enzyme activities in the p-fluorophenylalanine resistant strain were much higher than those of the parent. Berlin *et al.* also found that a parent strain of *C. roseus* produced catharanthine only in the production medium but its tryptophan analog resistant mutant accumulated the same alkaloid even in the growth medium. Among several types of analogues tested, 4-fluorotryptophan was found to be the most efficient of them.

Increase of metabolite levels using regulatory mutants is theoretically possible and selection of suitable analogues for this purpose could be an important factor in order to produce a variety of products.

Several research groups have used mutagens such as N-methyl-N'-nitro-N-nitrosoguanidine, ethylmethane sulfonate, N-ethyl-N-nitrosourea or X-rays to induce high yielding strains.

In China, a fine callus strain of *Anisodus acutangulus* was derived through irradiation with 4000 R of X-ray, and the level of scopolamine in the cells was 0.177 mg/g d.wt., which was about 30% higher than of the parent. The productivity was stable. Deus treated *C. roseus* with X-rays and obtained a cell line having a high producing activity of serpentine whose level was 2%.

A cell line of *Lavendula vera* producing a high level of free biotin was obtained by gamma ray irradiation for 1 hr. with ^{60}Co (dose 10 KR h) by Watanabe *et al.*. The line was found to contain 7 times the amount, 0.425 μg/g-fresh wt., of free biotin compared with the original unselected cells, 0.061 μg/g fresh wt., and 4.5 times that found in the leaves. In spite of the difficulty of obtaining auxotrophic mutants in plant cells, several groups have been actively working with this approach using haploid cells or protoplasts although their aim is not always for plant metabolite production.

Induction of a mutant having altered permeability could also be important, because plant cells generally accumulate their metabolites intracellularly, which is disadvantageous in commercial production because the amount of compounds produced is usually low.

If the cells excreted products in large amounts, the product cost would be reduced. According to Berlin's results, *Thuja occidentalis* excreted monoterpenoids, but the levels in the medium were only 5% of those in the mother plant.

The same group reported that *Macleya microcarpa* cells excreted nearly all the alkaloids detectable in the culture flask. researchers cultivated *Tinospora rumphii* cells in 14 ml medium and found 0.57 (5.3% in dry weight cells) of isoquinoline alkaloids in the cells and 0.5 mg in the culture filtrate after 7 days cultivation.

By replacement of the medium with fresh medium after 3 days of cultivation, 0.50 mg of the alkaloids in the cells, and 1.02 mg in the filtrate were accumulated. It seems then that the products must be excreted to some extent. Unfortunately, the secretion mechanisms for secondary products in higher plant cells have not yet been elucidated and extensive fundamental studies are required before meaningful manipulation can take place.

MORPHOLOGICAL DIFFERENTIATION AND ROOT CULTURE

Organ Culture

It is desirable to use morphologically undifferentiated cells for the production of useful metabolites in ways similar to microorganisms and there are many examples which show high productive ability of such cells compared with intact plants as already described in this review. In fact, the author has a callus of *Phytolacca americana* which was induced from a stem tissue more than 10 years ago. This morphologically undifferentiated cells still produce a high level of an alkaloid, betanine. However, a putative link between differentiation and secondary metabolite accumulation has been proposed by many researchers in this field. Wienmann discussed that a close correlation existed between the expression of secondary metabolism and morphological and cytological differentiation, but he concluded that it is not yet clear to what extent secondary metabolism depends on the development of specific structures, it is unknown whether these two processes are genetically and/or physiologically linked.

The development of a certain level of differentiation is considered to be important in the successful production of phytochemicals by cell cultures. There are many examples in the literature demonstrating a relationship between differentiation and secondary metabolic accumulation. Hiraoka and Tabata successively transferred the callus of *Datura meteloides* from a medium with auxins to one without and then cultivated continuously.

Relationship between Productivity of Alkaloids and Differentiations

Plants	*Alkaloid concentration (% dry wt.)*
Callus	1×10^{-2}
Shoots-forming callus	1.5×10^{-2}
Growing shoots	2×10^{-2}
Roots-forming shoots	3×10^{-2}
Leaf of young plant	1×10^{-1}
Leaf of matured plant	1×10^{-1}

In *Digitalis purpurea* cultures, researchers showed stimulation of digitalis cardenolides production by organ redifferentiation in callus tissues. A similar phenomena was also found in rotenone formation using *Derris elliptica* and morphinane alkaloid production using *Papaver somniferum*. Furuya *et al.* investigated the correlation between the stage of morphological differentiation and producing ability of the alkaloids using *P. somniferumi*, and found a green callus which differentiates epidermis or vascular bundles produced the alkaloids. A limited degree of tissue differentiation occurred and the cell contained codeine as a main alkaloid while the level of morphine increase as differentiation progressed.

Root cultures derived from suspension cultured cells of *P. bracteatum* were shown to produce thebaine in 0.03% yield. They also reported that axenic callus and shoot cultures of

Pyrethrum cinerarifolium had an ability to produce pyrethrin. They isolated a few high yielding strains which were derived from high yielding plant selections. One isolate accumulated 11.3 mg total pyrethrins per 100 g dry weight but it subsequently differentiated into a shoot culture following the first analysis. Therefore, researchers concluded that differentiated culture tended to produce more pyrethrins than did callus cultures. Using an established shoot culture derived from the disc floret of the plant, 341.8 mg of pyrethrins per 100 g wt., were obtained.

The relationship between differentiation and anthocyanin production using *Daucus carota* cells. The cells were fractionated by Ficoll density gradient centrifugation. In the density fraction (>14% of Ficoll) somatic embryos were formed in a medium containing 10^{-7} M zeatin but anthocyanin was scarcely produced. On the other hand, the cells in the lower density fraction (>12% of Ficoll) synthesized anthocyanin in the same medium but formed few embryos. 40 to 50% of the total cells in the higher cell fraction synthesized anthocyanin at a maximum.

The use of organs as opposed to cells or cell aggregates might necessitate an adaptation of cultured scale-up technologies, but in general these are not considered to be insurmountable. Indeed, root cultures of *Panax ginseng* have successfully been grown up to a volume of 20 KL and high levels of ginsenosides were obtained. A semi-continuous production system using differentiated cultures has been suggested by Fuller, in which a series of vats with a 10% aliquot being transferred to the next whilst still in the dividing stage, with the remainder being left to grow and accumulate product.

Hairy Root Culture

An alternative possibility is to induce biochemical differentiation, but suppress morphological differentiation. This would be difficult with an initially heterogenous population and the cells would have to be first selected for homogeneity in shape and metabolism. In fact, using a range of species, selection of regular green aggregates with a spherical shape and with cells of a regular morphology has been achieved. Such aggregates were found to enable high flow rates and easy medium removal, superior to those obtained with more dispersed cultures.

Two reports are worth noting with respect to differentiated cell growth and phytochemical production. It has been observed that the insertion of a very fine platinum or titanium wire into a disorganized callus of *Helianthus tuberousus* brings about morphological differentiation, whereas control, untreated tissue remained in an undifferentiated state. Should this phenomenon be reproducible in other species it might well serve as a well-defined means of controlling differentiation and possibly secondary metabolism. It was suggested that a charge transfer mechanism was responsible for these observations.

A second discovery (possibly acting by a similar mechanism) has shown that electric currents (1-2 μA) bring about shoot regeneration in callus culture at a rate five times greater than in controls. This has been patented as a process for the stimulation of growth and differentiation of plant tissue and for increasing the accumulation of secondary metabolites. The use of *Agrobacterium rhizogenes* has been receiving attention recently in secondary metabolism research. It inserts the Ri plasmid into wounded tissue, causing the growth of very fine adventitious roots, so-called "hairy-roots". These roots can be cultured in hormone-free medium and there are several examples of enhanced accumulation of secondary products, relative to non-transformed tissue.

Flores in the U.S. is a leading scientist in hairy root culture studies, and reported in 1987 that all hairy root clones of *Hyoscyamus* plants grew faster than ordinary root cultures and produced the similar level of tropane alkaloids to that accumulated in the intact plants. Scientists have shown that 17 day-old cultured hairy roots of *Beta vulgaris* had twice as much betacyanin and three times as much betaxanthin as seedling roots. On a mg/g dry wt. basis, the concentrations of these betalains were equal to or greater than those reported for storage roots.

The hairy root cultures of *Lupinus polyphyllus* and *L. hartweigii* produced higher amounts of isoflavine glucosides than those of hormone-dependent cells. They also found that hairy root cultures of *Peganum harmala* synthesized higher levels of β-carboline glucoid, ruine and serotonin. *Valeriana officinalis* var. *sambucifolia* hairy roots produced 44.3 mg/g-cells d.w. of valepotriates having spasmolytic and sedative activities. The productivity was 0.9 mg/g/day and the concentration was approximately 4 times higher than that of normal roots. Eilert and his colleague transformed *Ruta gaveolens* leaflets using *A. rhizogenes* and obtained the hairy root tissue. The tissue produced psoralen, isopimpirellin (methyoxylated furanocoumarins), xanthotoxin, bergapten, dictamunine, α-fagarine, kokusaginine, edulinine and hydroxyrutacridone epoxide. The concentration of sucrose in the medium affected the levels of these secondary metabolites.

Researchers in U.K. has been employing hairy root culture systems for production of various chemicals. The levels of nicotine in *Nicotiana rustica* hairy roots and of betanine in *Beta vulgaris* were shown by his group to be at comparable or slightly higher than their intact plants. They also regenerated hairy roots from protoplasts of *N. rustica* hairy root tissues. Hairy root cultures of *Datura stramonium* and related *Datura* species were reported by Rhodes *et al.* to produce hyoscyamine as the major tropane alkaloid and small amounts of other tropanes including atropine and hyoscine (scopolamine). To cultivate hairy roots in large-scale fermentors. At the start of the fermentation process, the fermentation vessel is inoculated with suitable small lengths of hairy roots which then grow to substantially fill the vessel. It has been found to be highly advantageous if the lengths of roots which form the inoculant are distributed throughout the vessel. To achieve this, a space-filling lattice of inoculation points is provided in the fermentation vessel. The inoculating lengths are suspended in a suitable medium which is then passed into the vessel. The inoculant lengths lodge at the inoculation points and thereafter grow in a conventional fashion.

Recently, scientists compared hairy root cultures with suspension cultures in production of isoflavonoids by *Lupinus* species and that of harmane alkaloid and serotonin by *Peganum* species, and concluded the hairy root cultures are the superior to suspension cultures. The biotechnological application of hairy root cultures is promising for a number of reasons: (1) stable, high level production; (2) fast auxin-independent growth; and, (3) the suitability for adaptation to fermentor systems. It is, therefore one of the most feasible techniques from an industrial point of view.

MICRO-PROPAGATION OF TISSUE CULTURE PLANTS

Micro propagation is the practice of rapidly multiplying stock plant material to produce a large number of progeny plants, using modern plant tissue culture methods. Micro propagation is used to multiply novel plants, such as those that have been genetically modified or bred through conventional plant breeding methods. It is also used to provide a sufficient number of plantlets for planting from a stock plant which does not produce seeds, or does not respond well to vegetative reproduction.

Establishment

Micro propagation begins with the selection of plant material to be propagated. Clean stock materials that are free of viruses and fungi are important in the production of the healthiest plants. Once the plant material is chosen for culture, the collection of explants(s) begins and is dependent on the type of tissue to be used; including stem tips, anthers, petals, pollen and others plant tissues. The explants material is then surface sterilized, usually in multiple courses of bleach and alcohol washes and finally rinsed in sterilized water. This small portion of plant tissue, sometimes only a single cell, is placed on a growth medium, typically containing sucrose as an energy source and one or more plant growth regulators (plant hormones). Usually the medium is thickened with agar to create a gel which supports the explants during growth. Some plants are easily grown on simple media but others require more complicated media for successful growth; The plant tissue grows and differentiates into new tissues depending on the medium. For example, media containing cytokines are used to create branched shoots from plant buds. and it happens in a vegetative form.

Multiplication

Multiplication is the taking of tissue samples produced during the first stage and increasing their number. Following the successful introduction and growth of plant tissue, the establishment stage is followed by multiplication. Through repeated cycles of this process, a single explants sample may be increased from one to hundreds or thousands of plants. Depending on the type of tissue grown, multiplication can involve different methods and media. If the plant material grown is callus tissue, it can be placed in a blender and cut into smaller pieces and recultured on the same type of culture medium to grow more callus tissue. If the tissue is grown as small plants called plantlets, hormones are often added that cause the plantlets to produce many small offshoots that can be removed and recultured, these are all 5 types.

Transfer from Culture

In the final stage of plant micro propagation, the plantlets are removed from the plant media and transferred to soil or (more commonly) potting compost for continued growth by conventional methods. This stage is often combined with the "pretransplant" stage.

Pretransplant

This stage involves treating the plantlets/shoots produced to encourage root growth and "hardening." It is performed in vitro, or in a sterile "test tube" environment.

"Hardening" refers to the preparation of the plants for a natural growth environment. Until this stage, the plantlets have been grown in "ideal" conditions, designed to encourage rapid growth. Due to lack of necessity, the plants are likely to be highly susceptible to disease and often do not have fully functional dermal coverings and will be inefficient in their use of water and energy.

In vitro conditions are high in humidity and plants grown under these conditions do not form a working cuticle and stomata that keep the plant from drying out, when taken out of culture the plantlets need time to adjust to more natural environmental conditions.

Hardening typically involves slowly weaning the plantlets from a high-humidity; low light, warm environment to what would be considered a normal growth environment for the species in question. This is done by moving the plants to a location high in humidity.

Advantages

Micro propagation has a number of advantages over traditional plant propagation techniques: The main advantage of micro propagation is the production of many plants that are clones of each other.

- Micro propagation can be used to produce disease-free plants.
- Micro propagation produces rooted plantlets ready for growth, saving time for the grower when seeds or cuttings are slow to establish or grow.
- It can have an extraordinarily high fecundity rate, producing thousands of prop gules while conventional techniques might only produce a fraction of this a number.
- It is the only viable method of regenerating genetically modified cells or cells after protoplast fusion.
- It is useful in multiplying plants which produce seeds in uneconomical amounts, or when plants are sterile and do not produce viable seeds or when seed can't be stored.
- Micro propagation often produces more robust plants, leading to accelerated growth compared to similar plants produced by conventional methods - like seeds or cuttings.

- Some plants with very small seeds, including most orchids, are most reliably grown from seed in sterile culture.
- A greater number of plants can be produced per square meter and the prop gules can be stored longer and in a smaller area.

Disadvantages

Micro propagation is not always the perfect means of multiplying plants. Conditions that limit its use include:

- It is very expensive, and can have a labour cost of more than 70%.
- A monoculture is produced after micro propagation, leading to a lack of overall disease resilience, as all progeny plants may be vulnerable to the same infections.
- Mechanization of the process could reduce labour costs, but has proven difficult to achieve, despite active attempts to develop technological solutions.

3

Plant Cell Culture

The complexity of higher plants has inevitably led workers, concerned with investigating particular aspects of plant physiology, to the use of systems which are of reduced complexity. Hence, the early and continuing use by plant physiologists of isolated plant organs (*e.g.* seedling roots, leaves), complex tissue systems (*e.g.* discs cut from leaves and storage organs) organ segments (*e.g.* segments of coleoptiles and hypocotyls) and isolated cell organelles. However, isolated organs and organ fragments are still systems of very considerable complexity and they are, from the beginning, systems of declining viability and favourable sites for colonization by microorganisms.

The concept that the aseptic *culture* of isolated organs, tissues and cells would 'give some interesting insight into the properties and potentialities which the cell as an elementary organism possesses' and 'would provide information about the inter-relationships and complementary influences to which cells within the multicellular whole organism are exposed' was formulated as early as 1902 by Haberlandt. Then, after a lapse of more than 30 years, White (1934) described successful root cultures initiated from the root tips of tomato seedlings, and White (1939) and Gautheret (1939) demonstrated that the parenchymatous wound callus which frequently forms at the exposed surfaces of organ segments could be removed and grown indefinitely as a relatively undifferentiated tissue (callus) culture. From this period there has been rapid progress in organ and tissue culture. Root cultures have been developed from many species. Cultures of stem apices (meristem culture) and of leaf, flower and fruit primordia have been successfully established. These organ cultures as experimental systems differ from isolated organs in two important respects; they are sterile (free from microorganism contamination) and are handled aseptically, and they are sytems where unimpaired viability is evidenced by growth involving both cell division and cell expansion. Such cultures have contributed to our knowledge of the specific nutritional and hormonal requirements essential for the growth and development of the separate organs of the whole plant and of their specific physiology and biosynthetic activities. Callus cultures have also now been established from a very wide range of species and have been used in studies on the initiation of root and shoot primordia, on cytodifferentiation, on the induction of division in quiescent tissue cells, on the nature of plant tumour cells and on the synthesis of a diversity of secondary plant products.

Researcher reported that if fragments of callus cultures of *Tagetes erecta* or *Nicotiana tabacum* were transferred to liquid medium and agitated on a reciprocal shaker, then the callus fragments broke up to give a suspension of single cells and small aggregates of cells and that this suspension contained actively dividing cells and hence could be propagated by serial subculture. Such liquid cell suspension cultures have now been obtained from calluses of a number of species and this chapter will outline the development of more sophisticated techniques for their culture and assess their value for studies on the control of growth, metabolism and differentiation in higher plant cells.

HISTORY OF PLANT CELL, TISSUE AND ORGAN CULTURES

Historically, Henri-Louis Duhamel du Monceau (1756) pioneered the experiments on wound healing in plants through spontaneous callus (unorganised mass of cells) formation on decorticated region of elm plants. But the science of cell and tissue culture could be advanced after propounding the cell theory by Schleiden and Schwann (1839). Trecul (1853) observed callus formation in a number of plants. Vochting (1878) suggested the presence of polarity as a key feature that guide the development of plant fragments. He observed that the upper portion of a piece of a stem always produced buds and the basal region produced callus or roots. In 1902, a German Botanist Gottlieb Haberlandt developed the concept of culture of isolated cells of Tradescantia in artificial condition. Though his experiment failed to induce the cells to divide.

He did not succeed because by that time even auxin was not discovered. But he lent a foundation to plant physiology. He described the cultivation of mesophyll cells of Lamium purpureum and Eichhornia crassipes, epidermal cells of Ornithogalum and hair cells of Pumonaria. Cell survived for 3-4 weeks. Due to this endeavour, Hamberlandt is regarded as the father of tissue culture. Basically, he suggested the concept of totipotency.

From 1902 to 1930 attempts were made for organ culture. Scientist isolated embryos of some crucifers and successfully grew on mineral salts and sugar solutions. Scientist successfully regenerated a bulky callus, buds, roots from a poplar tress on the surface of medium containing IAA which proliferated cell division. P.R. Gautheret at the University of Sorbonne, Paris (France) tried for several years to cultivate the isolated cells and root tips but failed. In 1939, he reported first the propagation of carrot by using indole acetic acid.

Then the possibility for cultivation of plant tissues for unlimited period was announced simultaneously by researchers, an American scientist, reported first time the successful continuous cultures of tomato root tips in liquid medium and in vitro cultivation of viruses on excised roots.

During 1940 to 1970, suitable nutrient media were developed for culture of plant cells, tissue, protoplasts, anthers, roots tips and embryos. In vitro morphogenesis (*i.e.* regeneration of complete plant from cultured tissue) of plants was always successfully done. In 1941, researchers and co-workers used coconut milk (embryo sac fluid) for embryo development and callus formation in Datura.

The concept of cellular totipotency was further advanced in subsequent years by various researchers. In 1958, scientists obtained regeneration in callus tissue culture of Duccus carrota. They took out small pieces of phloem of carrot roots and kept in liquid medium containing coconut water. The medium was shaken so that the cluster of cells could not be formed. Beside, some of cells multiplied arid formed 'rooting clumps'.

When these were transferred onto a semisolid medium containing similar nutrients, they developed into the new plantlets. When these plantlets were transferred to pots, they developed into a new plant. The foundation of commercial plant tissue culture was laid in 1960 with the discovery, of G.M. Morel for a million fold increase in clonal multiplication of an orchid, Cymbidium.

In 1959, discovery of kinetin promoted and co-workers and demonstration of induction of regeneration of shoots in tobacco callus paved the way for multiplication of plant by tissue culture. In 1960s, E. Cooking for the first time developed a method for isolation of protoplasts in large quantities using the fungal enzyme obtained from *Myrothecieum* sp.

In India, work on tissue culture was started during mid 1950s at the Department of Botany (University of Delhi) by Panchanan Maheshwari who is regarded as father of embryology in India. Different tissue culture methodologies were involved for morphogenic studies involving ovary, embryo, endosperm, ovules, etc. At the University of Delhi, for the first time developed the haploid through anther and pollen cultures.

Discovery of haploid production was a landmark in the development of plant tissue culture. In 1952, the Pfizer Inc., New York (U.S.A) got the US Patent and started producing industrially the secondary metabolites of plants. The first commercial production of a natural product shikonin by cell suspension culture was obtained.

The advancements made in cell and tissue culture technology are due to the development in composition of culture media. Based on the success of plant cell culture techniques many recent advances have been done in the area of micropropagation, production of secondary metabolites and pathogen-free plants, genetic manipulation (*e.g. in vitro* pollination, somatic hybridation/cybridisation, induction of haploid, genetic transformation and production of transgenic plants).

The ability of tot potency of plant tissues can be exploited for:

- Rapid propagation of important plants,
- Propagation of rare and endangered plants in which plants fail to grow from seeds,
- Rapid propagation of new varieties of crop plants.
- Production of virus-free crop plants, and
- Induction and selection of mutants.

During 1980, recombinant DNA technology made possible to transform artificially cultured plant cells by introducing foreign genes. The gene revolution has made the second green revolution. Now it is possible to develop plants of desired genetic characters.

METABOLISM OF PLANT CELLS IN BATCH CULTURE

Plant cells in batch culture, *i.e.* cultures in a fixed volume of culture medium, increase in biomass by cell division and cell growth until a factor in the culture environment becomes limiting and sends them into a stationary phase. When such stationary phase cells are subcultured they pass in succession through a lag phase, a short-lived period of exponential growth, a period of declining relative growth rate and then again enter stationary phase. Traditionally such cultures are initiated by an inoculum establishing a relatively high initial cell density and only accomplish a very limited number of divisions before entering stationary phase. For example cell cultures of sycamore (*Acer pseudoplatanus*) initiated at *ca.* 2×10^5 cells ml^{-1} will reach a final cell density of *ca.* 3×10^6 cells ml^{-1} corresponding to 4 successive doublings of the initial population.

The degree of cellular aggregation in these cell cultures depends upon the species of cell, or cell line within a species, and the culture conditions, but always shows a basically similar pattern of change during the growth cycle of a batch culture. The culture at stationary phase contains the highest proportion of free cells and mean cell volume is at its maximum value. When subcultured to new medium, the cells first embark upon a massive synthesis of new cytoplasm and associated organelles and then begin to divide. For a short time cell division proceeds at a specific growth rate (μ) which is constant and maximal (μ_{max}) for that culture environment. During this phase mean cell volume declines sharply and the proportion of cells in aggregates rises. Then the specific growth rate begins to decline (slowly at first and later at an ever increasing rate) mean cell volume increases and, associated with this cell expansion, the aggregates break up and release free cells. Associated with these growth and structural changes are changes in physiological activity. Measurements, on a per cell basis, of respiration, of the levels of individual cell constituents and of the activities of individual enzymes show that peaks of activity occur. These may be quite sharp and are not coincidental. Different metabolic patterns emerge and decline during the progress of batch culture. Thus RNA synthesis is initiated prior to cell division, proceeds for a time at a greater rate than cell number increase and then ceases whilst cell division is still. Free nucleotides (mainly UDP-glucose and ATP in sycamore cells) are synthesized rapidly during lag phase, presumably an essential preparation for subsequent synthesis of cell-wall polysaccharides and as an energy source for the endergonic processes of cell division, but their net synthesis ceases very shortly after the onset of division.

Similar transient high activity in carbohydrate oxidation by the pentose phosphate pathway during lag phase has been interpreted as providing the necessary NADPH for the massive biosynthesis achieved during the lag phase of the growth cycle. By contrast, the very sharp peak in ethylene production in sycamore cell cultures occurs late in the cell division phase when the cells are beginning to increase in mean cell volume and may be responsible for initiating aggregate breakdown.

An essentially similar pattern of ethylene production has been reported for cell cultures of *Rosa* spp., *Glycine max, Triticum monococcum, Melilotus alba, Haplopappus gracilis* and *Ruta graveolens*.

Large changes in the activity of phenylalanine ammonia-lyase (PAL) and in *p*-coumarate: CoA ligase occur prior to stationary phase in cultures of *Glycine max*. A similar peak of PAL activity has been reported in cell cultures of *Rosa* sp.. These changes coincide with maximum production of total phenols by the cultures. Other secondary products are produced by cell cultures, the time of maximum synthesis being restricted to a phase in the growth cycle and often being markedly influenced in its intensity by the plant growth hormone composition of the culture medium. Thus during the progress of batch culture the cells pass through a series of contrasted physiological states which encompass cells becoming meristematic, cells expressing high meristematic activity, cells undergoing expansion and becoming either metabolically quiescent or in which certain restricted metabolic pathways are emphasized.

Are these large changes in cellular structure and metabolic activity observed in batch-propagated cell cultures examples of cellular differentiation? This important question cannot at present be satisfactorily answered. Certainly cultured cells do not correspond closely, either structurally or physiologically, with particular tissue cells of the plant body. To reproduce in culture the complete pattern of differentiation of selected specialized tissue cells is thus an objective not yet realized. Nevertheless the study of the origin in culture of particular physiological states and their cytological basis *may* advance our understanding of the molecular basis of cytodifferentiation in plants.

A recent book on cytodifferentiation in animal cells advances the widely accepted concept that the changes involved are consequent upon the activation of different sets of genes in different cell types and that this activation is expressed in terms of the synthesis of enzymes and other cellular proteins. Further, the differentiation process is regarded as a relatively permanent and irreversible change. In support of this it is possible to quote studies such as those of Cahn and Cahn (1966) on the culture of retina cells; such cells continue to produce the characteristic pigment granules during prolonged culture under conditions conducive to active cell division whereas *in vivo* such cells are non-dividing. If under certain secondary conditions of culture pigment granules were lost, nevertheless when the cells were returned to the primary conditions of culture the pigmentation returned. To distinguish more minor and readily reversible changes in physiology from cytodifferentiation the former are described as modulations and are considered to reflect the operation of allosteric and other 'fine' processes of metabolic regulation. However, scientist concedes that 'it is not at all easy to draw a distinction between those enzymes which are fundamental to differentiation and those which represent very short-term modulations in the activity of cells' and in considering cytodifferentiation in liver cells states that 'differentiation and modulation do not represent distinct processes but are merely the extreme ends of a spectrum of changes that can occur'.

Although from a number of plant species, cell cultures can be readily initiated from different organs (roots, stems, leaf petiole or lamina, cotyledons etc.) or from different living tissues within an organ (parenchymatous cells of pith, cortex, or mesophyll, cambial and other meristematic cells, immature vascular cells etc.) there is no very convincing evidence that they retain, in culture, characteristics of their *in vivo* origin although, they may not have undergone, during culture induction, the required degree of dedifferentiation necessary to express their totipotency (*i.e.* the capacity to generate a new plant in the way normally achieved from the fertilized egg). Such observations suggest that cytodifferentiation in higher plants, provided it has not proceeded to the point where cell death is inevitable, is a more readily reversible process than in the cells of higher animals.

Hence the readily reversible physiological states observed in plant cell cultures may be basically identical with the states involved in normal cytodifferentiation. Further, it raises the possibility that cytodifferentiation does not depend on the transcriptional activity of different sets of genes for each kind of tissue cell but that the 'specialized' physiology of such cells may represent the influence of cytoplasmic factors (plant hormones?) on the stability and transport of RNA species and other aspects of the translational steps in gene expression. It may be possible to examine such hypotheses experimentally with plant cell cultures.

STEADY STATES OF GROWTH

The short period of exponential growth observed in batch cultures. However, even during this phase of the growth cycle, the cells do not achieve a steady state (a state of balanced growth); cell division is uncoupled from increase in cell dry weight and protein content so that the cells are changing in size and composition despite the constancy of the double time of the culture. Such observations raised the question of whether balanced growth could be achieved in plant cell cultures if a constant culture environment could be established by developing open continuous culture systems (systems in which inflow of fresh medium is balanced by outflow of an equal volume of culture). Scientists (1971) have developed such a system providing conditions of aeration and agitation appropriate to plant cell cultures, capable of long-term aseptic operation and functional either as a chemostat or as a turbidostat.

CHEMOSTAT CULTURES SYSTEM

Subsequent work with this system operated as a chemostat (where equilibrium is established at a fixed rate of imput of a growth-limiting nutrient) has shown that long-term steady states of growth can be achieved with plant cell cultures and that such cultures conform to the chemostat theory developed from work with microorganisms.

In a chemostat, the relationship between cell density, x (cells per unit volume of culture), dilution rate, D (volume of new medium added per unit time expressed as a fraction of the total culture volume), specific growth rate, μ (increase in biomass per unit biomass per unit time) and time is given by the equation

$$Dx/dt = \mu x - Dx$$

When equilibrium is reached and a steady state established $dx/dt = 0$, $\mu = D$ and x has a value characteristic of the dilution rate. Further, the nutritive environment remains constant, each nutrient achieving an equilibrium concentration which is related to its input concentration and the rate of its consumption by the culture. The equilibrium achieved in a chemostat culture results from one particular nutrient (depending upon the composition of the culture medium) becoming the limiting nutrient and determining the specific growth rate (μ) of the cells.

The nature of these steady states can be illustrated from work involving sycamore cell cultures growing in a synthetic medium in which the supply of nitrogen is the limiting factor. Data for one such steady state ($D = 0.194$ day^{-1}).

This shows that the cells are in a balanced state of growth and metabolism (as illustrated by the values for cell number, packed cell volume, cell dry weight, protein, DNA and RNA, and oxygen demand) and that the nutrient medium within the culture vessel is constant in composition (as illustrated by constancy of culture pH and the levels of glucose, phosphate and nitrate).

Such steady state cells also display constant levels of metabolites and constant levels of activity of individual enzymes.

Such chemostat cultures can be operated from very low growth rates (*i.e.* low dilution rates) to growth rates approaching the maximum growth rate (μ_{max}) for the culture medium chosen, provided dilution rate is such that the cells can still achieve a matching growth rate. Of course if dilution rate is further increased, cell density does not stabilize and the culture suffers wash-out. Cells in balanced growth but highly contrasted in growth rate (and hence in cytology and metabolism) can therefore be obtained by chemostat culture.

The range of change in certain cell parameters in sycamore cell cultures at different dilution rates (and hence specific growth rates) over the range D = 0.06–0.236 day^{-1} (corresponding to double times over the range 280–70 hr). What this means is that it is possible to stabilize at will, by fixing dilution rate at an appropriate level, the individual physiological states which have only a transient existence in batch culture. Work with chemostat cultures has shown that the same cell population can be taken through a series of steady states and then if the dilution rate is returned to that of an earlier steady state the cells again achieve not only the new predictable growth rate but also the physiological activities earlier recorded as characteristic.

Such experiments demonstate the full reversibility of the cytological and physiological changes invoked. Interest will now focus on detailed studies of the kinetics of the transition between steady states in terms of enzyme activities and metabolite levels.

Preliminary studies along these lines have already shown that during these transitions there are pronounced oscillations in enzyme activity levels (characteristic for each enzyme monitored) which gradually decline in amplitude as the new steady state is established. How far this behaviour is to be explained in terms of changes in rates of enzyme synthesis and degradation has yet to be determined. Clearly study of these transitions will yield entirely new data on metabolic regulation in higher plant cells; whether it will yield the key to expose the changes underlying cytodifferentiation is less certain.

CONSTANCY OF TURBIDOSTAT CULTURES

The constancy of culture opacity in the steady state has formed the basis for a second form of continuous culture—the turbidostat system (a continuous system in which inflow of new medium occurs in response to an increase in the opacity-decrease in the light transmission of the culture). The turbidostat culture system developed for work with sycamore cell cultures. Here, each time the population density exceeds a pre-selected value as determined by the optical density continuously monitored by the photocell, an electronically operated valve opens to admit a pulse of new medium.

This reduces the optical density of the culture and the valve closes. These imputs of new medium are balanced by periodic harvesting of small volumes of culture in response to an electronically controlled level detector which controls the output valve.

The effect is to produce a culture of constant volume and constant population density growing at a constant rate. Whereas in the chemostat growth rate must always be below μ_{max} (the culture growth being limited by the supply of a chosen nutrient) here in the turbidostat growth can safely proceed under non-limiting nutrient conditions and one can study the effect of physical factors (*e.g.* temperature, light regime, CO_2 tension) and growth regulators, in particular plant growth hormones, on growth rate, and by appropriate techniques on the duration of the different phases of the cell cycle. This is the system where one can attempt to achieve conditions under which biomass increase expresses the maximum genetic potential for cell growth. Such a system offers an entirely new approach to studies on the molecular basis of the hormonal control of cell growth.

SYNCHRONOUS CELL CULTURES

Plant cell cultures are routinely propagated by batch cultures initiated at a relatively high initial cell density (2×10^5 cells ml^{-1}) and subcultured when they enter stationary phase. It is, however, possible to initiate such batch cultures of sycamore cells at much lower cell densities and to use as inoculum cells maintained in stationary phase as long as possible without suffering decline in viability. When this is done using an enriched synthetic medium the cultures show a more extended lag phase and then embark upon a succession of highly synchronous divisions as evidenced by the data for cell counts, mitotic index (percentage cells in a recognizable stage of mitosis) determinations and estimations of nuclear

DNA content (by microdensity following Feulgen staining).

By using for such synchronous batch cultures the 4-litre culture vessel developed for the continuous culture systems but modified by adding a stainless-steel sampling valve automatically operated by a timing device it has been possible to show the synchrony of a number of metabolic events in the cell cycle.

The period during which DNA is doubled takes place during a restricted period of the interphase between successive mitoses. Scientists termed this the S phase and distinguished the interphase period before S phase as G1 (the first gap) and the period after completion of S phase and before mitosis (M) as G2 (the second gap).

Cell cleavage (cytokinesis) usually follows directly upon mitosis so that G1 can be timed from the origin of the daughter cells although, as originally defined, G1 begins as soon as nuclear division is complete. These stages in the cell cycle can be determined in exponential asynchronous cultures by determinations of doubling time (cell count data), mitotic index, labelling index (per cent nuclei and mitoses labelled following flash label with tritiated thymidine—^{3}H-Tdr), fraction of labelled mitoses, microdensitomitry and autoradiography, achieved by the single slide technique of Mak (1965).

These methods have been applied to cultures of sycamore cell lines during the phase of exponential growth in batch cultures and to steady state chemostat cultures growing at different rates (doubling times ranging from 22 to 85 hr). This has revealed that the phases S (7.0 ± 0.2 hr), G2 (8.7 ± 0.6 hr) and M (2.9 ± 0.3 hr) are relatively constant whereas, according to the cell doubling time, G1 varies widely (4–60 hr). This observation that G1 varies with different cycle times, whereas S + G2 is relatively constant has also been observed in work with mammalian cells both in culture and *in vivo*. Certain critical events in G1 may be essential to the initiation of S phase and may be rate limiting. In the work with sycamore cells growing at reduced rates, nitrogen supply is the limiting factor and when cells enter stationary phase in batch culture, they are arrested in G1.

The value of synchronous cultures for studies on the cell cycle is that they enable particular metabolic events to be monitored. Work along these lines with plant cells has only recently been undertaken. In a study involving synchronous sycamore cell cultures it was shown that total extractable protein and RNA rise throughout interphase but at an increased rate during S + G2.

This was supported by studies of the rate of incorporation of labelled amino acids and uridine into these fractions. Respiration rate similarly rose throughout interphase but with two peaks of activity during S phase and cytokinesis. When, however, changes in the activity of extracted enzymes were studied different patterns emerged. Thymidine kinase and aspartate transcarbamoylase showed single and separated peaks of activity, succinic dehydrogenase showed two well separated peaks of activity, and glucose-6-phosphate dehydrogenase activity rose continuously throughout interphase.

Whilst the content of total extractable histone rose parallel with total protein, study of the rates of incorporation of ^{3} H-labelled lysine and ^{14} C-labelled arginine into this fraction pointed to greatly enhanced histone turn-over associated with S-phase. It is not known whether the changes in enzyme activity detected in these studies reflected changes in rates of enzyme synthesis. Researcher in work on cell synchrony in explants of Jerusalem artichoke tubers has shown however, by using the deuterium labelling technique, that changes in the activity of glucose-6-phosphate dehydrogenase during interphase do result from changes in rate of synthesis of the enzyme.

If future work along these lines enables the many separate metabolic events of the cell cycle of plant cells to be chartered, we will then have a number of 'markers' (points where particular metabolic events are initiated or terminated). This will enable us to identify those events along the interphase plateau whose initiation or pace is affected by nutritional factors and plant hormones, to determine whether certain events only occur when their controlling genes (which could be 'mapped') are exposed during DNA replication and whether other processes which proceed continuously show gene dosage effects as evidenced by increases in their rate after the points in DNA replication when their controlling genes are duplicated.

TOTIPOTENCY

The ability of a single cell to divide and produce all the differentiated cells in an organism, including extraembryonic tissues. Totipotent cells formed during sexual and asexual reproduction include spores and zygotes. In some organisms, cells can dedifferentiate and regain totipotency. For example, a plant cutting or callus can be used to grow an entire plant. Mammalian development commences when an oocyte is fertilized by a sperm forming a single celled embryo, the zygote. Consistent with the definition, the zygote is totipotent, meaning that this single cell has the potential to develop into an embryo with all the specialized cells that make up a living being, as well as into the placental support structure necessary for fetal development.

Thus, each totipotent cell is a self-contained entity that can give rise to the whole organism. This is said to be true for the zygote and for early embryonic blastomeres up to at least the 4-cell stage embryo. Experimentally, totipotency can be demonstrated by the isolation of a single blastomere from a preimplantation embryo and subsequently monitoring its ability to support a term birth following transfer into a suitable recipient. This approach was pioneered in rats and has been realized in several mammalian species including nonhuman primates. In the latter case, we confirmed the ability of isolated blastomeres from 2- and 4-cell stage, IVF produced embryos of the rhesus monkey to support term pregnancies and to produce live animals. As embryo development progresses to the 8-cell stage and beyond depending on the species, the individual blastomeres that comprise the embryo gradually lose their totipotency. It is generally believed that this restriction in developmental potential indicates irreversible differentiation and specialization of early embryonic cells into the first two lineages, the inner cell mass (ICM) that includes cells that will give rise to the fetus and the trophectoderm (TE), and an outer layer of cells that is destined to an extraembryonic fate.

A complication in assessing the state of potency of blastomeres isolated from more advanced stages of development is insufficient cytoplasmic volume. Thus, although the blastomeres may in fact be totipotent, embryonic development of relatively small isolated blastomeres arrests at or near the time of blastulation. Recall that the zygote and early blastomeres undergo several unusual mitotic or cleavage divisions that are not accompanied by a corresponding growth of cytoplasm, that is, there is no change in embryo size despite the presence of more cells or blastomeres and each individual blastomere becomes smaller. The embryonic genome at these early stages is transcriptionally quiescent and development is regulated by maternally inherited factors present at the time of fertilization in the oocyte. The transition in developmental regulation with activation of the embryonic genome and a complete loss of dependence on oocyte factors occurs before the blastocyst stage in a species-specific manner. Additionally, by the late morula or early blastocyst stage the embryo ceases cleavage divisions and resumes normal mitotic divisions with concomitant increases in cell volume during the S-phase. The likelihood that early blastomeres retain totipotency for a major part of preimplantation development but experimentally we cannot prove it is directly supported by the fact that the addition of oocyte cytoplasm to a blastomere of the 8- to 16-cell stage embryo can restore, or perhaps more appropriately allow expression of, its full developmental potential. This approach, embryonic cell nuclear transfer, has been employed in the monkey to demonstrate the totipotency of 8- to 16-cell stage blastomeres whereby reconstructed embryos when transferred to a recipient resulted in a term birth.

It is also known that conglomerates of embryonic cells at a later stage of development can develop into an organism. An experimental manipulation that supports this concept involves blastocyst splitting. Cutting the embryo into halves with an approximately equal distribution of TE and ICM cells can lead to the production of viable infants. Obviously, embryo splitting that creates demi embryos with highly distorted ratios of ICM to TE cells is inconsistent with the production of live births.

THE CONCEPT OF TOTIPOTENCY

Many somatic plant cells, including some fully differentiated types (*e.g.* leaf mesophyll), provided they contain intact nuclear, plastid and mitochondrial genomes, have the capacity to regenerate into whole plants. This phenomenon is *totipotency*, an amazing developmental plasticity that sets plant cells apart from most of their animal counterparts, and was first demonstrated by Steward and Reinert in the 1950s. Often totipotency is revealed when cells or tissues are disturbed or removed from their normal environment and, for example, placed onto artificial media in tissue culture. A differentiated plant cell that is selectively expressing its genetic information can instead initiate expression of the programme required for generation of an entire new plant.

Many plants have been regenerated from single cells, but not all plant cells are totipotent; some are terminally differentiated, often because of partial or complete genome loss. We can generalise by saying that most plants at most stages of the life cycle have some populations of cells that are totipotent. Totipotency is of course also a property of normal undifferentiated cells, for example in meristems.

The first step in expression of regenerative totipotency is for mature cells to re-enter the cell cycle and resume cell division — a process known as *dedifferentiation*. This may lead directly to organised development, such as occurs in the epidermal cells of immature hypocotyls of *Trifolium* where somatic embryos develop (*direct embryogenesis*), or formation of shoots or roots (*direct organogenesis*). Alternatively, there may be an intervening callus stage from which organised structures can later be induced to develop — referred to as *indirect organogenesis*.

Expression of totipotency depends on *competence*, by which we mean the ability of cells to be induced along a particular developmental pathway, and *determination*, in which cells become irreversibly committed to a particular pathway. *Convolvulus* explants display an initial competence to follow two possible developmental pathways – root or shoot formation.

Later, once induction of, say, shoots has begun, cells become determined and transfer to conditions that normally induce root formation are now ineffective. However, formation of callus does not necessarily guarantee subsequent organogenesis or that the direction of organogenesis can be controlled. Commitment of root primordia in cereal callus cultures often seems to be irreversible and a high proportion of cells become terminally differentiated root cap cells that secrete the mucus normally associated with caps of intact roots. Calluses which do not lead to regeneration are a common occurrence.

One intriguing question is whether expression of totipotency is a phenomenon of a single cell or normally results from the collective interaction of a cluster of cells. We might expect somatic embryogenesis to be an ideal experimental system because normal zygotic embryogenesis always starts from a single cell, the fertilised egg. Perhaps surprisingly, groups of hypocotyl cells from very young embryos may contribute collectively to formation of an embryo 'bud'; on the other hand, single epi-dermal cells from more mature tissues can divide to produce an embryo. The ability to undergo direct organogenesis may be linked to developmental age of explant tissue, with cells progressively losing this potential as they mature. Fully mature cells, if they retain any capacity for dedifferentiation, tend to exhibit totipotency via indirect organogenesis. Loss of totipotency is probably due to genetic (physical changes to chromosomes, for example loss of DNA, nucleotide sub-stitution, endopolyploidy) or epigenetic (changes in gene expression as a consequence of development, for example DNA methylation) blocks.

TYPES OF DIFFERENTIATION

Differentiation implies development of organised structures, usually from undifferentiated tissue but also from previously specialised cells that would not normally give rise to organised multicellular growth (*e.g.* epidermal cells, pollen grains). In plant tissue culture, undifferentiated tissue is referred to as callus although a callus can contain meristematic nodules that may not be obvious to the naked eye but which never develop further unless suitable conditions are supplied. Development of organised structures can follow one of three pathways:

1. Shoot regeneration, based on a unipolar structure with a shoot apical meristem
2. Root regeneration, essentially a unipolar structure with a root apical meristem
3. Somatic embryogenesis in which there is a bipolar structure.

Repeated division of immature post-meiotic pollen grains (microspores) leads to production of haploid plants, and is another type of embryogenesis. The phenomenon was first discovered in 1966 by the researchers when studying meiosis *in vitro* in *Datura innoxia* anthers. Sometimes differentiation takes place in the absence of cell division: in tissue culture systems, such as *Zinnia elegans,* we commonly find xylem elements appearing among otherwise undifferentiated cells. This form of xylogenesis represents the acquisition of a specific metabolic competence that is quite different from that of the parental cell. Clearly, differentiation *in vitro* can take several forms.

INDIRECT ORGANOGENESIS: PLANT GROWTH REGULATORS AND DIFFERENTIATION

An understanding of the mechanisms underlying regeneration of whole plants, or parts of plants, from cells has come some way since the classic observations of Skoog and Miller that the direction of differentiation could be influenced by the ratio of the exogenously supplied growth regulators auxin and cytokinin. They observed in tobacco stem pith cultures that a high ratio of auxin to cytokinin led to initiation of roots whereas a low ratio led to development of shoots. Although there are many species for which this simple manipulation will not work, in general auxins (*e.g.* IAA (indoleacetic acid), NAA (a-naphthaleneacetic acid) and IBA indolebutyric acid)) will stimulate regeneration of roots, and cytokinins (*e.g.* BAP (6-benzylaminopurine) and kinetin) will promote regeneration of shoots or embryos.

It is now obvious that the two groups of growth regulators play an important role in unlocking totipotent expression. Dedifferentiation and callus formation occur naturally in response to wounding. Indeed, wound responses involve auxin and cytokinins and seem to be the biological trigger for plant regeneration from somatic cells. However, *sustained* callus growth *in vitro* requires addition of one or more growth regulators. Prior to the chemical characterisation of IAA in 1934, attempts to obtain long-term callus cultures failed. With very few exceptions, auxin is essential for dedifferentiation and commonly 2,4-dichlorophenoxyacetic acid (2,4-D) is used to promote callus; cytokinin often enhances this process.

In tissues with a high endogenous level of auxin, culture of explants on a medium containing cytokinin as the only growth regulator may lead to development of shoots with very little callus. Not all living cells respond to auxin and this is particularly true of mature cells of grasses. Without dedifferentiation, it is not possible to move to the next stage of totipotent expression — plant regeneration. Until the late 1980s, grasses, especially the economically important cereals, were regarded as recalcitrant *in vitro*. Since that time, researchers have developed methods of regeneration for most of these species. This includes work on sugar cane, sorghum, wheat and barley in several Australian laboratories.

The first example of a single *isolated* cell dividing directly to produce an embryo was recorded in 1970 in a suspension culture of *Daucus carota*. However, even in this carrot system, the phenomenon is rare and normally somatic embryogenesis is indirect via an initial callus phase. Protoplasts capable of undergoing cell division seldom give rise directly to organised structures but first synthesise a new cell wall, then produce a callus from which shoots or embryos can later regenerate.

Although auxin stimulates initial cell division in quiescent cells, continued presence of auxin can inhibit organised outgrowth. This is a typical example of the sequential functions of a single hormone through a developmental progression. In practical terms, cultures are usually transferred onto low or zero auxin media to permit or speed up shoot organogenesis. Sometimes 'removal' of auxin occurs when auxin in the medium is degraded either by the tissue itself or via chemical reactions such as photo-oxidation. Cytokinins promote outgrowth of shoots but are normally kept at very low concentration when root regeneration is wanted.

THE ROLE OF GROWTH REGULATORS

Direct organogenesis bypasses the need for a callus phase. A good example is the formation of somatic embryos. Most evidence suggests that direct embryogenesis proceeds from cells which were already embryogenically competent while they were part of the original, differentiated tissue. These pre-embryogenic cells appear only to require favourable conditions (such as wounding or application of exogenous growth regulators) to allow release into cell division and expression of embryogenesis. Such cells tend to be much more responsive than those involved in indirect organogenesis and do not seem to require the same auxin 'push' to initiate division; indeed, the cells may never have left the cell cycle and growth regulator application has some more subtle role. In *Trifolium repens* hypocotyl epidermis, we see that BAP (a cytokinin) promotes reorientation of the plane of cell division, leading to initiation of a promeristemoid. An analogous response occurs in cotyledon explants of *Abies amabilis* where subepidermal cells develop into shoots. In haploid embryos developed from *Brassica napus* anther cultures, cytokinin actually suppresses secondary embryoid formation and instead promotes normal leafy shoots. This suggests a role for cytokinin in switching between shoot development and embryogenesis. Similarly, researchers, working with thin-layer explants only three to six epidermal cells deep from floral branches of *Nicotiana tabacum*, revealed an absolute effect of growth regulators on the direction of differentiation. Although sucrose concentration and light modify the response, structures produced depend mainly on the auxin to cytokinin ratio. At 0.1:1, vegetative shoot buds form and at 100:1 roots are generated, but a 1:1 ratio promotes floral bud initiation. Incidentally, this remains a classic example of formation of new floral meristems *in vitro*.

4

Applications of Biotechnology in Horticulture

The requirement of fruits and vegetables is increasing proportionally with the increasing population in the country. How do we keep horticultural production on par with the burgeoning population?

Although conventional plant breeding techniques have made considerable progress in the development of improved varieties, they have not been able to keep pace with the increasing demand for vegetables and fruits in the developing countries. Therefore an immediate need is felt to integrate biotechnology to speed up the crop improvement programmes.

Biotechnological tools have revolutionized the entire crop improvement programmes by providing new strains of plants, supply of planting material, more efficient and selective pesticides and improved fertilizers. Many genetically modified fruits and vegetables are already in the market in developed countries. Modern biotechnology encompasses broad areas of biology from utilization of living organisms or substances from those organisms to make or to modify a product, to improve plant or animal or to develop micro-organisms for specific use. It is a new aspect of biological and agricultural science which provides new tools and strategies in the struggle against world's food production problem. The major areas of biotechnology which can be adopted for improvement of horticultural crops.

TISSUE CULTURE

One of the widest applications of biotechnology has been in the area of tissue culture and micro propagation in particular. It is one of the most widely used techniques for rapid asexual in vitro propagation. This technique is economical in time and space affords greater output and provides disease free and elite propagules. It also facilitates safer and quarantined movements of germplasm across nations. When the traditional methods are unable to meet the demand for propagation material this technique can produce millions of uniformly flowering and yielding plants. Micropropagation of almost all the fruit crops and vegetables is possible now. Production of virus free planting material using meristem culture has been made possible in many horticultural crops. Embryo rescue is another area where plant breeders are able to rescue their crosses which would otherwise abort.

Culture of excised embryos of suitable stages of development can circumvent problems encountered in post zygotic incompatibility. This technique is highly significant in intractable and long duration horticultural species. Many of the dry land legume species have been successfully regenerated from cotyledons, hypocotyls, leaf, ovary, protoplast, petiole root, anthers, etc., Haploid generation through anther/pollen culture is recognized as another important area in crop improvement. It is useful in being rapid and economically feasible. Complete homozygosity of the offspring helps in phenotype selection for quantitative characters and particularly for qualitatively inherited characters making breeding much easier successful isolation, culture and fusion of plant protoplasts has been very useful in transferring cytoplasmic male sterility for obtaining hybrid vigour through mitochondrial recombination and for genetic transformation in plants.

In vitro germplasm conservation is of great significance in providing solutions and alternative approaches to overcoming constrains in management of genetic resources. In crops which are propagated vegetatively and which produce recalcitrant seeds and perennial crops which are highly heterozygous seed storage is not suitable. In such crops especially, *in vitro* storage is of great practical importance. These techniques have successfully been demonstrated in a number of horticultural crops and there are now various germplasm collection centres. In vitro germplasm also assures the exchange of pest and disease free material and helps in better quarantine.

Plant breeders are continually searching for new genetic variability that is potentially useful in cultivar improvement. A portion of plants regenerated by tissue culture often exhibits phenotypic variation atypical of the original phenotype. Such variation, termed somaclonal variation may be heritable *i.e.* genetically stable and passed on to the next generation. Alternatively, the variation may be epigenetic and disappear following sexual reproduction. These heritable variation are potentially useful to plant breeders.

GENETIC ENGINEERING OF PLANTS

Genetic Engineering involves three major steps:

- Identification and isolation of suitable genes for transfer
- Delivery system to insert desired gene into recipient cells.
- Expression of new genetic information in recipient cells.

Using techniques of genetic engineering many useful genes have been introduced into plants and many transgenic plants have been developed in which the foreign DNA has been stably integrated and resulted in the synthesis of appropriate gene product. Transgenic plants have covered about 52.6 m hectares in the Industrial and developing countries upto 2001. Genes for the following traits have been introduced to the crop plants.

Herbicide Tolerance

Transgenic plants are developed that are resistant to herbicides allowing farmers to spray crops so as to kill only weeds but not their crops. Many herbicide tolerant plants have been developed in tomato, tobacco, potato, soybean, cotton, corn oilseed rape, petunia, etc. Glyphosate is one of the most potent broad spectrum environment friendly herbicide known, it is marketed under the trade name Round up. Glyphosate kills plants by blocking the action of an enzyme (5-enolpyruvyl shikimate-3-phosphate synthase) (EPSPS) an essential enzyme in the biosynthesis of aromatic amino acids, tyrosine, phenylalanine and tryptophan. Amino acids are building blocks of protein. Transgenic plants resistant to Glyphosate have been developed by transferring gene of EPSPS that over prodoce this enzyme thus inhibiting the effect of Glyphosate. A number of detoxifying enzymes have been identified in plants as well as in microbes. Some of these include glutahthione-s-transferase or GST in maize and other plants which detoxifies the herbicide bromoxynil and phosphinothricin acetyl transferase (PAT) which detoxifies the herbiside PPT (L-phosphinothricine). Transgenic plants using *bxn* gene from Klebsiella and *bar* gene from Strepotomyces have been obtained in potato, oilseed, sugarbeet, soybean, cotton and corn and are found to be herbicide resistance. These transgenic plants reduce the use of weeding labour, farmers cost and increase yield.

Engineering Pathogen Resistance

Viruses are the major pests of crop plants which cause considerable yield losses. Many strategies have been applied to control virus infection using coat protein and satellite RNA. Viruses are submicroscopic pockets of nucleic acid (DNA or RNA) enclosed in a protein coat and can multiply within a host cell. Use of viral coat protein as a transgene for producing virus resistant plants is one of the most spectacular successes achieved in plant biotechnology. Coat protein gene from tobacco mosaic virus (TMV) classified as a positive strand RNA virus has been transferred to tobacco, making it nearly resistant against TMV. Using gene for nucelocapsid protein resistance has been introduced in crops like tomato, tobacco, lettuce, groundnut, pepper and in ornaments like *Impatiens, Ageratum* and *Crysnathemum* against tomato spotted wilt virus. Use of satellite RNA (SATRNA) makes many transgenic plants resistant to Cucumber Mosaic Virus (CMV). Transgenic resistant plants have also been developed against alfalfa mosaic virus, potato virus X, Rice tungro virus, tobacco rattle virus and Papaya ring spot virus.

During the Past decade many resistance genes whose products are involved in recognizing the invading pathogens have been identified and cloned. A number of signaling pathways which follow the pathogen infection have been dissected. Many of the antifungal compounds synthesized by plants which combat fungal infections have been identified. The major strategies for developing fungal resistance have been production of transgenic plants with antifungal molecules like proteins and toxins, and generation of hypersensitive response through R genes or by manipulating genes of SAR pathway. A chitinase gene from bean plants in tobacco and *Brassica napus* showed enhanced resistance to *Rhizoctonia solani.* In another case chitinase gene obtained from *Serratia marcescens* (soil bacterium) is introduced in tobacco making it resistant to *Alternaria longipes* which causes brown spot diseases. Acetyl transferase gene is introduced in tobacco making it resistant to *Pseudomonas syringea,* a causal agent of wild fire disease.

Stress Resistance

A number of genes responsible for providing resistance against stresses such as to water stress heat, cold, salt, heavy metals and phytohormones have been identified. Studies are also being conducted on metabolites like proteins and betains that have been implicated in stress tolerance. Resistance against chilling was introduced into tobacco plants by introducing gene for glycerol-1-phosphate acyl-transferase enzyme from *Arabidopsis.* Many plants respond to drought stress by synthesizing a group of sugar derivatives called polyols (Mannitol, Sorbitol and Sion). Plants that have more polyols are more resistant to stress. Using a bacterial gene capable of synthesizing mannitols it is possible to raise the level of mannitol very high making plants resistant to drought.

Fruit Quality

Tomatoes which ripen slowly are helpful in transportation process. Transgenic tomato with reduced pectin methyl esterase activity and increased level of soluble solids and higher pH increases processing quality. Tomatoes exhibiting delayed ripening have been produced either by using antisense RNA against enzymes involved in ethylene production (e.g. ACC synthase) or by using gene for deaminase which degraded l-aminocyclopropane-l-carboxylic acid (ACC) an immediate precursor of ethylene. This increases the shelf life of tomatoes. These tomatoes can also stay on the plant long giving more time for accumulation of sugars and acids for improving flavour. It is produced at commercial level in European and American countries. Tomatoes with elevated sucrose and reduced starch could also be produced using sucrose phosphate synthase gene. Starch content in potatoes has been increased by 20-40% by using a bacterial ADP glucose pyrophosphorylase gene.

Pest Resistance

The insecticidal beta endotoxin gene (Bt gene) has been isolated from *Bacillus thuringiensis* the commonly occurring soil bacteria and transferred to number of plants such as cotton, tobacco, tomato, soybean, potato, etc. to make them resistant to attack by insects. These genes produce insecticidal crystal proteins which affect a range of lepidopteran, coleopteran, dipteran insects. These crystals upon ingestion by the insect larva are solubilised in the highly alkaline midgut into individual protoxins which vary from 133 to 136 kDa in molecular weight. Insecticidal crystal protein produced during vegetative growth of the cells (VIP) are also found to be highly effective against insect control. Bt resistant plants are already in the market.

Male Sterility and Fertility Restoration

This is helpful in hybrid seed production. Transgenic

plants with male sterility and fertility restoration genes have become available in *Brassica napus*. It facilitates production of hybrid seed without manual emasculation and controlled pollination as often done in maize.

In 1990, scientists have successfully used a gene construct having another specific promoter from TA29 gene of tobacco and bacterial coding sequence for a ribonuclease gene from *Bacillus* Sp. (barnase gene) for production of transgenic plants in *Brassica napus*. Here the translated gene prevented normal pollen development leading to male sterilily.

MOLECULAR DIAGNOSTICS

Nucleic Acid Probes

It is now possible to detect the plant diseases even before onset of symptoms by using cDNA probes. Probes are nucleic acid sequences of pathogen causing organisms labelled with certain markers. cDNA probes corresponding to specific regions of the pathogens can be generated using standard recombinant DNA technique.

Monoclonal Antibodies (McAb)

Immunochemical techniques are extremely useful for the rapid and accurate routine detection of plant pathogens and ultimately the diagnosis of plant disease and their relatedness, The introduction of hybridoma technology has provided methods for the production of homologous and biochemically defined immunological reagents of identical specificity which are produced by a single cell line and are directed against a unique epitope of the immunizing antigen.

The great potential of McAbs in phytopathological diagnostics is essential because of homogeneous antibody preparations with defined activity and specificity can be produced in large quantities over long periods.

Even though hybridoma technology is a laborious and expensive enterprise compared to standard immunization procedures it is going to be widely used for large scale diagnosis.

MOLECULAR MARKERS

The possibilities of using gene tags of molecular makers for selecting agronomic traits has made the job of breeder easier. It has been possible to score the plants for different traits or disease resistance at the seedling stage itself. The use of RFLP (Restriction Fragment Length polymorphism), RAPD (Random Amplified Polymorphic DNA), AFLP (Amplified Fragment Length Polymorphism) and isozyme markers in plant breeding are numerous. RFLPs are advantageous over morphological and isozyme markers primarily because their number is limited only by genome size and they are not environmentally or developmentally influenced. Molecular maps now exist for a number of crop plants including corn, tomato, potato, rice, lettuce, wheat, Brassica species and barley. RFLPs have wide ranging applications including cultivar finger printing, identification of quantitative trait loci, analysis of genome organization, germplasm introgression and map-based cloning. AFLP is becoming the tool of choice for fingerprinting because of its reproducibility compared to RAPD. Microsatellile or simple sequence repeats (SSRS) markers have also become the choice for a wide range of applications in genotyping, genome mapping and genome analysis.

DEVELOPMENT OF MICROBIAL INOCULAN

Indiscriminate and injudicious use of chemical fertilizers and pesticides for the crop production and control of insect-pests has resulted in pollution of the environment deterioration of soil health and development of resistance by many insects and residue problems. Hence there is a great concern world wide to use safer biofertilisers and biopesticdies in the integrated nutrient management and pest management systems.

Biofertilizers are micro-organisms which fix atmospheric nitrogen or solubilise fixed phosphorus in the soil and make more nutrients available to the plant. Some of the organisms providing major inputs are the biological nitrogen fixing organisms such as *Rhizobium, Azotobacter, Azospirillum* and phosphate solubilising organisms such as *Bacillus polymyxa, B. magaterium, Pseudomonas striata* and certain fungal species of Aspergillus and *Penicillium.*

The benefits of using micro-organisms as fertilizers are many fold. They are less expensive, nontoxic to plants, do not pollute the ground water nor render the soil acidic and unfit for growth of plants. *Rhizobium* forms nodules on the roots of leguminous plants and help in fixing nitrogen from the atmosphere to ammonium irons which get converted to amino acids in the plant system. Inoculation with this bacteria helps in reducing addition of nitrogenous fertilizers to the soil. *Azospirillum* is also found colonizing inter cellular spaces inside the root system. These bacteria also contribute substantially to the nitrogen requirement of the plant. Phosphate solubilising bacteria are another group of micro-organisms which solubilise the insoluble phosphorus in the soil and make them readily available to the crop.

Mycorrhiza is the symbiotic association of the roots of crop plants with non-pathogenic fungus. They provide nutrients absorbed from deeper layers of soil to the plants. They help the plants in better plant establishment and growth when inoculated. Many fruit crops like papaya, mango, banana, citrus, pomegranate are found to be dependent on this association and are greatly benefited by its inoculation in procuring higher phosphate and other nutrient from the soil. These mycorrhizal associations help the plants in overcoming pathogen attack also. They improve soil characters too. Genetic modification of microbes: By using DNA recombination technique it has been possible to genetically manipulate different strains of these bacteria suitable to different environmental conditions and to develop strains with traits with capacity for better competitiveness and nodulation.

Biopesticides are biological organisms which can be formulated as that of the pesticides for the control of pests. Biopesticides are gaining importance in agriculture, horticulture and in public heatlh programmes for the control of pests. The advantages of using biopesticides are many. They are specific to target pests and do not harm the non target organisms such as bees, butterflies and are safe to humans and live stocks, they do not disturb the food-chain nor leave behind toxic residues. Some of the microbial pesticides used to control insect pests are *Bacillus thuringiensis* species to control various insect pests. Insecticidal property of these bacteria are due to crystals of insecticidal proteins produced during sporulation. These proteins are stomach poisons and are highly insect specific. Bt toxins could kill plant parasitic nematode too. Number of baculoviruses (BV) nuclear polyhedrosis virus (NPV) is being developed as microbial pesticides both nationally and internationally, A few examples of these are *Heliothis, Spodoptera, Plusia, Agrotis, Trichoplusia,* etc.

Biocontrol Agents

These are other microbes which are antagonistic to several pathogenic fungus and are good substitutes to fungicides or insecticide. These are Bacillus sps. *Pseudomonas fluorescens, Trichoderma, Verticillium* sp., *Streptromyces* spp. etc. These organisms are commercially available.

The extent of commercial application of plant biotechnology is the important mark for measuring the vitality of this newly emerging technology. Small and marginal farmers can adopt less expensive technologies like the use of biofertilizers and biopesticides while capital intensive technologies can be adopted by rich farmers

BIOTECHNOLOGY AND ITS APPLICATION TO AGRICULTURE AND HORTICULTURE

Biotechnology is broadly defined as any technique that uses live organisms *viz.* bacteria, viruses, fungi, yeast, animal cells, plant cells etc. to make or modify a product, to improve plants or animals or to engineer micro-organisms for specific uses. It encompasses genetic engineering, inclusive of enzyme and protein engineering plant and animal tissue culture technology, biosensors for biological monitoring, bioprocess and fermentation technology. Biotechnology is essentially and interdisciplinary are consisting of biochemistry, molecular chemistry, molecular and microbiology, genetics and immunology etc. it is concerned with upgradation of quality and also utilization of livestock and resources for the well being of both animals and plants.

Modern biotechnology holds considerable promise to meet challenges in agricultural production. It makes use of life sciences, chemical sciences and engineering sciences in achieving and improving the technological applications of the capabilities of the living organism of their derivates to make products of value to man and society. It is used in living systems to develop commercial processes and products which also includes the techniques of Recombinant DNA, gene transfer, embryo manipulation, plant regeneration, cell culture, monoclonal antibodies and bio-processed engineering. These techniques can transform ideas into practical applications, viz., certain crops can be genetically altered to increase their tolerance to certain herbicides. Biotechnology can be used to develop safer vaccines against viral and bacterial diseases. It also offers new ideas and techniques applicable to agriculture and also develops a better understanding of living systems of our environment and ourselves. It has a tremendous potential fir improving crop production, animal agriculture and bio-processing.

New approaches in biotechnology can develop high yielding and more nutritious crop varieties, improve resistance to disease and also reduce the need for fertilizer and other expensive agricultural chemicals. It could also improve forestry and its products, fibre crops and chemical feedstocks. Plant biotechnologies an play a key role in the massive production of improved crop varieties (through in vitro tissue culture followed by clonal propagation), as well as in their genetic improvement. They can also help in propagating plant species which contain useful and biologically active substances, e.g., food additive, pigment, pharmaceuticals, biopesticides, etc. Organ tissue and cell culture could be more efficient than conventional extraction.

Biotechnology helps to isolate the gene, study its function and regulation, modify the gene and reintroduce it into its natural host of another organism. It help unlocking the secrets of diseases resistance, regulates growth and development or manipulates communication among cells and among other organisms. It is a comparatively new technique and is used in the field of agriculture and horticulture. This mainly involves manipulation in the genetic code (which includes processes like gene transfer), tissue culture, monoclonal antibody preparation protoplast fusion.

The gene transfer technology is to locate the relevant gene(s) among the tens of thousands that make up the genome. This is done by reducing the lengths of an organism's genomic DNA equivalent to one or several genes. These smaller segments can be stored and then cloned to produce a quantity of genetic material for further analysis. Cloned genes are necessary research tools for studies of the structure, function and expression of the genes. They are also used as diagnostic test probes in medicine and agriculture to detect specific diseases.

The transfer of genes from one organism to another is a natural process that creates variation in biological traits. It under lies all attempts to improve agricultural species whether through traditional agricultural breeding or through the techniques of molecular biology. The molecular biological methods of gene transfer alleviate the process to manipulated one gene at a time. They can also control the way in which these genes express themselves in the new variety of plant and animal. This can shorten the time required to develop new varieties and give greater precision. This can also be used to exchange genes.

Tissue Culture is the science of cultivating animal/plant tissue in a prepared medium. Technologies based on this can be harnessed to achieve crop improvement objectives.

The application of tissue culture are in the filed of multiplying bamboos, mass multiplication, micro propagation etc.

- *Multiplication of bamboos*. In general, it takes a long period to flower in bamboos. It has been reported that bamboos can be induced to flower in tissue culture in relatively lesser time. This opens up vast possibilities of selective breeding of improved bamboo varieties and thus replacing the vegetative propagation by speed propagation.

- *Mass multiplication* is carried out with a number of ornamental and field crops which have shown that the use of this fully mechanized procedure of multiplication, distribution and transfer is suited to commercial micropropagation.
- *Micropropagation* has been carried out in several crop which include, potato, sweet potato, yams, garlic, lime, banana, pineapple and papaya; spices including ginger, small cardamom, turmeric, black pepper and several aromatic and medicinal plants such as sarpgandha and antamul. Elite genotypes of banana, papaya, coconut, small cardamom and oil palm have been multiplied on a commercial scale by private seed companies. Micropropagation of ornamental plants such as gladioli, orchids and bougainvillea which have tremendous export value has been achieved.

Tissue culture technology is the most disseminated. These techniques have been known in India since the thirties. Indian Scientists are well recognized internationally for the significant contribution they have made in the development in this field.

Among the tissue culture techniques, plant-propagation is the only area of biotechnology commercially exploited in India. Massive multiplication of plants have been conducted by private companies since the middle sixties. The recent Indian economical policies have favoured the development of agro-industries, including biotechnological companies. Since 1992, emerging private companies have successfully multiplied hundreds of thousands of ornamental plants for both the local and international markets.

Biofertilisers

Certain micro-organisms and minute plants which can absorb gaseous nitrogen and phosphorous directly from the atmosphere and make it available to the plants can be identified, multiplied in the laboratories and introduced into the root zone of crop plants to supply nitrogen and phosphorous. Materials containing such organisms are called biofertilisers. Some of the biofertiliser are Rhizobium, Azotobacter, Azispir illiumm Blue-green algae, Azolla etc.

World Scenario

In world scenario immunization of seeds and predators and production of pharmaceuticals are covered in the countries like America, China, Philippines, Madagascar, Australia. Successful immunization of cucumber seedlings against the Anthracnose fungus have been achieved. And the acquired immunity can be extended to predators as well.

Approximately 119 pure chemical substance extracted from higher plants were used in medicine throughout the world. The market potential for herbal drugs in the Western world could range from Rs. 186.20 billion in the next ten years to Rs. 1,786 billion by the year 2000 if the AIDS epidemic continued unchecked. Utilization of plant biotechnologies for the production of pharmaceuticals, however, faced certain problems like rare occurrences of highly productive cell lines, difficulty in including the cells to produce the desired compound, vulnerability of slow- growing tissue to bacterial and fungal infections, laborious excretion between different genes and general shuffling of chromosomes. In Philippines, intensive work has been done on identification of medicinal plants where new medicines processing factory has been setup based on more than 300 identified medicinal plants. Similarly nearly 40, 000 different kinds of traditional plant drugs have been produced in 57 factories. Commercial usefulness of medicinal plants can be illustrated by Catharanthus roseus which has been widely grown on commercial scale in Madagascar and is even exported. Many new products like human and veterinary vaccines, chemicals and pharmaceuticals have been extensively developed in Australia.

Hairy root culture, derived from callus tissue, infected by Agrobacterium rhizogenes, gives a natural defence against infection and considerable work has been done on this. Application of biotechnology in crop improvement is noteworthy. The example of which are:

- Improved malting quality of barley by gene transfer, Finland;
- Insect resistant plant seeds by transgenesis, California;
- Mass test tube reproduction of genetically improved banana plants, St.Paulo;
- Genetic engineering of cut flowers (pink to white chrysanthemum), Netherlands;
- Herbicide resistant crop (engineered plants) to resist the toxic effect of weed killer.

Indian Scenario

Indian scenario is also studded with examples of several ongoing biotechnology research projects *viz.*, genetic changes in the Indian mustard, genetic diversity in some indica cultivators, production of rice hybrid tolerant to saline conditions using tissue culture, wide hybridization and use of pollen as a system for screening disease resistance, development of chickpea strains with improved acronomic traits etc.

Commercial application of the results however has yet to wait till such time the elaborate fields tests are undertaken, results calibrated and processes standardized. Setting up of national Gene Banks with the objective of conserving species of medicinal and aromatic plants under endangered/ threatened categories is an important developed. Some of the achievements include the procedures for isolation of BT plasmid DNA, preparation of plasmid DNA library, probing of ICP gene and purification of toxic crystal protein from Bacillus cultures which have been standardized.

Preferred Options

The technologies suitable in the Indian context are as follows:

- Recombinant DNA manipulation technology is the construction of a strech of DNA sequence consisting of components derived from different sources.

- Gene transfer technology is the ability to identify a particular gene one that encodes a desired trait in an organism.
- Tissue Culture is the science of cultivating animal/ plant tissue in a prepared medium. Technologies based on this can be harnessed to achieve crop improvement objectives.
- The application of tissue culture are in the filed of multiplying bamboos, mass multiplication, micro-propagation etc.
- Biofertilisers: Certain micro-organisms and minute plants which can absorb gaseous nitrogen and phosphorous directly from the atmosphere and make it available to the plants can be identified, multiplied in the laboratories and introduced into the root zone of crop plants to supply sitrogen and phosphorous. Materials containing such organisms are called biofertilisers. Some of the biofertlisers are Rhizobium, Azotobacter, Azispirillium, Blue-green algae, Azolla etc.
- Areas related medicines and health, chemical industry, mineral beneficiation and extractive metallurgy and to no less extent the agriculture, forestry, horticulture, aquaculture, poultry and food industry together with environment protection pursuit will derive the benefits of biotechnology.
- R&D organizations and industrial establishments involved in the development, production and marketing of activities/products relating to glucose, poultry, hormones, pharmaceuticals, sugar, agriculture, biomedical, horticulture, environment and acquaculture as also administrative/planning departments both in private and government sectors will be restlessly busy with the applied aspects of the various options that the biotechnology will unfold near future.
- Lack of awareness, incentive, trained manpower and realization by the potential users of the advantage

of biotechnology options over conventional processing routes and more so the absence of case histories developed on promotional basis are some of the main deterrents in adaptability of biotechnology.

APPLICATION OF PLANT TISSUE CULTURE TO AGRICULTURE AND FORESTRY

Plant tissue culture technique offers an excellent opportunity for mass propagation of plants in laboratory test tubes, which are transferred to the field. Besides crop plants, the technique is also applied to regenerate saplings for plantation and regeneration of dwindled forests. Some rare and nearly extinct plant species can be rescued and propagated by this technique. Embryos produced by incompatible crosses also are rescued, seed dormancy is overcome, life cycle is shortened and much more.

This technique is amalgamated with genetic engineering to regenerate plants with novel characters and combine two or more beneficial characters into a single plant. Things, once seemed impossible, have been made possible. We shall discuss about four elementary applications of this technique, namely, (1) micro-propagation; (2) organogenesis; (3) somatic embryogenesis and (4) protoplast culture and fusion.

MICRO-PROPAGATION

Basically, micro propagation is similar to rooting of plant cuttings and is, in a way, another method of vegetative propagation of plants. However, it differs from the conventional procedure in that it is carried out in an aseptic condition and requires a unique recipe *i.e.* an artificial nutrient medium. It is used for forestry improvement and is an example of direct laboratory to land transfer of biotechnological benefits A small plant cutting or explant (usually an axillary bud) is surface sterilized and inoculated into a culture vessel containing a semi-solid nutrient medium. The inoculated culture vessel is incubated at room temperature.

In a day or two, a large number of shoots develop from the axillary bud in a process known as axillary bud proliferation. Each growing point is sub-cultured to give rise to shoot. This phenomenon is known as adventitious shoot formation. Each shoot is stimulated by an auxin to develop roots. The new plantlet is transferred to the field.

Organogenesis

Organogenesis, in essence, refers to differentiation of organs, such as shoot and root from an undifferentiated mass of cells. The cells of an explant are highly differentiated. When an explant is placed in an artificially enriched nutrient medium, its differentiated cells first de-differentiate and form a mass of unorganized cells known as callus. The cells of the callus then re-differentiate and produced the desired tissue and then an organ or organs under the influence of specific growth regulators (hormones). Single cells also can be cultured and made to develop shoot and root one followed by the other. Plant growth regulators (hormones) play an important role in this regard.

There are two important groups of plant hormones: cytokinins and auxins. Cytokinins such as kinetin and adenine promote shoot differentiation, while auxins, such as indole acetic acid (IAA) and naphthalene acetic acid (NAA) promote root differentiation. It has been established that shoo root differentiation depends upon the ratio or quantitative interaction betwee cytokinins and auxins. For example, two molecules of kinetin or 15,000 molecule of adenine are required to neutralize one molecule of IAA. Thus, shoot/10 differentiations is a function of the quantitative interaction between cytokinin an auxin.

This principle is applied to plant cells or tissues cultured in vitro. Kinetin and IA are added to the in vitro culture in required amounts, one following the others- promote shoot and root differentiation.

Somatic Embryogenesis

In flowering plants, an embryo is the product of the zygote

and the zygote is the product of the fusion of two gametes. The embryo undergoes a preprogrammed development and forms a plantlet. In a nutshell, under a normal circumstance, a embryo is the result of sexual reproduction. Such embryos are known as zygoti embryos. However, plant tissue culture technique offers a method of producing; embryos from somatic cells bypassing sexual reproduction such embryos a known as somatic embryos. The process of formation of somatic embryos is known as somatic embryogenesis.

Somatic embryo formation starts with a mass of single cells or a tissue grown on a semirsolid nutrient medium. A cell repeatedly divides and forms a cell aggregate. The cell aggregate passes through different stages, such as globular, heart shaped and torpedo shaped stages.

The torpedo shaped stage is the mature stage. The culture is initially started on a semi-solid medium and the callus so formed is transferred to a liquid medium in an agitated and aerated bioreactor.

The cells breaking off from the callus develop into somatic embryos. Mature stages (torpedo shaped stages) are sorted out and grown to maturity on a semi-solid medium. Dormancy is induced before these are processed for transfer to the field. There are four methods, by which the somatic embryos are transferred to the field.

- These are germinated in the laboratory, transplanted in pots and then transferred to the field.
- The dormant embryos are encapsulated in a gel containing an adequate nutrient for the embryo. These encapsulated embryos are known as artificial or synthetic seeds such seeds can be planted in the field.
- This method involves the germination of the embryos under a controlled condition and then mixing of the seedlings is mixed with a gel like medium. The seedling- gel mix is sown in the field.
- The embryos are germinated and then fluid drilled.

The major advantages of this process are: (1) rescue of zygotic embryos formed by: incompatible crosses and (2) overcoming seed sterility and dormancy.

PROTOPLAST CULTURE AND FUSION

Protoplasts are plant cells, whose cell wall is digested. The cell is bound by a plasma membrane. For the isolation and culture of protoplast, isolated protoplasts from two different species of plants have been successfully fused to produce a single protoplast containing the genetic material and the cytoplasm of both the fusing protoplasts. The process of fusion is not straightforward It is facilitated by some agents, known as fusogens. Fusogens are of two types: chemical and electrical. Poly ethylene glycol (PEG) is a chemical fusogen.

It is not used as a universal fusogen, since it is toxic to protoplasts of some plants; alternately, pulses of electric current (direct current) are applied to the fusing protoplasts. This method is known as electro-fusion. The depicts the sequential fusion of two protoplasts, resulting in a synkaryon. There are three steps in this process. First, two protoplasts come in close proximity. Then the plasma membranes of the two fuse and then the two nuclei lie in the mingled cytoplasm. This stage is known as a heterokaryon. In the third stage, the two nuclei fuse forming a synkaryon.

The cell wall of the fused protoplast is regenerated and the cell is cultured in an artificially enriched nutrient medium. The following sequence of events is same as that in the callus culture. This process is also known as somatic hybridization and the products as somatic hybrids. This method bypasses the fusion of gametes of two unrelated plant species. Scientists obtained the first somatic hybrid by fusing the isolated protoplasts of *Nicotiana glauca* with *N. langsdorfii*. However, sometimes, due to cellular incompatibility, two nuclei can not co-exist. Consequently, one nucleus is eliminated and a protoplast containing the nucleus of one species and the cytoplasm of both results.

The ensuing hybrid is known as a cytoplasmic hybrid or cybrid. Somatic hybridization is attempted in plant species, which are sexually incompatible. The well known example of a somatic hybrid is 'pomato' obtained from the protoplasts of potato and tomato. However, this hybrid is of little commercial value.

ADVANCES IN PLANT BIOTECHNOLOGY

APPLICATIONS IN AGRICULTURE

Many of the foods that are already common in our diet are obtained from plant varieties that were developed using conventional genetic techniques of breeding and selection.

Today, by inserting one or more genes into a plant, scientists are able to produce a plant with new, advantageous characteristics. The new gene splicing techniques are being used to achieve many of the same goals and improvements that plant breeders historically have sought through conventional methods. They give scientists the ability to isolate genes and introduce new traits into foods without simultaneously introducing undesirable traits. This is an important improvement over traditional breeding. Because of the increased precision offered by the bioengineered methods, the risk of introducing detrimental traits is actually likely to be reduced.

GENE AND GENOME ANALYSIS

Plant genome and physical and genetic maps are available for several plants. As an example of studies on genome the rice genome. Rice has a much smaller genome (430 Mbp per haploid genome) than many other crops that belong to the Poaceae family. Due to the genome colinearity, high similarity in gene order and gene content, among the Poaceae family, the importance of rice genetics has been emphasized, and comparative analyses among rice, wheat, and maize have been intensively studied. As a result, rice becomes the model crop for the molecular genetic approach. This crop is available for many applications, including the construction of a high dense map, expressed sequence tag (EST) and full genomic sequence database, bacterial and yeast artificial chromosome (BAC and YAC) libraries, quantitative traits loci (QTL) mapping for yield and morphology, functional genomics by knockout mutagenesis using T-DNA insertion, map-based cloning, and genetically modified rice using transformation techniques.

State-of-the-art Genome Profiling (GP)

The traditional approach for species identification is exclusively based on phenotypic traits such as morphological, anatomical, chemical properties and others, which are often affected by environmental factors and thus are difficult to analyse and unreliable. Interspecies homogeneity, intraspecies variability and the existence of undescribed species often lead to phenotypic misidentification. Moreover, species, which are phenotypically far less prominent, cannot be always identified in this way. To overcome these problems, genotypebased (nucleic acid-based) techniques have been employed as an alternative or complementary approach and have continuously been developed including RFLP, AFLP, RAPD, 16S rRNA or 16S-23S internal transcribed spacer (ITS) sequence analysis and others. These methods provide a possible way to identify species directly based on their genomic sequences but none of them have been shown to identify species in general, mainly because of the insufficiency in the amount of information which they can provide. In this stream, the whole genome sequencing is surely the most definitive solution for species identification though simply too redundant for such purposes and impossible in practice to analyse all the constituents of a heavily dense population. On the other hand, the information obtained from the comparison of a single gene is often not sufficient to place a species at the appropriate position on the phylogenetic tree. A realistic solution conforming to the notion of the amount of information sufficient for species identification and demonstrated this by inventing a novel method called Genome Profiling (GP), which is a temperature-gradient gel electrophoresis (TGGE) analysis of random-PCR products. Next, the complexity of the generated data, genome profiles, can be simplified by extracting feature points in GP, *i.e.*, species identification dots (spiddos) which can be used for further processing of measuring the similarity of two species by calculating Pattern Similarity Score (PaSS). Further, the technical advances by constructing internet-based GP databases (named On-web GP), and developing a highly reproducible and miniaturized system (micro-TGGE) have moved this technology towards being a universal, general and global tool for species identification.

RECOMBINANT DNA TECHNOLOGY

Gene Targeting (GT)

Gene targeting (GT) is a key technology for the rational, accurate and safe exploitation of plantsthrough genetic manipulation. Moreover, it offers the potential to completely knockout the expression of target genes or to make specific changes to gene function, objectives that cannot be achieved by conventional transgenesis. The ability to target DNA integration would permit the locus-specific integration of a transgene into a predetermined site of the host genome, avoiding the accidental inactivation of an endogenous gene localized at the insertion site or the unexpected expression profiles of the transgene itself, the so-called position effect. Systematic isolation and sequencing of genomic DNA flanking the insertion sites.

The plastid genome transformation technique has gained prominence due to its better integration and less chances of random spread. The genome propagated by higher plant plastids, the plastome, is typically a double stranded DNA molecule of 130 to 160 kb. Over one hundred copies of this genome can be present in a single plastid. It is ideally represented as a circular monomer containing 2 inverted repeats, even though reality is more complex since linear and circular multimers have been frequently detected. The complete sequence of this highly polyploidy genome is available for about 20 different species of angiosperms. The first successful transformation of tobacco was performed using as marker a mutant plastid DNA fragment covering the 16SrRNA gene derived from a line resistant to spectinomycin and streptomycin. Major improvements in the selection process were soon obtained with the dominant aadA marker gene, inactivating spectinomycin or streptomycin. When fused to GFP, this marker can be used to track the selection process.

Genes encoding resistance to kanamycin, nptII and more recently aphA-6 are also possible options, and could be more appropriate for some species.

There are three different fates for the external DNA to get integrated into the native genome. They are homologous recombination, illegitimate recombination or nonhomologous end joining, and single-strand annealing.. Single-strand annealing (SSA), a third path of repair, requires the presence of repeated sequences on both sides of a break. After exonuclease degradation of the 5′ ends, repair occurs by annealing of the two complementary sequences, a process leading to the loss of the genetic information contained between these repeats. With respect to the species preferential DSB repair pathway, HR but also IR mediates transgene integration. This second aspect explains the inefficiency of GT in higher plants, which use HR as a minor pathway of repair. Thus, despite the fact that transgene integration processes are still unclear in plants transgenic DNA would be preferentially integrated by end joining whether or not sharing homology within the host genome.

GM Crops

The U.S. Food and Drug Administration (FDA) has found no evidence to indicate that either ordinary plant deoxyribonucleic acid (DNA) or the DNA inserted into plants using bioengineering presents food safety problems. Nor are the small amounts of the newly expressed proteins likely to change dramatically the safety profile of the plant. If safety concerns should arise, however, they would most likely fall into one of three broad categories: allergens, toxins, or anti-nutrients. FDA has extensive experience in evaluating the safety of such substances in food. It is important to note that the kinds of food safety testing typically conducted by developers of a bioengineered food crop to ensure that their foods meet all applicable requirements of the Food, Drug and Cosmetics Act (FD&C Act) address these potential concerns. In the event that something unexpected does occur, this testing provides a way to detect such changes at the developmental stage and defer marketing until any concern is resolved.

As aforementioned, some of the food safety concerns that could arise include:

Allergens: Foods normally contain many thousands of different proteins. While the majority of proteins do not cause allergic reactions, virtually all known human allergens are proteins. Since genetic engineering can introduce a new protein into a food plant, it is possible that this technique could introduce a previously unknown allergen into the food supply or could introduce a known allergen into a "new" food.

Toxins: It is possible that a new protein, as introduced into a crop as a result of the genetic modification, could cause toxicity.

Anti-nutrients: It is possible that the introduction of anti-nutrients, such as molecules like phytic acid, could reduce essential dietary minerals such as phosphorus.

The use of genetic engineering techniques could also result in unintended alterations in the amounts of substances normally found in a food, such as a reduction of Vitamin C or an increase in the concentration of a naturally occurring toxicant in the plant food.

5

Organic Manures and Biofertilizers

INTRODUCTION

BIOFERTILIZER

Biofertilizers are ready to use live formulates of such beneficial microorganisms which on application to seed, root or soil mobilize the availability of nutrients by their biological activity in particular, and help build up the micro-flora and in turn the soil health in general. With the introduction of green revolution technologies the modern agriculture is getting more and more dependent upon the steady supply of synthetic inputs (mainly fertilizers), which are products of fossil fuel (coal+ petroleum). Adverse effects are being noticed due to the excessive and imbalanced use of these synthetic inputs. This situation has lead to identifying harmless inputs like biofertilizers. Use of such natural products like biofertilizers in crop cultivation will help in safeguarding the soil health and also the quality of crop products.

Benefits of Biofertilizers

- Increase crop yield by 20-30%.
- Replace chemical nitrogen and phosphorus by 25%.
- Stimulate plant growth.
- Activate the soil biologically.
- Restore natural soil fertility.

- Provide protection against drought and some soil borne diseases.
- Cost effective.
- Suppliment to fertilizers.
- Eco-friendly (Friendly with nature).
- Reduces the costs towards fertilizers use, especially regarding nitrogen and phosphorus.

For Nitrogen :

- Rhizobium for legume crops.
- Azotobacter/Azospirillum for non legume crops.
- Acetobacter for sugarcane only.
- Blue –Green Algae (BGA) and Azolla for low land paddy.

For Phosphorous :

- Phosphatika for all crops to be applied with Rhizobium,
- Azotobacter, Azospirillum and Acetobacter

For enriched compost :

- Cellulolytic fungal culture
- Phosphotika and Azotobacter culture

What biofertilizers are recommended for crops?

- Rhizobium + Phosphotika at 200 g each per 10 kg of seed as seed treatment are recommended for pulses such as pigeonpea, green gram, black gram, cowpea etc., groundnut and soybean.
- Azotobacter + Phosphotika at 200 gm each per 10 kg of seed as seed treatment are useful for wheat, sorghum, maize, cotton, mustard etc.
- For transplanted rice, the recommendation is to dip the roots of seedlings for 8 to 10 hours in a solution of Azospirillum + Phosphotika at 5 kg each per ha.

Biofertilizers are Applied to Crops

- *Seed treatment:* 200 g of nitrogenous biofertilizer and 200 g of Phosphotika are suspended in 300-400 ml of water and mixed thoroughly. Ten kg seeds are treated with this paste and dried in shade. The treated seeds have to be sown as soon as possible.

- *Seedling root dip:* For rice crop, a bed is made in the field and filled with water. Recommended biofertilizers are mixed in this water and the roots of seedlings are dipped for 8-10 hrs.
- *Soil treatment:* 4 kg each of the recommended biofertilizers are mixed in 200 kg of compost and kept overnight. This mixture is incorporated in the soil at the time of sowing or planting.

Good Response to Biofertilizer Application

- Biofertilizer product must contain good effective strain in appropriate population and should be free from contaminating microorganisms.
- Select right combination of biofertilizers and use before expiry date.
- Use suggested method of application and apply at appropriate time as per the information provided on the label.
- For seed treatment adequate adhesive should be used for better results.
- For problematic soils use corrective methods like lime or gypsum pelleting of seeds or correction of soil pH by use of lime.
- Ensure the supply of phosphorus and other nutrients.

Response from the Application of Biofertilizers

On account of quality of product :

- Use of ineffective strain.
- Insufficient population of microorganisms.
- High level of contaminants.

On account of inadequate storage facilities :

- May have been exposed to high temperature.
- May have been stored in hostile conditions.

On account of usage :

- Not used by recommended method in appropriate doses.
- Poor quality adhesive.
- Used with strong doses of plant protection chemicals.

On account of soil and environment :

- High soil temperature or low soil moisture.
- Acidity or alkalinity in soil.
- Poor availability of phosphorous and molybdenum.
- Presence of high native population or presence of bacteriophages.

Precautions one should take for Using Biofertilizers

- Biofertilizer packets need to be stored in cool and dry place away from direct sunlight and heat.
- Right combinations of biofertilizers have to be used.
- As Rhizobium is crop specific, one should use for the specified crop only.
- Other chemicals should not be mixed with the biofertilizers.
- While purchasing one should ensure that each packet is provided with necessary information like name of the product, name of the crop for which intended, name and address of the manufacturer, date of manufacture, date of expiry, batch number and instructions for use.
- The packet has to be used before its expiry, only for the specified crop and by the recommended method of application.
- Biofertilizers are live product and require care in the storage
- Both nitrogenous and phosphatic biofertilizers are to be used to get the best results.
- It is important to use biofertilizers along with chemical fertilizers and organic manures.
- Biofertilizers are not replacement of fertilizers but can supplement plant nutrient requirements.

ORGANIC MANURE

Organic manures are natural products used by farmers to provide food (plant nutrients) for the crop plants. There are a number of organic manures like farmyard manure, green manures, compost prepared from crop residues and other farm wastes, vermicompost, oil cakes, and biological wastes - animal bones, slaughter house refuse.

Organic Manures Beneficial in the Cultivation of Crops

Organic manures increase the organic matter in the soil. Organic matter in turn releases the plant food in available from for the use of crops. However, organic manures should not be seen only as carriers of plant food. These manures also enable a soil to hold more water and also help to improve the drainage in clay soils. They provide organic acids that help to dissolve soil nutrients and make them available for the plants.

Organic Manures differing from Fertilizers

Organic manures have low nutrient content and therefore need to be applied in larger quantities. For example, to get 25 kg of NPK, one will need 600 to 2000 kg of organic manure where as the same amount of NPK can be given by 50 kg of an NPK complex fertilizer. The nutrient content of organic manures is highly variable from place to place, lot to lot, and method of preparation. The composition of fertilizers is almost constant. For example, urea contain 46% N regardless of which factory makes it any where in the world.

Plant Nutrients are Provided by Organic Manures

Just as different fertilizers contain different amounts of plant nutrients, organic manures are also not alike. Average quality of farmyard manure provides 12 kg nutrients per ton and compost provides 40 kg per ton. Most of the legume green manures provide 20 kg of nitrogen per ton.

Each ton of sorghum/rice/maize straw can be expected to add 26 kg of nutrients.

Green Manuring

Green manuring is the practice of growing a short duration, succulent and leafy legume crop and ploughing the plants in the same field before they form seeds.

Green Leaf Manuring

Green leaf manuring refers to adding the loppings from legume plants or trees to a field and then incorporating them into the soil by ploughing.

Green Manure Crops are Beneficial

Sesbania, Crotalaria, 'Pillipesara', Cowpea etc. are good for green manuring.

Popular Green Leaf Manuring Plants

Glyricidia, Pongamia, Leucina are common green leaf manuring plants.

Compost

Compost is well decomposed organic wastes like plant residues, animal dung, and urine earth from cattle sheds, waste fodder etc.

Good Compost is Prepared

Compost making is the process of decomposing organic wastes in a pit. Site for compost making is selected should be at a high level and water should not pond during monsoon season. Pit should be of 3′ depth and 6′ to 8′ width. Length may be of any convenient size. The process is as follows:

- Make slurry of the cattle dung with water.
- Prepare 6" layer of organic wastes – plant residues, sweepings from the cattle shed, waste fodder, dried plants stalks and leaves etc. and sprinkle water to just moisten it. (Over watering should be avoided).
- Cover with the layer with urine earth and cattle dung slurry.
- Add 5 to 10 kg of super phosphate for every 10 tons of organic wastes.
- Repeat the process of putting such layers till the pit is full.
- Close the pit with urine earth, waste fodder and then heap the soil till it gets convex shape (about 1 to 1.5′ above the ground) so that the rainwater rolls away.

- After six months compost is ready to apply to the fields.

The pit can be filled up if sufficient organic wastes are available. Otherwise a temporary partition can be made in the pit with bamboos or stalks and the pit can be filled up over time filling each partitioned area as and when the material is available for composting.

Compost Making

Due to quick heating and drying during the decomposition of organic wastes, nitrogen in the organic wastes will be lost due to volatilization. Addition of super phosphate decreases such nitrogen losses. It will also increase the phosphate content of compost.

Vermicomposting

Vermicomposting is a type of compost making in which earthworms are used to convert organic wastes into valuable material to supply nutrients for crops.

ORGANIC FARMING AND MANURES

MANURES

Manures are plant and animal wastes that are used as sources of plant nutrients. They release nutrients after their decomposition. The art of collecting and using wastes from animal, human and vegetable sources for improving crop productivity is as old as agriculture.

Manures are the organic materials derived from animal, human and plant residues which contain plant nutrients in complex organic forms. Naturally occurring or synthetic chemicals containing plant nutrients are called fertilizers. Manures with low nutrient, content per unit quantity have longer residual effect besides improving soil physical properties compared to fertilizer with high nutrient content. Major sources of manures are:

- Cattle shed wastes-dung, urine and slurry from biogas plants

- Human habitation wastes-night soil, human urine, town refuse, sewage, sludge and sullage
- Poultry Jitter, droppings of sheep and goat
- Slaughterhouse wastes-bone meal, meat meal, blood meal, horn and hoof meal, Fish wastes
- Byproducts of agro industries-oil cakes, bagasse and press mud, fruit and vegetable processing wastes etc.
- Crop wastes-sugarcane trash, stubbles and other related material
- Water hyacinth, weeds and tank silt, and
- Green manure crops and green leaf manuring material.

Manures can also be grouped, into bulky organic manures and concentrated organic manures based on concentration of the nutrients.

Bulky Organic Manures

Bulky organic manures contain small percentage of nutrients and they are applied in large quantities. Farmyard manure (FYM), compost and green-manure are the most important and widely used bulky organic manures. Use of bulky organic manures has several advantages:

- They supply plant nutrients including micronutrients
- They improve soil physical properties like structure, water holding capacity etc.,
- They increase the availability of nutrients
- Carbon dioxide released during decomposition acts as a CO_2 fertilizer and
- Plant parasitic nematodes and fungi are controlled to some extent by altering the balance of microorganisms in the soil.

Farmyard Manure

Farmyard manure refers to the decomposed mixture of dung and urine of farm animals along with litter and left over material from roughages or fodder fed to the cattle. On an average well decomposed farmyard manure contains 0.5 per cent N, 0.2 per cent P_2O_5 and .0.5 per cent K_2O. The present method of preparing farmyard manure by the farmers is defective. Urine, which is wasted, contains one per cent nitrogen and 1.35 per cent potassium. Nitrogen present in urine is mostly in the form of urea which is subjected to volatilization losses.

Even during storage, nutrients are lost due to leaching and volatilization. However, it is practically impossible to avoid losses altogether, but can be reduced by following improved method of preparation of farmyard manure. Trenches of size 6 m to 7.5 m length, 1.5 m to 2.0 m width and 1.0 m deep are dug.

All available litter and refuse is mixed with soil and spread in the shed so as to absorb urine. The next morning, urine soaked refuse along with dung is collected and placed in the trench. Trench from one end should be taken up for filling with daily collection. When the section is filled up to a height of 45 cm to 60 cm above the ground level, the top of the heap is made into a dome and plastered with cow dung earth slurry. The process is continued and when the first trench is completely filled, second trench is prepared.

The manure becomes ready for use in about four to five months after plastering. If urine is not collected in the bedding, it can be collected along with washings of the cattle shed in a cemented pit from which it is later added to the farmyard manure pit. Chemical preservatives can also be used to reduce losses and enrich farmyard manure.

The commonly used chemicals are gypsum and superphosphate. Gypsum is spread in the cattle shed which absorbs urine and prevents volatilization loss of urea present in the urine and also adds calcium and sulphur. Superphosphate also acts similarly in reducing losses and also increases phosphorus content.

Partially rotten farmyard manure has to be applied three to four weeks before sowing while well rotten manure can be applied immediately before sowing. Generally 10 to 20 t/ha is applied, but more than 20 t/ha is applied to fodder grasses and vegetables. In such cases farmyard manure should be applied at least 15 days in advance to avoid immobilization of nitrogen. The existing practice of leaving manure in small heaps scattered in the field for a very long period leads toloss of nutrients.

These losses can be reduced by spreading the manure and incorporating by ploughing immediately after application. Vegetable crops such as potato, tomato, sweet-potato, carrot, raddish, onion etc., respond well to the farmyard manure. The other responsive crops are sugarcane, rice, napier grass and orchard crops like oranges, banana, mango and plantation crop like coconut.

The entire amount of nutrients present in farmyard manure is not available immediately. About 30 per cent of nitrogen, 60 to 70 per cent of phosphorus and 70 per cent of potassium are available to the first crop.

Sheep and Goat Manure

The droppings of sheep and goats contain higher nutrients than farmyard manure and compost. On an average, the manure contains 3 per cent N, 1 per cent P_2O_5 and 2 per cent K_2O.It is applied to the field in two ways. The sweeping of sheep or goat sheds are placed in pits for decomposition and it is applied later to the field. The nutrients present in the urine are *wasted* in this method. The second method is sheep penning, wherein sheep and goats are kept overnight in the field and urine and fecal matter added to the soil is incorporated to a shallow depth by working blade harrow or cultivator or cultivator.

Poultry Manure

The excreta of birds ferment very quickly. If left exposed, 50 percent of its nitrogen is lost within 30 days. Poultry manure contains higher nitrogen and phosphorus compared to other bulky organic manures. The average nutrient content is 3.03 per cent N; 2.63 per cent P_2O_5 and 1.4 per cent K_2O.

Concentrated Organic Manures

Concentrated organic manures have higher nutrient content than bulky organic manure. The important concentrated organic manures are oilcakes, blood meal, fish manure etc. These are also known as organic nitrogen fertilizer. Before their organic nitrogen is used by the crops, it is converted through bacterial action into readily usable ammoniacal nitrogen and nitrate nitrogen. These organic fertilizers are, therefore, relatively slow acting, but they supply available nitrogen for a longer period.

Oil Cakes

After oil is extracted from oilseeds, the remaining solid portion is dried as cake which can, be used as manure. The oil cakes are of two types:

- Edible oil cakes which can be safely fed to livestock; *e.g.* Groundnut cake, Coconut cake etc., and
- Non edible oil cakes which are not fit for feeding livestock; *e.g.*: Castor cake, *Neem cake, Mahua cake* etc.

Both edible and non-edible oil cakes can be used as manures. However, edible oil cakes are fed to cattle and non-edible oil cakes are used as manures especially for horticultural crops.

Nutrients present in oil cakes, after mineralization, are made available to crops 7 to 10 days after application. Oilcakes need to be well powdered before application for even distribution and quicker decomposition.

The average nutrient content of different oil-cakes is presented in the following table.

Average nutrient content of oil cakes

Oil-cakes	*Nutrient content (%)*		
	N	*P_2O_5*	*K_2O*
Non edible oil-cakes			
Castor cake	4.3	1.8	1.3
Cotton seed cake (undecorticated)	3.9	1.8	1.6
Karanj cake	3.9	0.9	1.2
Mahua cake	2.5	0.8	1.2
Safflower cake (undecorticated)	4.9	1.4	1.2
Edible oil-cakes			
Coconut cake	3.0	1.9	1.8

Cotton seed cake (decorticated)	6.4	2.9	2.2
Groundnut cake	7.3	1.5	1.3
Linseed cake	4.9	1.4	1.3
Niger cake	4.7	1.8	1.3
Rape seed cake	5.2	1.8	1.2
Safflower cake (decorticated)	7.9	2.2	1.9
Sesamum cake	6.2	2.0	1.2

OTHER CONCENTRATED ORGANIC MANURES

Blood meal when dried and powdered can be used as manure. The meat of dead animals is dried and converted into meat meal which is a good source of nitrogen. Average nutrient content of animal based concentrated organic manures is given in the following table.

Average Nutrient Content of Animal Based Concentrated Organic Manures

Organic Manures	*Nutrient Content (%)*		
	N	P_2O_5	K_2O
Blood meal	10 - 12	1 - 2	1.0
Meat meal	10.5	2.5	0.5
Fish meal	4 - 10	3 - 9	0.3 - 1.5
Horn and Hoof meal	13	-	-
Raw bone meal	3 - 4	20 - 25	-
Steamed bone meal	1 - 2	25 - 30	-

ROLE OF ORGANIC MATTER IN SOIL FERTILITY

Organic matter forms a very small but an important portion and it is obtained from dead plant roots, crop residues, various organic manures like farmyard manure, compost and green manure, fungi, bacteria, worms and insects.

FUNCTIONS OF ORGANIC MATTER

- Organic matter improves the physical condition of the soil, particularly the structure.
- Decaying organic matter acts as a food material for bacteria, fungi and other organisms.

- Presence of organic matter dissolves many insoluble soil minerals and make them available to plants
- It plays an important role in the nutrient supplying power of soil as it has got high cation exchange capacity (CEC)
- It increases the water holding capacity of the soil, particularly in sandy soils.
- It improves aeration and infiltration in heavy soils.
- It reduces loss of soil by water and wind erosion
- It regulate soil temperature
- It serves as an important source of certain plant of food element (N, P, S etc.).
- The buffering nature of the organic matter is considered to be advantageous in the residue management of pesticides, herbicide and other heavy metals.

ORGANIC AND INORGANIC FERTILIZERS

A fertilizer is any material, organic or inorganic, natural or synthetic, that supplies plants with the necessary nutrients for plant growth and optimum yield. Organic fertilizers are natural materials of either plant or animal origin, including livestock manure, green manures, crop residues, household waste, compost, and woodland litter. Inorganic (or mineral) fertilizers are fertilizers mined from mineral deposits with little processing (*e.g.*, lime, potash, or phosphate rock), or industrially manufactured through chemical processes (*e.g.*, urea). Inorganic fertilizers vary in appearance depending on the process of manufacture. The particles can be of many different sizes and shapes (crystals, pellets, granules, or dust) and the fertilizer grades can include straight fertilizers (containing one nutrient element only), compound fertilizers (containing two or more nutrients usually combined in a homogeneous mixture by chemical interaction) and fertilizer blends (formed by physically blending mineral fertilizers to obtain desired nutrient ratios).

SPECIFIC PROPERTIES OF ORGANIC FERTILIZERS

Organic nutrient sources are highly heterogeneous and vary in quality and quantity. The quality aspect is important in determining the nutrient release potential of the organic fertilizer. Microorganisms that decompose organic fertilizers use the carbon in such materials as an energy source for growth. Required in even bigger quantities by microorganisms for growth and reproduction is nitrogen (N). Commonly available materials are often particularly low in N content. For organic fertilizers with low N contents (such as cereal straw and most smallholder farmyard manures), microorganisms themselves will consume much of the available N for their own growth. Consequently, insignificant amounts of N will be released for the crop. Thus, on their own, poor quality materials have limited potential to enhance productivity. The effectiveness of such materials can be improved by combining them with mineral N fertilizers such as ammonium-nitrate or urea. Mineral fertilizers may be used more efficiently by crops growing on soils with adequate amounts of soil organic matter supplied by organic fertilizers.

DIFFERENCES BETWEEN ORGANIC AND INORGANIC FERTILIZERS IN TERMS OF THEIR USE

Organic Fertilizers

Soil fertility on smallholder farms is almost entirely dependant on locally available resources. Cattle manure, cereal and legume stover, and woodland litter are the commonly used organic fertilizers, but these are rarely applied in sufficient quantities to impact on crop yields. The use of high quality organic fertilizers is rarely practised, although through research and extension activities in Africa, some farmers now include legume green manures or legume-based fallows in crop sequences. The main advantage of using organic fertilizers is that, compared to mineral fertilizers, they are usually available on or near the farm at very little or no cost other than labour costs of handling, transportation, or opportunity costs of land used for their production.

Inorganic (Mineral) Fertilizers

Mineral fertilizers need to be applied to crop at least two times within a growing season (split application), either basally at planting or top-dressed during vegetative growth. The amount of inorganic fertilizer used in most smallholder farming systems falls far below standard extension recommendations, due to poor purchasing power, risk aversion due to poor and unreliable rainfall, and lack of significant returns. When available, fertilizer use is not overly labour intensive, thus allowing time for other tasks (or for earning income elsewhere).

Differences between Organic and Inorganic Fertilizers in Terms of Application

The method and timing of fertilizer application is an essential component of good farming. For organic materials, decomposition rate and timing of application influence the release of nutrients to the crop. Organic fertilizer application methods include broadcasting, banding, and spot application (or side-dressing). Broadcasting requires less labour and helps to evenly cover the field surface before incorporation into soil through plowing or hand-hoeing. Incorporation generally increases the fertility status of the whole plow layer. If the quantity of organic fertilizer is limited, it may be banded along furrows or spot applied, but the seed needs to be placed away from the fertilizer. Side-dressed organic fertilizers are not likely to have much immediate effect due to delayed nutrient release.

Mineral fertilizers can be applied by hand or with application equipment. When hand applied, it is essential to distribute the fertilizers uniformly and at the recommended rates to avoid over- or under-fertilization. Application equipment needs proper adjustment to ensure uniform spreading. Broadcast fertilizer should be incorporated after application to enhance effectiveness or to avoid evaporation losses of N. With banding or spot application, take care that no fertilizer is placed too close to either the seed or the germinating plant, to avoid damage to the seedling or roots.

Differences in Terms of their Effectiveness

Continued use of organic fertilizers results in increased soil organic matter, reduced erosion, better water infiltration and aeration, higher soil biological activity as the materials decompose in soil, and increased yields after the year of application (residual effects). Proper handling of organic fertilizers enhances their quality and effectiveness. For example, with the exception of green manures, there is significant crop response if organic fertilizers are combined with N-based mineral fertilizers or other N-rich organic materials. Mineral fertilizers on the other hand immediately supply nutrients needed by crops. Basal fertilizers contain elements required for good crop establishment and early growth while top-dressing can be done through split applications depending on visible hunger signs and/or moisture availability. In risky environments, spot application of small amounts of N fertilizers improves fertilizer effectiveness. The best response to fertilizer use is obtained if the soil has a high inherent fertility level (high organic matter status). Building inherent fertility requires practices such as retaining crop residues on the field.

TYPES OF ORGANIC MANURES

HUMUS

In soil science, humus (coined 1790–1800; < *Latin*: earth, ground) refers to any organic matter that has reached a point of stability, where it will break down no further and might, if conditions do not change, remain as it is for centuries, if not millennia. In agriculture, humus is sometimes also used to describe mature compost, or natural compost extracted from a forest or other spontaneous source for use to amend soil. It is also used to describe a topsoil horizon that contains organic matter (humus type, humus form, humus profile).

HUMIFICATION

Transformation of Organic Matter into Humus

The process of "humification" can occur naturally in soil, or in the production of compost. The importance of chemically stable humus is thought by some to be the fertility it provides to soils in both a physical and chemical sense, though some agricultural experts put a greater focus on other features of it, such as its ability to suppress disease. It helps the soil retain moisture by increasing microporosity, and encourages the formation of good soil structure.

The incorporation of oxygen into large organic molecular assemblages generates many active, negatively charged sites that bind to positively charged ions (cations) of plant nutrients, making them more available to the plant by way of ion exchange. Humus allows soil organisms to feed and reproduce, and is often described as the "life-force" of the soil. Yet, it is difficult to define humus precisely; it is a highly complex substance, which is still not fully understood. Humus should be differentiated from decomposing organic matter in that the latter is rough-looking material, with the original plant remains still visible, whereas fully humified organic matter is uniform in appearance (a dark, spongy, jelly-like substance) and amorphous in structure, and may remain such for millennia or more.

It has no determinate shape, structure or character. However, humified organic matter, when examined under the microscope may reveal tiny plant, animal or microbial remains that have been mechanically, but not chemically, degraded. This suggests a fuzzy boundary between humus and organic matter. In most literature, humus is clearly considered as an integral part of soil organic matter.

Plant remains (including those that passed through an animal gut and were excreted as feces) contain organic compounds: sugars, starches, proteins, carbohydrates, lignins, waxes, resins, and organic acids.

The process of organic matter decay in the soil begins with the decomposition of sugars and starches from carbohydrates, which break down easily as detritivores initially invade the dead plant organs, while the remaining cellulose and lignin break down more slowly.

Simple proteins, organic acids, starches and sugars break down rapidly, while crude proteins, fats, waxes and resins remain relatively unchanged for longer periods of time. Lignin, which is quickly transformed by white-rot fungi, is one of the main precursors of humus, together with by-products of microbial and animal activity. The end-product of this process, the humus, is thus a mixture of compounds and complex life chemicals of plant, animal, or microbial origin that has many functions and benefits in the soil. Earthworm humus (vermicompost) is considered by some to be the best organic manure there is.

Stability of Humus

Compost that is readily capable of further decomposition is sometimes referred to as effective or active humus, though scientists would say that, if it is not stable, it is not humus at all. This kind of compost, rich in plant remains and fulvic acids, is an excellent source of plant nutrients, but of little value with respect to long-term soil structure and tilth.

Stable (or passive) humus consists of humic acids and humins, which are so highly insoluble, or so tightly bound to clay particles and hydroxides, that they cannot be penetrated by microbes and are greatly resistant to further decomposition. Thus stable humus adds few readily available nutrients to the soil, but plays an essential part in providing its physical structure. Some very stable humus complexes have survived for thousands of years. The most stable humus is that formed from the slow oxidation of black carbon, after the incorporation of finely powdered charcoal into the topsoil. This process is at the origin of the formation of the fertile Amazonian dark earths or Terra preta do Indio.

BENEFITS OF SOIL ORGANIC MATTER AND HUMUS

- The process that converts raw organic matter into humus feeds the soil population of microorganisms and other creatures, thus maintains high and healthy levels of soil life.

- The rate at which raw organic matter is converted into humus promotes (when fast) or limits (when slow) the coexistence of plants, animals, and microbes in soil.
- Effective humus and stable humus are further sources of nutrients to microbes, the former provides a readily available supply, and the latter acts as a longer-term storage reservoir.
- Decomposition of dead plant material causes complex organic compounds to be slowly oxidized (lignin-like humus) or to break down into simpler forms (sugars and amino sugars, aliphatic, and phenolic organic acids), which are further transformed into microbial biomass (microbial humus) or are reorganized, and further oxidized, into humic assemblages (fulvic and humic acids), which bind to clay minerals and metal hydroxides. There has been a long debate about the ability of plants to uptake humic substances from their root systems and to metabolize them. There is now a consensus about how humus plays a hormonal role rather than simply a nutritional role in plant physiology.
- Humus is a colloidal substance, and increases the soil's cation exchange capacity, hence its ability to store nutrients by chelation. While these nutrient cations are accessible to plants, they are held in the soil safe from being leached by rain or irrigation.
- Humus can hold the equivalent of 80–90% of its weight in moisture, and therefore increases the soil's capacity to withstand drought conditions.
- The biochemical structure of humus enables it to moderate – or buffer – excessive acid or alkaline soil conditions.
- During the humification process, microbes secrete sticky gum-like mucilages; these contribute to the crumb structure (tilth) of the soil by holding particles

together, and allowing greater aeration of the soil. Toxic substances such as heavy metals, as well as excess nutrients, can be chelated (that is, bound to the complex organic molecules of humus) and so prevented from entering the wider ecosystem.

- The dark colour of humus (usually black or dark brown) helps to warm up cold soils in the spring.

GREEN MANURE

In agriculture, a green manure is a type of cover crop grown primarily to add nutrients and organic matter to the soil. Typically, a green manure crop is grown for a specific period of time, and then ploughed under and incorporated into the soil while green or shortly after flowering.

Green manure crops are commonly associated with organic agriculture, and are considered essential for annual cropping systems that wish to be sustainable. Traditionally, the practice of green manuring can be traced back to the fallow cycle of crop rotation, which was used to allow soils to recover.

FUNCTIONS OF GREEN MANURE CROPS

Green manure crops may include legumes such as cowpeas, soybeans, annual sweet clover, vetch, sesbania, and velvet beans, as well as non-leguminous crops such as sudangrass, millet, sorghum, and buckwheat. Legumes are often used as green manure crops for their nitrogen fixing abilities, while non-leguminous crops are used primarily for weed suppression and addition of biomass to the soil. Green manures usually perform multiple functions, that include soil improvement and soil protection:

- Leguminous green manures such as clover and vetch contain nitrogen-fixing symbiotic bacteria in root nodules that fix atmospheric nitrogen in a form that plants can use.
- Green manures increase the percentage of organic matter (biomass) in the soil, thereby improving water retention, aeration, and other soil characteristics.

- The root systems of some varieties of green manure grow deep in the soil and bring up nutrient resources unavailable to shallower-rooted crops.
- Common cover crop functions of weed suppression and prevention of soil erosion and compaction are often also taken into account when selecting and using green manures.
- Some green manure crops, when allowed to flower, provide forage for pollinating insects.

Incorporation of cover crops into the soil is immediately followed by an increase in abundance of soil microorganisms that aid in the decomposition of this fresh material. The degradation of plant material allows the nutrients held within the green manure to be released and made available to the succeeding crop. This additional decomposition also allows for the re-incorporation of nutrients that are found in the soil on a particular farm such as nitrogen (N), potassium (K), phosphorus (P), calcium (Ca), magnesium (Mg), and sulfur (S). Microbial activity in the soil also leads to the formation of mycelium and viscous materials which benefit the health of the soil by increasing its soil structure (*i.e.* by aggregation). Soil that is well-aggregated has increased aeration and water infiltration rates, and is more easily turned or tilled than non- aggregated soil. Further aeration of the soil results from the ability of the root systems of many green manure crops to efficiently penetrate compact soils. The amount of humus found in the soil also increases with higher rates of decomposition, which is beneficial for the growth of the crop succeeding the green manure crop.

Green manure crops are also useful for weed control, erosion prevention, and reduction of insect pests and diseases. The deep rooting properties of many green manure crops make them efficient at suppressing weeds. Green manure crops often provide habitat for many native pollinators as well as predatory beneficial insects, which allow for a reduction in the input of insecticides where cover crops are planted. Some green manures are also successful at suppressing plant diseases, especially Verticillium wilt in potato. Incorporation of green manures into a farming system can drastically reduce, if not eliminate, the need for additional products such as supplemental fertilizers and pesticides.

NUTRIENT CREATION

Green manure is broken down into plant nutrient components by heterotrophic bacteria that consumes organic matter. Warmth and moisture contribute to this process, similar to creating compost fertilizer. The plant matter releases large amounts of carbon dioxide and weak acids that react with insoluble soil minerals to release beneficial nutrients. Soil that are high in calcium minerals, for example, can be given green manure to generate a higher phosphate content in the soil, which in turn acts as a fertilizer.

The ratio of carbon to nitrogen in a plant is a crucial factor to consider, since it will impact the nutrient content of the soil and may starve a crop of nitrogen, if the incorrect plants are used to make green manure. The ratio of carbon to nitrogen will differ from species to species, and depending upon the age of the plant. The ratio is referred to as C : N. The value of N is always one, whereas the value of carbon or carbohydrates is expressed in a value of about 10 up to 90; the ratio must be less than 30:1 to prevent the manure bacteria from depleting existing nitrogen in the soil. Rhizobium are soil organisms that interact with green manure to retain atmospheric nitrogen in the soil. Legumes, such as beans, alfalfa, clover and lupines, have root systems rich in rhizobium, often making them the preferred source of green manure material.

Green Manure Crops

Another important contribution of green manure to an agricultural field is the nitrogen fixing ability and consequent nitrogen accumulation in the soil, particularly of those leguminous crops used. Depending on the species of cover crop grown, the amount of nitrogen released into the soil lies between 40 and 200 pounds per acre. With green manure use, the amount of nitrogen that is available to the succeeding crop is usually in the range of 40-60% of the total amount of nitrogen that is contained within the green manure crop.

Average biomass yields and nitrogen yields of several legumes by crop	*Biomass tons acre^{-1}*	*N lbs acre^{-1}*
Sweet clover	1.75	120
Berseem clover	1.10	70
Crimson clover	1.40	100
Hairy vetch	1.75	110

Use in Organic Farming

Organic farming relies on soil health and cycling of nutrients through the soil using natural processes. Green manures perform the vital function of fertilization, in concert with the addition of animal manures if those are used. While there are a variety of beneficial aspects of the use of green manure, there are also limitations to consider. Time, energy, and resources (monetary and natural) are required to successfully grow and utilize these cover crops. Consequently, it is important to choose green manure crops based on the growing region and annual precipitation amounts to ensure efficient growth and use of the cover crop(s).

Green manure also brings other organic advantages with it depending upon the plant type used. Buckwheat, for example, prevents the spread of weeds, and Winter wheat and Winter rye can also be used for grazing.

6

Biofertilizers: Pollution and Contamination of Soil

One of the major concerns in today's world is the pollution and contamination of soil. The use of chemical fertilizers and pesticides has caused tremendous harm to the environment. An answer to this is the biofertilizer, an environmentally friendly fertilizer now used in most countries. Biofertilizers are organisms that enrich the nutrient quality of soil. The main sources of biofertilizers are bacteria, fungi, and cynobacteria (blue-green algae). The most striking relationship that these have with plants is symbiosis, in which the partners derive benefits from each other.

Plants have a number of relationships with fungi, bacteria, and algae, the most common of which are with mycorrhiza, rhizobium, and cyanophyceae. These are known to deliver a number of benefits including plant nutrition, disease resistance, and tolerance to adverse soil and climatic conditions. These techniques have proved to be successful biofertilizers that form a health relationship with the roots.

Biofertilizers will help solve such problems as increased salinity of the soil and chemical run-offs from the agricultural fields. Thus, biofertilizers are important if we are to ensure a healthy future for the generations to come.

MYCORRHIZA

Mycorrhizae are a group of fungi that include a number of types based on the different structures formed inside or outside the root. These are specific fungi that match with a number of favourable parameters of the the host plant on which it grows. This includes soil type, the presence of particular chemicals in the soil types, and other conditions.

These fungi grow on the roots of these plants. In fact, seedlings that have mycorrhizal fungi growing on their roots survive better after transplantation and grow faster. The fungal symbiont gets shelter and food from the plant which, in turn, acquires an array of benefits such as better uptake of phosphorus, salinity and drought tolerance, maintenance of water balance, and overall increase in plant growth and development. While selecting fungi, the right fungi have to be matched with the plant. There are specific fungi for vegetables, fodder crops, flowers, trees, etc.

Mycorrhizal fungi can increase the yield of a plot of land by 30%-40%. It can absorb phosphorus from the soil and pass it on to the plant. Mycorrhizal plants show higher tolerance to high soil temperatures, various soil- and root-borne pathogens, and heavy metal toxicity.

LEGUME-RHIZOBIUM RELATIONSHIP

Leguminous plants require high quantities of nitrogen compared to other plants. Nitrogen is an inert gas and its uptake is possible only in fixed form, which is facilitated by the rhizobium bacteria present in the nodules of the root system. The bacterium lives in the soil to form root nodules (*i.e.* outgrowth on roots) in plants such as beans, gram, groundnut, and soybean.

Blue-green Algae

Blue-green algae are considered the simplest, living autotrophic plants, i.e. organisms capable of building up food materials from inorganic matter. They are microscopic. Blue-green algae are widely distributed in the aquatic environment. Some of them are responsible for water blooms in stagnant water.

They adapt to extreme weather conditions and are found in snow and in hot springs, where the water is 85 °C. Certain blue-green algae live intimately with other organisms in a symbiotic relationship. Some are associated with the fungi in form of lichens. The ability of blue-green algae tophoto-synthesize food and fix atmospheric nitrogen accounts for their symbiotic associations and also for their presence in paddy fields.

Blue-green algae are of immense economic value as they add organic matter to the soil and increase soil fertility. Barren alkaline lands in India have been reclaimed and made productive by inducing the proper growth of certain blue-green algae.

BIOFERTILIZERS TECHNOLOGY

BIOFERTILIZERS PREPARATION

Biofertilizers are defined as preparations containing living cells or latent cells of efficient strains of microorganisms that help crop plants' uptake of nutrients by their interactions in the rhizosphere when applied through seed or soil. They accelerate certain microbial processes in the soil which augment the extent of availability of nutrients in a form easily assimilated by plants.

Very often microorganisms are not as efficient in natural surroundings as one would expect them to be and therefore artificially multiplied cultures of efficient selected microorganisms play a vital role in accelerating the microbial processes in soil.

Sl. No.	*Groups*	*Examples*
N. fixing Biofertilizers		
1.	Free-living	*Azotobacter, Beijerinkia, Clostridium, Klebsiella, Anabaena, Nostoc,*
2.	Symbiotic	*Rhizobium, Frankia, Anabaena azollae*
3.	Associative Symbiotic	*Azospirillum*
P Solubilizing Biofertilizers		
1.	Bacteria	*Bacillus megaterium* var. *phosphaticum, Bacillus subtilis Bacillus circulans, Pseudomonas striata,*
2.	Fungi	*Penicillium sp, Aspergillus awamori*

P Mobilizing Biofertilizers		
1.	Arbuscular mycorrhiza	*Glomus* sp.,*Gigaspora sp.,Acaulospora* sp., *Scutellospora* sp. & *Sclerocystis* sp.
2.	Ectomycorrhiza	*Laccaria* sp., *Pisolithus* sp., *Boletus* sp., *Amanita* sp.
3.	Ericoid mycorrhizae	*Pezizella ericae*
4.	Orchid mycorrhiza	*Rhizoctonia solani*
Biofertilizers for Micro nutrients		
1.	Silicate and Zinc solubilizers	*Bacillus* sp.
Plant Growth Promoting Rhizobacteria		
1.	Pseudomonas	*Pseudomonas fluorescens*

Use of biofertilizers is one of the important components of integrated nutrient management, as they are cost effective and renewable source of plant nutrients to supplement the chemical fertilizers for sustainable agriculture. Several microorganisms and their association with crop plants are being exploited in the production of biofertilizers. They can be grouped in different ways based on their nature and function.

DIFFERENT TYPES OF BIOFERTILIZERS

Rhizobium

Rhizobium is a soil habitat bacterium, which can able to colonize the legume roots and fixes the atmos-pheric nitrogen symbiotically. The morphology and physiology of Rhizobium will vary from free-living condition to the bacteroid of nodules. They are the most efficient biofertilizer as per the quantity of nitrogen fixed concerned. They have seven genera and highly specific to form nodule in legumes, referred as cross inoculation group. *Rhizobium* inoculant was first made in USA and commercialized by private enterprise in 1930s.

Initially, due to absence of efficient bradyrhizobial strains in soil, soybean inoculation at that time resulted in bumper crops but incessant inoculation during the last four decades by US farmers has resulted in the build up of a plethora of inefficient strains in soil whose replacement by efficient strains of bradyrhizobia has become an insurmountable problem.

Azotobacter

Of the several species of *Azotobacter, A. chroococcum* happens to be the dominant inhabitant in arable soils capable of fixing N_2 (2-15 mg N_2 fixed/g of carbon source) in culture media. The bacterium produces abundant slime which helps in soil aggre-gation. The numbers of *A. chroococcum* in Indian soils rarely exceeds 105/g soil due to lack of organic matter and the presence of antagonistic microorganisms in soil.

Azospirillum

Azospirillum lipoferum and *A. brasilense* (*Spirillum lipoferum* in earlier literature) are primary inhabitants of soil, the rhizosphere and intercellular spaces of root cortex of graminaceous plants. They perform the associative symbiotic relation with the graminaceous plants. The bacteria of Genus *Azospirillum* are N_2 fixing organisms isolated from the root and above ground parts of a variety of crop plants. They are Gram negative, *Vibrio* or *Spirillum* having abundant accumulation of polybetahydroxybutyrate (70 %) in cytoplasm.

Five species of *Azospirillum* have been described to date *A. brasilense, A.lipoferum, A.amazonense, A.halopraeferens* and *A.irakense*. The organism proliferates under both anaerobic and aerobic conditions but it is preferentially micro-aerophilic in the presence or absence of combined nitrogen in the medium. Apart from nitrogen fixation, growth promoting substance production (IAA), disease resistance and drought tolerance are some of the additional benefits due to *Azospirillum* inoculation.

Cyanobacteria

Both free-living as well as symbiotic cyanobacteria (blue green algae) have been harnessed in rice cultivation in India. A composite culture of BGA having heterocystous *Nostoc, Anabaena, Aulosira* etc. is given as primary inoculum in trays, polythene lined pots and later mass multiplied in the field for application as soil based flakes to the rice growing field at the rate of 10 kg/ha. The final product is not free from extraneous contaminants and not very often monitored for checking the presence of desiredalgal flora.

Once so much publicized as a biofertilizer for the rice crop; it has not presently attracted the attention of rice growers all over India except pockets in the Southern States, notably Tamil Nadu. The benefits due to algalization could be to the extent of 20-30 kg N/ha under ideal conditions but the labour oriented methodology for the preparation of BGA biofertilizer is in itself a limitation. Quality control measures are not usually followed except perhaps for random checking for the presence of desired species qualitatively.

Azolla

Azolla is a free-floating water fern that floats in water and fixes atmospheric nitrogen in association with nitrogen fixing blue green alga *Anabaena azollae*. *Azolla* fronds consist of sporophyte with a floating rhizome and small overlapping bi-lobed leaves and roots. Rice growing areas in South East Asia and other third World countries have recently been evincing increased interest in the use of the symbiotic N2 fixing water fern *Azolla* either as an alternate nitrogen sources or as a supplement to commercial nitrogen fertilizers. *Azolla* is used as biofertilizer for wetland rice and it is known to contribute 40-60 kg N/ha per rice crop.

Phosphate Solubilizing Microorganisms (PSM)

Several soil bacteria and fungi, notably species of *Pseudomonas, Bacillus, Penicillium, Aspergillus etc.* secrete organic acids and lower the pH in their vicinity to bring about dissolution of bound phosphates in soil. Increased yields of wheat and potato were demonstrated due to inoculation of peat based cultures of *Bacillus polymyxa* and *Pseudomonas striata*. Currently, phosphate solubilizers are manufactured by agricultural universities and some private enterprises and sold to farmers through governmental agencies. These appear to be no check on either the quality of the inoculants marketed in India or the establishment of the desired organisms in the rhizosphere.

AM Fungi

The transfer of nutrients mainly phosphorus and also zinc and sulphur from the soil *milleu* to the cells of the root cortex is mediated by intracellular obligate fungal endosymbionts of the genera *Glomus, Gigaspora, Acaulospora, Sclerocysts* and *Endogone* which possess vesicles for storage of nutrients and arbuscles for funneling these nutrients into the root system. By far, the commonest genus appears to be *Glomus*, which has several species distributed in soil. Availability for pure cultures of AM (Arbuscular Mycorrhiza) fungi is an impediment in large scale production despite the fact that beneficial effects of AM fungal inoculation to plants have been repeatedly shown under experimental conditions in the laboratory especially in conjunction with other nitrogen fixers.

Silicate Solubilizing Bacteria (SSB)

Micro-organisms are capable of degrading silicates and aluminum silicates. During the metabolism of microbes several organic acids are produced and these have a dual role in silicate weathering. They supply H+ ions to the medium and promote hydrolysis and the organic acids like citric, oxalic acid, Keto acids and hydroxy carbolic acids which from complexes with cations, promote their removal and retention in the medium in a dissolved state.

The studies conducted with a Bacillus sp. isolated from the soil of granite crusher yard showed that the bacterium is capable of dissolving several silicate minerals under *in vitro* condition.

The examination of anthrpogenic materials like cement, agro inputs like super phosphate and rock phosphate exhibited silicate solubilizing bacteria to a varying degree. The bacterial isolates made from different locations had varying degree of silicate solubilizing potential. Soil inoculation studies with selected isolate with red soil, clay soil, sand and hilly soil showed that the organisms multiplied in all types of soil and released more of silica and the available silica increased in soil and water. Rice responded well to application of organic sliceous residue like rice straw, rice husk and black ash @ 5 t/ ha. Combining SSB with these residues further resulted in increased plant growth and grain yield. This enhancement is due to increased dissolution of silica and nutrients from the soil.

Plant Growth Promoting Rhizobacteria (PGPR)

The group of bacteria that colonize roots or rhizosphere soil and beneficial to crops are referred to as plant growth promoting rhizobacteria (PGPR). The PGPR inoculants currently commercialized that seem to promote growth through at least one mechanism; suppression of plant disease (termed Bioprotectants), improved nutrient acquisition (termed Biofertilizers), or phytohormone production (termed Biostimulants). Species of *Pseudomonas* and *Bacillus* can produce as yet not well characterized phytohormones or growth regulators that cause crops to have greater amounts of fine roots which have the effect of increasing the absorptive surface of plant roots for uptake of water and nutrients. These PGPR are referred to as Biostimulants and the phytohormones they produce include indole-acetic acid, cytokinins, gibberellins and inhibitors of ethylene production.

Recent advances in molecular techniques also are encouraging in that tools are becoming available to determine the mechanism by which crop performance is improved using PGPR and track survival and activity of PGPR organisms in soil and roots. The science of PGPR is at the stage where genetically modified PGPR can be produced. PGPR with antibiotic, phytohormone and siderophore production can be made. Despite of promising results, biofertilizers has not got widespread application in agriculture mainly because of the variable response of plant species or genotypes to inoculation depending on the bacterial strain used. Differential rhizosphere effect of crops in harbouring a target strain or even the modulation of the bacterial nitrogen fixing and phosphate solubilizing capacity by specific root exudates may account for the observed differences. On the other hand, good competitive ability and high saprophytic competence are the major factors determining the success of a bacterial strain as an inoculant.

Studies to know the synergistic activities and persistence of specific microbial populations in complex environments, such as the rhizosphere, should be addressed in order to obtain efficient inoculants. In this regards, research efforts are made at Agricultural College and Research Institute, Madurai to obtain appropriate formulations of microbial inoculants incorporating nitrogen fixing, phosphate- and silicate-solubilizing bacteria and plant growth promoting rhizobacteria which will help in promoting the use of such beneficial bacteria in sustainable agriculture.

LIQUID BIOFERTILIZERS

Biofertilizers are such as *Rhizobium, Azospirillum* and Phosphobacteria provide nitrogen and phosphorous nutrients to crop plants through nitrogen fixation and phosphorous solubilization processes. These Biofertilizers could be effectively utilized for rice, pulses, millets, cotton, sugarcane, vegetable and other horticulture crops. Biofertilizers is one of the prime input in organic farming not only enhances the crop growth and yield but also improves the soil health and sustain soil fertility. At present, Biofertilizers are supplied to the farmers as carrier based inoculants. As an alternative, liquid formulation technology has been developed in the Department of Agricultural Microbiology, TNAU, Coimbatore which has more advantages than the carrier inoculants.

Benefits

The advantages of Liquid Bio-fertilizer over conventional carrier based Bio-fertilizers are listed below:

- Longer shelf life -12-24 months.
- No contamination.
- No loss of properties due to storage upto 45º c.
- Greater potentials to fight with native population.

- High populations can be maintained more than 109 cells/ml upto 12 months to 24 months.
- Easy identification by typical fermented smell.
- Cost saving on carrier material, pulverization, neutralization, sterilization, packing and transport.
- Quality control protocols are easy and quick.
- Better survival on seeds and soil.
- No need of running Bio-fertilizer production units through out the year.
- Very much easy to use by the farmer.
- Dosages is 10 time less than carrier based powder Bio-fertilizers.
- High commercial revenues.
- High export potential.
- Very high enzymatic activity since contamination is nil.

Characteristics of Different Liquid Bio-fertilizers

Rhizobium

This belongs to bacterial group and the classical example is symbiotic nitrogen fixation. The bacteria infect the legume root and form root nodules within which they reduce molecular nitrogen to ammonia which is reality utilized by the plant to produce valuable proteins, vitamins and other nitrogen containing compounds.

The site of symbiosis is within the root nodules. It has been estimated that 40-250 kg N/ha/year is fixed by different legume crops by the microbial activities of *Rhizobium*. The percentage of nodules occupied, nodules dry weight, plant dry weight and the grain yield per plant the multistrain inoculant was highly promising.

Physical Features of Liquid Rhizobium

- Dull white in colour
- No bad smell
- No foam formation, pH 6.8-7.5.

Azospirllium

It belongs to bacteria and is known to fix the considerable quantity of nitrogen in the range of 20- 40 kg N/ha in the rhizosphere in non- non-leguminous plants such as cereals, millets, oilseeds, cotton etc. The efficiency of *Azospirillium* as a Bio-Fertilizer has increased because of its ability of inducing abundant roots in several pants like rice, millets and oilseeds even in upland conditions. Considerable quantity of nitrogen fertilizer up to 25-30 % can be saved by the use of *Azospirillum* inoculant. The genus *Azospirillum* has three species *viz., A. lipoferum, A. brasilense* and *A. amazonense*. These species have been commercially exploited for the use as nitrogen supplying Bio-Fertilizers.

One of the characteristics of *Azospirillum* is its ability to reduce nitrate and denitrify. Both *A. lipoferum,*and *A. brasilense* may comprise of strains which can actively or weakly denitrify or reduce nitrate to nitrite and therefore, for inoculation preparation, it is necessary to select strains which do not possess these characteristics. *Azospirllium lipoferum* present in the roots of some of tropical forage grasses uch as Digitaria, Panicum, Brachiaria, Maize, Sorghum, Wheat and Rye.

Physical Features of Liquid **Azospirillum**

- The colour of the liquid may be blue or dull white.
- Bad odours confirms improper liquid formulation and may be concluded as mere broth.
- Production of yellow gummy colour materials comfirms the quality product.
- Acidic pH always confirms that there is no Azospirillum bacteria in the liquid.

N_2 fixing capacity of *Azospirillum* in the roots of several plants and the amount of N2 fixed by them.

Plant	*Mg N_2 fixed/g of substrate*
Oryza sativa (Paddy)	28
Sorghum bicolour (Sorghum)	20
Zea mays (Maize)	20
Panicum sp.	24

Cynodon dactylon	36
Setaria sp	12
Amaranthus spinosa	16

Production of Growth Hormones

Azospirillum cultures synthesize considerable amount of biologically active substances like vitamins, nicotinic acid, indole acetic acids giberllins. All these hormones/chemicals helps the plants in better germination, early emergence, better root development.

Role of Liquid Azospirillum under Field Conditions

- Stimulates growth and imparts green colour which is a characteristic of a healthy plant.
- Aids utilization of potash, phosphorous and other nutrients.
- Encourage plumpness and succulence of fruits and increase protein percentage.

Sign of Non-Functioning of Azospirillum in the Field

- No growth promotion activity
- Yellowish green colour of leaves, which indicates no fixation of Nitrogen.

Azotobacter

It is the important and well known free living nitrogen fixing aerobic bacterium. It is used as a bio-Fertilizer for all non leguminous plants especially rice, cotton, vegetables etc. *Azotobacter* cells are not present on the rhizosplane but are abundant in the rhizosphere region. The lack of organic matter in the soil is a limiting factor for the proliferation of *Azotobaceter* in the soil.

Field experiments were conducted during the pre-kharif wet seasons to find out the influence on rice grain yield by the combined use of N- fixing organisms and inorganic nitrogen fertilizer which recorded increase in was yield.

Physical Features of Liquid Azotobacter

The pigmentation that is produced by Azotobacter in aged

culture is melanin which is due to oxidation of tyrosine by tyrosinase an enzyme which has copper. The colour can be noted in liquid forms.

- *A. chroococcum*: Produces brown-black pigmentation in liquid inoculum.
- *A. beijerinchii*: Produces yellow- light brown pigementation in liquid inoculum
- *A. vinelandii*: Produces green fluorescent pigmentation in liquid inoculum.
- *A. paspali*: Produces green fluorescent pigmentation in liquid inoculum.
- *A. macrocytogenes*: Produces, pink pigmentation in liquid inoculum.
- *A. insignis*: Produces less, gum less, grayish-blue pigmentation in liquid inoculum.
- *A. agilies*: Produces green-fluorescent pigmentation in liquid inoculum.

Role of Liquid Azotobacter in Tissue Culture

The study was conducted on sugarcane variety CO 86032 in Tissue culture Laboratories of Rajashree Sugars and Chemicals Ltd, Varadarajnagar, Theni, Tamil Nadu. The liquid bioinoculants were provided Regional Director, RCOF, Bangalore to evaluate their growth promoting effects on sugarcane micropropagation. He recorded Biometric observations like Plant height, leaf length, width, root length, no of roots. Chemical parameters –Protein, Carbohydrates, N, P, K total biomass and concluded as follows:

- The performance of *Azotobacter* liquid inoculant was c
- omparatively better than all the treatments in 10 % MS medium followed Azospirillum.
- The performance of *Azotobacter* liquid inoculant was comparatively better than all the treatments followed by Azosopirillum for the growth of the polybag sugarcane seedlings.

Role of Liquid Azotobacter as a Bio-control Agent

Azotobacter have been found to produce some antifungal

substance which inhibits the growth of some soil fungi like *Aspergillus, Fusarium, Curvularia, Alternaria, Helminthosporium, Fusarium* etc.

Acetobaceter

This is a sacharophillic bacteria and associate with sugarcane, sweet potato and sweet sorghum plants and fixes 30 kgs/N/ha year. Mainly this bacterium is commercialized for sugarcane crop. It is known to increase yield by 10-20 t/acre and sugar content by about 10-15 percent.

Effect of Liquid Acetobacter diazotrophicus on Sugarcane

In South India use of Azospirillum and Phosphobacterium on the cash crop sugarcane is a regular practice for the past few years with a saving of nearly 20% of chemical nitrogen and phosphate applications. Now, it has been reported that a bacteria *Acetobacter diazotrophicus* which is present in the sugarcane stem, leaves, soils have a capacity to fix up to 300 kgs of nitrogen. This bacteria first reported in brazil where the farmers cultivate sugarcane in very poor subsoil fertilized with Phosphate, Potassium and micro elements alone, could produce yield for three consecutive harvests, without any nitrogen fertilizer. They have recorded yield 182-244 tones per ha. This leads to the assumption that active nitrogen fixing bacteria has associated within the plant.

Do's and Don't for Entrepreneurs, Dealers and farmers

Do	*Don't*
Keep Bio-fertilizers bottles away from direct heat and sunlight. Store it in cool and dry place.	Don't store Bio-fertilizers bottles under heat and sunlight
Sell only Bio-fertilizers bottles which contain batch number, the name of the crop on which it has to be used, the date of manufacture and expiry period.	Don't sell Bio-fertilizers bottles after their expiry period is over.
If the expiry period is over, then discard it as it is not effective.	Don't prick holes into the bottles or puncture them to pour the content
Keep Bio-fertilizers bottles away from fertilizer or pesticide containers and they should not be mixed directly.	Do not mix the Bio-fertilizers with fungicides, insecticides, herbicides, herbicides and chemical fertilizers.

Liquid Bio-fertlizer Application Methodology

There are three ways of using Liquid Bio-fertilizers:

Seed Treatment

Seed Treatment is a most common method adopted for all types of inoculants. The seed treatment is effective and economic. For small quantity of seeds (up to 5 kg quantity) the coating can done in a plastic bag. For this purpose, a plastic bag having size (21" × 10") or big size can be used. The bag should be filled with 2 kg or more of seeds. The bag should be closed in such a way to trap the airs as much as possible. The bag should be squeezed for 2 minutes or more until all the seed are uniformly wetted. Then bag is opened, inflated again and shaked gently. Stop shaking after each seeds gets a uniform layer of culture coating. The bag is opened and the seed is dried under the shade for 20-30 minutes. For large amount of seeds coating can be done in a bucket and inoculant can be mixed directly with hand. Seed Treatment with *Rhizobium, Azotobacter, Azospirillum,* along with PSM can be done.

The seed treatment can be done with any of two or more bacteria. There is no side (antagonistic) effect. The important things that has to be kept in mind are that the seeds must be coated first with *Rhizobium, Azotobacter* or *Azospirillum*. When each seed get a layer of above bacteria then PSM inoculant has to be coated as outer layer. This method will provide maximum number of each bacteria required for better results. Treatments of seed with any two bacteria will not provide maximum number of bacteria on individual seed.

Root Dipping

For application of *Azospirillum*//PSM on paddy transplating/vegetable crops this method is used. The required quantity of *Azospirillum*//PSM has to be mixed with 5-10 litres of water at one corner of the field and the roots of seedlings has to be dipped for a minimum of half-an-hour before transplantation.

Soil Application

Use 200ml of PSM per acre. Mix PSM with 400 to 600 kgs of Cow dung FYM along with ½ bag of rock phosphate if available. The mixture of PSM, cow dung and rock phosphate have to be kept under any tree or under shade for over night and maintain 50% moisture. Use the mixture as soil application in rows or during leveling of soil.

Dosage of Liquid Bio-fertilizers in Different Crops

Recommended Liquid Bio-fertilizers and its application method, quantity to be used for different crops are as follows:

Crop	Recommended Bio-fertilizer	Application method	Quantity to be used
Field crops Pulses Chickpea, pea, Groundnut, soybean, beans, Lentil, lucern, Berseem, Green gram, Black gram, Cowpea and pigeon pea	*Rhizobium*	Seed treatment	200ml/acre
Cereals Wheat, oat, barley	*Azotobacter/ Azospirillum*	Seed treatment	200ml/acre
Rice	*Azospirillum*	Seed treatment	200ml/acre
Oil seeds Mustard, seasum, Linseeds, Sunflower, castor	*Azotobacter*	Seed treatment	200ml/acre
Millets Pearl millets, Finger millets, kodo millet	*Azotobacter*	Seed treatment	200ml/acre
Maize and Sorghum	*Azospirillum*	Seed treatment	200ml/acre
Forage crops and Grasses Bermuda grass, Sudan grass, Napier Grass , ParaGrass, StarGrass etc.	*Azotobacter*	Seed treatment	200ml/acre
Other Misc. Plantation Crops Tobacco	*Azotobacter*	Seedling treatment	500ml/acre
Tea, Coffee	*Azotobacter*	Soil treatment	400ml/acre
Rubber, Coconuts	*Azotobacter*	Soil treatment	2-3 ml/plant
Agro-ForestRY/Fruit Plants All fruit/agro-forestry (herb,shrubs, annuals and perennial) plants for fuel wood fodder, fruits,gum,spice,leaves,flowers,nuts and seeds puppose	*Azotobacter*	Soil treatment	2-3 ml/plant at nursery
Leguminous plants/ trees	*Rhizobium*	Soil treatment	1-2 ml/plant

Note: Doses recommended when count of inoculum is 1 × 108 cells/

ml then doses will be ten times more besides above said Nitrogen fixers, Phosphate solubilizers and potash mobilizers at the rate of 200 ml/acre could be applied for all crops.

Equipments Required for Biofertilizer Production

In biofertilizer production industry, equipments are the major infrastructure, which involves 70 percent of capital investment.

Any compromise on the usage of the following mentioned equipments may finally decline in the quality of biofertilizer.

After studying the principle behind the usage of all instruments, some of the instruments can be replaced with a culture room fitted with a U.V. Lamp. Autoclaves, Hot Air Oven, Incubators and sealing machines are indigenously made with proper technical specifications. The correct use of equipments will give uninterrupted introduction with quality inoculum.

It is an apparatus in which materials are sterilized by air free saturated steam (under pressure) at a temperature above 100°C. If the steam pressure inside the autoclave is increased to 15 psi, the temperature will rise to 121°C. this is sufficient to destroy all vegetative cells. Normally all growth medium are sterilized in the autoclave.

Laminar Air Flow Chamber

Laminar air flow chamber provides a uniform flow of filtered air. This continuous flow of air will prevent settling of particles in the work area.Air borne contamination is avoided in this chamber. Culture transfers and inoculation can be done here.

BOD Incubators

Incubators providing controlled conditions (light, temperature, humidity, etc.) required for the growth and development of microorganisms. Multiplication of starter culture can be done in this instrument.

Rotary Shaker

It is used for agitating culture flasks by circular motion under variable speed control. Shaking provides aeration for growth of cultures. Shakers holding upto 20-50 flasks are generally used. The capacity of the shaker may be increased if it is a double-decker type.

Hot Air Oven

Hot air oven is meant for sterilizing all glassware materials. Dry heat is used in this apparatus to sterilize the materials. Normally 180°C is used for two hours for sterilizing glasswares.

pH Meter

An instrument for measuring pH of the solution using a 0-14 scale in which seven represents neutral points, less than seven is acidity (excess of H′ over OH^-) and more than seven is alkality (excess of OH^- over H′) useful in adjusting the pH of the growth medium.

Refrigerator

This equipment is used preserving all mother cultures used for biofertilizer production. The mother culture is periodically sub-cultured and stored in the refrigerator for long- term usage.

Fermentor

A fermentor is the equipment, which provides the proper environment for the growth of a desired organism. It is generally a large vessel in which, the organism may be kept at the required temperature, pH, dissolved oxygen concentration and substrate concentration. Different models of fermentors are available depending upon the necessity. A simple version model contains steam generator, sterilization process devices and agitator. A sophisticated fermentor contains pH regulator, oxygen level regulator, anti-foam device, temperature controller, etc.

Mass Production of Bacterial Biofertilizer

Biofertilizers are carrier based preparations containing efficient strain of nitrogen fixing or phosphate solubilizing microorganisms. Biofertilizers are formulated usually as carrier based inoculants. The organic carrier materials are more effective for the preparation of bacterial inoculants. The solid inoculants carry more number of bacterial cells and support the survival of cells for longer periods of time.

- The mass production of carrier based bacterial biofertilizers involves three stages.
- Culturing of microorganisms
- Processing of carrier material
- Mixing the carrier and the broth culture and packing.

Culturing of Microorganisms

Although many bacteria can be used beneficially as a biofertilizer the technique of mass production is standardizedfor *Rhizobium, Azospirillum, Azotobacter* and phosphobacteria.

The media used for mass culturing are as follows:

Rhizobium : Yeast extract mannitol broth.

Add 10 ml of Congo red stock solution (dissolve 250 mg of Congo red in 100ml water) to 1 liter after adjusting the PH to 6.8 and before adding agar.

Rhizobium forms white, translucent, glistening, elevated and comparatively small colonies on this medium. Moreover, *Rhizobium* colonies do not take up the colour of congo red dye added in the medium. Those colonies which readily take up the congo red stain are not rhizobia but presumably *Agrobacterium,* a soil bacterium closely related to *Rhizobium.*

Azospirillum : Dobereiner's malic acid broth with NH_4Cl (1g per liter).

The broth is prepared in flasks and inoculum from mother culture is transferred to flasks. The culture is grown under shaking conditions at 30±2°C as submerged culture. The culture is incubated until maximum cell population of 1010 to 1011 cfu/ml is produced. Under optimum conditions this population level could be attained with in 4 to 5 days for *Rhizobium;* 5 to 7 days for *Azospirillum;* 2 to 3 days for phosphobacteria and 6-7 days for *Azotobacter*. The culture obtained in the flask is called starter culture. For large scale production of inoculant, inoculum from starter culture is transferred to large flasks/seed tank fermentor and grown until required level of cell count is reached.

Inoculum Preparation

- Prepare appropriate media for specific to the bacterial inoculant in 250 ml, 500 ml, 3 litre and 5 litre conical flasks and sterilize.
- The media in 250 ml flask is inoculated with efficient bacterial strain under aseptic condition
- Keep the flask under room temperature in rotary shaker (200 rpm) for 5-7 days.
- Observe the flask for growth of the culture and estimate the population, which serves as the starter culture.
- Using the starter culture (at log phase) inoculate the larger flasks (500 ml, 3 litre and 5 litre) containing the media, after obtaining growth in each flask.
- The above media is prepared in large quantities in fermentor, sterilized well, cooled and kept it ready.
- The media in the fermentor is inoculated with the log phase culture grown in 5 litre flask. Usually 1 -2% inoculum is sufficient, however inoculation is done up to 5% depending on the growth of the culture in the larger flasks.
- The cells are grown in fermentor by providing aeration (passing sterile air through compressor and sterilizing agents like glass wool, cotton wool, acid etc.) and given continuous stirring.
- The broth is checked for the population of inoculated organism and contamination if any at the growth period.
- The cells are harvested with the population load of 109 cells ml^{-1} after incubation period.

- There should not be any fungal or any other bacterial contamination at 10^{-6} dilution level
- It is not advisable to store the broth after fermentation for periods longer than 24 hours. Even at 4°C number of viable cells begins to decrease.

Processing of Carrier Material

The use of ideal carrier material is necessary in the production of good quality biofertilizer. Peat soil, lignite, vermiculite, charcoal, press mud, farmyard manure and soil mixture can be used as carrier materials.

The neutralized peat soil/lignite are found to be better carrier materials for biofertilizer production The following points are to be considered in the selection of ideal carrier material.

- Cheaper in cost
- Should be locally available
- High organic matter content
- No toxic chemicals
- Water holding capacity of more than 50%
- Easy to process, friability and vulnerability.

Preparation of Carrier Material

- The carrier material (peat or lignite) is powdered to a fine powder so as to pass through 212 micron IS sieve.
- The pH of the carrier material is neutralized with the help of calcium carbonate (1:10 ratio), since the peat soil/lignite are acidic in nature (pH of 4 - 5)
- The neutralized carrier material is sterilized in an autoclave to eliminate the contaminants.

Mixing the Carrier and the Broth Culture and Packing

Inoculant packets are prepared by mixing the broth culture obtained from fermentor with sterile carrier material:

Preparation of Inoculants Packet

- The neutralized, sterilized carrier material is spread in a clean, dry, sterile metallic or plastic tray.

- The bacterial culture drawn from the fermentor is added to the sterilized carrier and mixed well by manual (by wearing sterile gloves) or by mechanical mixer. The culture suspension is to be added to a level of 40 – 50% water holding capacity depending upon the population.
- The inoculant packet of 200 g quantities in polythene bags, sealed with electric sealer and allowed for curing for 2-3 days at room temperature (curing can be done by spreading the inoculant on a clean floor/ polythene sheet/by keeping in open shallow tubs/ trays with polythene covering for 2-3 days at room temperature before packaging).

Specification of the Polythene Bags

- The polythene bags should be of low density grade.
- The thickness of the bag should be around 50-75 micron.
- Each packet should be marked with the name of the manufacturer, name of the product, strain number, the crop to which recommended, method of inoculation, date of manufacture, batch number, date of expiry, price, full address of the manufacturer and storage instructions etc.,

Storage of Biofertilizerpacket

- The packet should be stored in a cool place away from the heat or direct sunlight.
- The packets may be stored at room temperature or in cold storage conditions in lots in plastic crates or polythene/gunny bags.
- The population of inoculant in the carrier inoculant packet may be determined at 15 days interval. There should be more than 109 cells/g of inoculant at the time of preparation and107 cells/g on dry weight basis before expiry date.

Mass Production of Mycorrhizal Biofertilizer

The commercial utilization of mycorrhizal fungi has

become difficult because of the obligate symbiotic nature and difficulty in culturing on laboratory media. Production of AM inoculum has evolved from the original use of infested field soils to the current practice of using pot culture inoculum derived from the surface disinfected spores of single AM fungus on a host plant grown in sterilized culture medium. Several researches in different parts of the world resulted in different methods of production of AM fungal inoculum as soil based culture as well as carrier based inoculum. Root organ culture and nutrient film technique provide scope for the production of soil less culture.

Vermiculite Contained raised AM Infected Maize Plants

- A trench (1m × 1m × 0.3m) is formed and lined with black polythene sheet to be used as a plant growth tub.
- Mixed 50 kg of vermiculite and 5 kg of sterilized soil and packed in the trench up to a height of 20 cm
- Spread 1 kg of AM inoculum (mother culture) 2-5 cm below the surface of vermiculite
- Maize seeds surface sterilized with 5% sodium hypochlorite for 2 minutes are sown
- Applied 2 g urea, 2 g super phosphate and 1 g muriate of potash for each trench at the time of sowing seeds. Further 10 g of urea is applied twice on 30 and 45 days after sowing for each trench
- Quality test on AM colonization in root samples is carried out on 30th and 45th day
- Stock plants are grown for 60 days (8 weeks). The inoculum is obtained by cutting all the roots of stock plants. The inoculum produced consists of a mixture of vermiculite, spores, pieces of hyphae and infected root pieces.
- Thus within 60 days 55 kg of AM inoculum could be produced from 1 sq meter area. This inoculum will be sufficient to treat 550 m2 nursery area having 11,000 seedlings.

AM Fungi

Nursery application: 100 g bulk inoculum is sufficient for one metre square. The inoculum should be applied at 2-3 cm below the soil at the time of sowing. The seeds/cutting should be sown/planted above the VAM inoculum to cause infection. For polythene bag raised crops: 5 to 10 g bulk inoculum is sufficient for each packet. Mix 10 kg of inoculum with 1000 kg of sand potting mixture and pack the potting mixture in polythene bag before sowing.

For out-planting: Twenty grams of VAM inoculum is required per seedling. Apply inoculum at the time of planting. For existing trees: Two hundred gram of VAM inoculum is required for inoculating one tree. Apply inoculum near the root surface at the time of fertilizer application.

Mass Production and Field Application of Cyanobacteria

Blue green algal inoculation with composite cultures was found to be more effective than single culture inoculation. A technology for mass scale production of composite culture of blue green algae under rice field condition was developed at TNAU and the soil based BGA inoculum could survive for more than 2 years. At many sites where algal inoculation was used for three to four consecutive cropping seasons, the inoculated algae establish well and the effect persisted over subsequent rice crop. Technologies for utilizing nitrogen fixing organisms in low land rice were the beneficial role of blue green algal inoculation in rice soils of Tamil Nadu.

The blue green algal inoculum may be produced by several methods *viz.*, in tubs, galvanized trays, small pits and also in field conditions. However the large-scale production is advisable under field condition which is easily adopted by farmers.

Multiplication in Trays

- Big metallic trays (6′ × 3′ × 6" lbh) can be used for small scale production
- Take 10 kg of paddy field soil, dry powder well and spread

- Fill water to a height of 3"
- Add 250 g of dried algal flakes (soil based) as inoculum
- Add 150 g of super phosphate and 30 g of lime and mix well with the soil
- Sprinkle 25 g carbofuran to control the insects
- Maintain water level in trays
- After 10 to 15 days, the blooms of BGA will start floating on the water sources
- At this stage stop watering and drain. Let the soil to dry completely
- Collect the dry soil based inoculum as flakes
- Store in a dry place. By this method 5 to 7 kg of soil based inoculum can be obtained.

Multiplication under Field Condition

Materials

- Rice field
- Super phosphate
- Carbofuran
- Composite BGA starter culture

Procedure

Select an area of 40 m2 (20m × 2m) near a water source which is directly exposed to sunlight. Make a bund all around the plot to a height of 15 cm and give it a coating with mud to prevent loss of water due to percolation.

- Plot is well prepared and levelled uniformly and water is allowed to a depth of 5-7.5 cm and left to settle for 12 hrs.
- Apply 2 kg of super phosphate and 200 g lime to each plot uniformly over the area.
- The soil based composite starter culture of BGA containing 8-10 species @ 5 kg/plot is powdered well and broadcasted.
- Carbofuran @ 200 g is also applied to control soil insects occurring in BGA.

- Water is let in at periodic intervals so that the height of water level is always maintained at 5 cm.
- After 15 days of inoculation, the plots are allowed to dry up in the sun and the algal flakes are collected and stored.

Observations

The floating algal flasks are green or blue green in colour. From each harvest, 30 to 40 kg of dry algal flakes are obtained from the plot.

Method of Inoculation of BGA in Rice Field

Blue green algae may be applied as soil based inoculum to the rice field following the method described below.

- Powder the soil based algal flakes very well.
- Mix it with 10 kg soil or sand (10kg powdered algal flakes with 10 kg soil/sand).
- BGA is to be inoculated on 7-10 days after rice transplanting.
- Water level at 3-4" is to be maintained at the time of BGA inoculation and then for a month so as to have maximum BGA development.

Observation

A week after BGA inoculation, algal growth can be seen and algal mat will float on the water after 2-3 weeks. The algal mat colour will be green or brown or yellowish green.

Mass Production and Field Application of *Azolla*

Azolla is a free-floating water fern that floats in water and fixes atmospheric nitrogen in association with nitrogen fixing blue green alga *Anabaena azollae*. *Azolla* fronds consist of sporophyte with a floating rhizome and small overlapping bi-lobed leaves and roots. Rice growing areas in South East Asia and other third World countries have recently been evincing increased interest in the use of the symbiotic N_2 fixing water fern *Azolla* either as an alternate nitrogen sources or as a supplement to commercial nitrogen fertilizers. *Azolla* is used as biofertilizer for wetland rice and it is known to contribute 40-60 kg N ha^{-1} per rice crop. The agronomic potential of *Azolla* is quite significant particularly for rice crop and it is widely used as biofertilizer for increasing rice yields. Rice crop response studies with *Azolla* biofertilizer in the People's Republic in China and in Vietnam have provided good evidence that *Azolla* incorporation into the soil as a green manure crop is one of the most effective ways of providing nitrogen source for rice. The utilization of *Azolla* as dual crop with wetland rice is gaining importance in Philippines, Thailand, Sri Lanka and India. The important factor in using *Azolla* as a biofertilizer for rice crop is its quick decomposition in soil and efficient availability of its nitrogen to rice. In tropical rice soils the applied *Azolla* mineralizes rapidly and its nitrogen is available to the rice crop in very short period. The common species of *Azolla* are *A. microphylla, A. filiculoides, A. pinnata, A. caroliniana, A. nilotica, A. rubra* and *A. mexicana*.

Mass Multiplication of *Azolla* under Field Conditions

A simple *Azolla* nursery method for large scale multiplication of *Azolla* in the field has been evolved for easy adoption by the farmers.

Materials

- One cent (40 sq.m) area plot
- Cattle dung
- Super phosphate
- Furadan
- Fresh *Azolla* inoculum

Procedure

- Select a wetland field and prepare thoroughly and level uniformly.
- Mark the field into one cent plots (20 x 2m) by providing suitable bunds and irrigation channels.
- Maintain water level to a height of 10 cm.
- Mix 10 kg of cattle dung in 20 litres of water and sprinkle in the field.

- Apply 100 g super phosphate as basal dose.
- Inoculate fresh *Azolla* biomass @ 8 kg to each pot.
- Apply super phosphate @ 100 g as top dressing fertilizer on 4th and 8th day after *Azolla* inoculation.
- Apply carbofuran (furadan) granules @ 100 g/plot on 7th day after *Azolla* inoculation.
- Maintain the water level at 10 cm height throughout the growth period of two or three weeks.
- Observations
- Note the *Azolla* mat floating on the plot. Harvest the *Azolla,* drain the water and record the biomass.

Method of Inoculation of *Azolla* to Rice Crop

The *Azolla* biofertilizer may be applied in two ways for the wetland paddy. In the first method, fresh *Azolla* biomass is inoculated in the paddy field before transplanting and incorporated as green manure. This method requires huge quantity of fresh *Azolla*. In the other method, *Azolla* may be inoculated after transplanting rice and grown as dual culture with rice and incorporated subsequently.

Azolla biomass incorporation as green manure for rice crop:

- Collect the fresh *Azolla* biomass from the *Azolla* nursery plot.
- Prepare the wetland well and maintain water just enough for easy incorporation.
- Apply fresh *Azolla* biomass (15 t ha-1) to the main field and incorporate the *Azolla* by using implements or tractor.

Azolla inoculation as dual crop for rice:

- Select a transplanted rice field.
- Broadcast the fresh *Azolla* in the transplanted rice field on 7th day after planting (500 kg/ha).
- Maintain water level at 5-7.5cm.
- Note the growth of *Azolla* mat four weeks after transplanting and incorporate the *Azolla* biomass by using implements or tranctor or during inter-cultivation practices.

- A second bloom of *Azolla* will develop 8 weeks after transplanting which may be incorporated again.
- By the two incorporations, 20-25 tonnes of *Azolla* can be incorporated in one hectare rice field.

BIOFERTILIZERS

TYPES, BENEFITS AND APPLICATIONS

Biofertilizers are the substances which make use of microorganisms to fertile the soil. These fertilizers are not harmful to crops or other plants like the chemical fertilizers. They are actually taken from the animal wastes along with the microbial mixtures. Microorganisms are used to increase the level of nutrients in the plants. They let the plants grow in a healthy environment. They are also environment friendly and do not cause the pollution of any sort. Use of biofertilizers in the soil, makes the plants healthy as well as protect them from getting any diseases.

Nitrogen Biofertilizers

This type of biofertilizers helps the agriculturists to determine the nitrogen level in the soil. Nitrogen is a necessary component which is used for the growth of the plant. Plants need a limited amount of nitrogen for their growth. The type of the crops also determines the level of nitrogen. Some crops need more nitrogen for their growth while some crops need fewer amounts. The type of the soil also determines that which type of biofertilizers is needed for this crop. For example, Azotobacteria is used for the non-legume crops; Rhizobium is needed for the legume crops. Similarly blue green algae are needed to grow rice while Acetobacter is used to grow sugarcane. It means almost all the crops need different types of biofertilizers depending on their needs.

Phosphorus Biofertilizers

Phosphorus biofertilizers are used to determine the phosphorus level in the soil. The need of phosphorus for the plant growth is also limited. Phosphorus biofertilizers make the soil get the required amount of phosphorus. It is not necessary that a particular phosphorus biofertilizers is used for a particular type of crop. They can be used for any types of the crops for example; Acetobacter, Rhizobium and other biofertilizers can use phosphotika for any crop type.

Compost Biofertilizers

Compost biofertilizers are those which make use of the animal dung to enrich the soil with useful microorganisms and nutrients. To convert the animals waste into a biofertilizers, the microorganisms like abcteria undergo biological processes and help in breaking down the waste. Cellulytic fungal culture and Azetobacter cultures can be used for the compost biofertilizers.

Advantages of Biofertilizers

- They help to get high yield of crops by making the soil rich with nutrients and useful microorganisms necessary for the growth of the plants.
- Biofertilizers have replaced the chemical fertilizers as chemical fertilizers are not beneficial for the plants. They decrease the growth of the plants and make the environment polluted by releasing harmful chemicals.
- Plant growth can be increased if biofertilizers are used, because they contain natural components which do not harm the plants but do the *vice-versa*.
- If the soil will be free of chemicals, it will retain its fertility which will be beneficial for the plants as well as the environment, because plants will be protected from getting any diseases and environment will be free of pollutants.
- Biofertilizers destroy those harmful components from the soil which cause diseases in the plants. Plants can also be protected against drought and other strict conditions by using biofertilizers.
- Biofertilizers are not costly and even poor farmers can make use of them.

- They are environment friendly and protect the environment against pollutants.

APPLICATIONS OF BIOFERTILIZERS TO CROP

Seedling Root Dip

This method is applied to the rice crop. A bed of water is spread on the land where the crop has to grow. The seedlings of rice are planted in the water and are kept there for eight to ten hours.

Seed Treatment

In this method, the nitrogen and phosphorus fertilizers are mixed together in the water. Then seeds are dipped in this mixture. After the applications of this paste to the seeds, seeds are dried. After they dry out, they have to be sown as soon as possible before they get damaged by harmful microorganisms.

Soil Treatment

All the biofertilizers along with the compost fertilizers are mixed together. They are kept for one night. Then the next day this mixture is spread on the soil where seeds have to be sown.

7

Mushroom Cultivation

Mushrooms are a source of high quality proteins, essential minerals and vitamins. Being low in starch content, they are good for diabetic patients. Mushroom is grown on agriculture residues like straw, leaves, and sticks which (after use) can be recycled back as organic manure. Mushroom cultivation demands no land but closed structure, which can even be a thatch-hut. it can be a remunerative cottage industry for rural women.

CULTIVATION

TISSUE CULTURE METHOD

Select fresh mature mushrooms (straight from the bed), wash them gently under running water to remove surface dirt. Blot it dry. Wipe the surface gently with 70 per cent alcohol. Using a sterile knife, cut a small slit at the bottom of the mushroom. Tear it into two halves and avoid touching the inner surface. Transfer a few pieces of tissue (Pseudoparenchyama) from the centre of the mushroom to the media in plants.

Spore Culture Method

The surface of a mature (open) mushroom should be disinfected by wiping gently with 70 percent alcohol. Remove the spore and place the cap with gills downwards on a piece of sterile white paper. Cut tiny piece of spore print and soak it in a few mi. of sterile tap water. Dip a sterile inoculating loop into this spore suspension and streak gently across the surface of an agar plate. Incubate the plate for a few days and a white mycelial (white thread like structure) mass resulting form the growth of germinated spores becomes evident.

Preparation of Spawn

Cook the grains (rye/sorghum/maize/wheat) in water until they are ready to burst. Drain off excess water. Mix in 2 percent (w/w) lime (calcium carbonate), fill loosely into glass bottles and plug with cotton. Sterilize them in an autoclave for 30 minutes at 121°C and allow it to cool. Inoculate the bottles with the prepared pure culture and incubate at 25° C for 10-15 days. When the whitish mycelium has spread over the Surface, the spawn is ready for use.

MATERIALS OF MUSHROOM PRODUCTION

For 100 kg Mushroom production - Dry paddy straw (not more than one year old) -100 kg; gram powder-2 kg; spawn bottles-l0; polythene *bag-i* kg; water and a shady structure.

PREPARATION OF SUBSTRATE

Use Dried paddy straw, 500 g per bed (Hulled maizecob, sugarcane bagasse, cotton waste, paper waste, etc., can also be used instead of paddy straw). Cut the paddy straw into small bits of 3 to 5 cm. and soak it in cold water for 6-8 hours.

Take it out and then immerse in boiling water for 15-30 minutes and drain off excess water. Dry the straw in the shade for 2 hours and then use. Remove the spawn from the bottle using a small iron rod with hook on one side. Dip the iron rod in antiseptic solution before use.

Separate the spawn into four lots. Fill the first layer with straw bits upto 5 cm height in the bottom of the polythene bag. Sprinkle spawn over the entire surface of the straw layer. Add second layer with the straw bits upto 10 cm height and sprinkle spawn as before. Similarly, repeat the spawning for third and fourth layers of straw bits. Then, fill the final layer with straw bits upto 5 cm height.

After spawning the beds keep the beds in the growing room for spawn running. Keep bags in the dark for a period of twenty days. White mycelial growth appears throughout the bed.

Cropping and Harvesting

After the spawn running period (*nearly* 15 days), remove the polythene cover and keep in the rack. The relative humidity is maintained above 75% by spraying water on the floor and gunny screens, but watering the beds is avoided for first two days.

After two days, sprinkle beds with water twice daily. Allow aeration and light for 20-30 minutes in morning and evening by opening windows of the growing room. First harvest can be made 24 to 26 days after spawning. Harvest fully-opened mushroom before the edge of the top rolls downward. Two to three harvests can be taken at 7-10 days interval. The yield is about 35 to 85 percent of the substrate (w/w).

HISTORY AND BACKGROUND OF MUSHROOM

FOLKLORE

Mushrooms, the plant of immortality? That's what ancient Egyptians believed according to the hieroglyphics of 4600 years ago. The delicious flavour of mushrooms intrigued the pharaohs of Egypt so much that they decreed mushrooms were food for royalty and that no commoner could ever touch them. This assured themselves the entire supply of mushrooms. In various other civilizations throughout the world, including Russia, China, Greece, Mexico and Latin America, mushroom rituals were practiced. Many believed that mushrooms had properties that could produce super-human strength, help in finding lost objects and lead the soul to the realm of the gods.

EARLY CULTIVATION

France was the leader in the formal cultivation of mushrooms. Some accounts say that Louis XIV was the first mushroom grower. Around this time mushrooms were grown in special caves near Paris set aside for this unique form of agriculture. From France, the gardeners of England found mushrooms a very easy crop to grow which required little labour, investment and space. Mushroom cultivation began gaining popularity in England with more experimentation with spawn and publicity in journals and magazines.

In the late 19th century, mushroom production made its way across the Atlantic to the United States where curious home gardeners in the East tried their luck at growing this new and unknown crop. However growers had to depend on spawn imported from England which, by the time it reached the U.S. was of poor quality.

This industry text suggested that mushroom growing was perfect for florists. Since they grew flowers on benches, florists could just slide mushroom beds right under their flower benches and gain a profit in growing two crops in the area of one. Falconer also thought that mushroom growing was ideal for farmers who had access to growing their own manure and spawn. At the time skilled labour was not a necessity of mushroom growing. It was recommended to house wives as well as a source of home income. Not only did Falconer's book develop target groups for which growing was suited. It also contained much practical advice on building beds for cultivation, the perfect growing temperature and where mushroom markets were developing.

The first producer of pure culture virgin spawn was the American Spawn Company of St. Paul Minnesota, headed by Louis F. Lambert, a French mycologist. He began the production of brick spawn and advertised it across the country as "Lambert's Pure Culture Spawn." It soon proved to be a very popular product. This spawn received a silver medal at the Universal Exposition in St. Louis in 1904. A measure of Lambert's success was that English spawn was soon being sold under the name "English Pure Culture Spawn."

By 1914, mushroom marketing began to play a much greater role in the industry. It was estimated in one publication that four to five million pounds of mushrooms were grown in the U.S. Cost to the mushroom grower was fifteen to twenty-five cents. At retail, the price was forty to sixty cents per pound. Marketing became very important with a popular theory being to bypass the middle man and aim directly at consumers. It was pointed out that attractive containers would move product and only good looking product would sell.

U.S. Mushroom Cultivation

In 1891, the first book on mushroom growing was published and it shed new light on the theory of cultivation. William Falconer, a mushroom grower and experimenter from Dosoris, Long Island agreed with the recommendations of agricultural journalists and compiled their theories in Mushrooms: How to Grow Them; A Practical Treatise on Mushroom Culture for Profit and Pleasure.

New Developments

At this time of budding industry developments, one problem continued to face farmers intent on perfecting the growing conditions–poor spawn quality. With such an important ingredient standing in the way of mushroom cultivation, the U.S. Department of Agriculture began work on manufacturing spawn as an alternative to the English product that had proven to be unreliable. In 1903, after much experimentation, two USDA scientists had produced the perfect pure-culture virgin spawn. The U.S. Mushroom Industry was finally freed from depending on imported spawn that had caused so many problems in the past.

Industry Growth

Moving from an easy back yard crop in the early days of cultivation, to a large money maker, the mushroom industry began to grow in certain parts of the country. Concentrated areas of industry growth were Long Island, Central Massachusetts, Chicago, Michigan and California. Southeastern Pennsylvania was (and still is today) the largest centre of mushroom production in the country. In 1924, the Pennsylvania Department of Agriculture boasted that 85% of U.S. mushrooms were grown in Pennsylvania. In 1930, the U.S.

Census Bureau revealed that there were 516 growers in the U.S. and that 350 were in Chester County, Pennsylvania.

After 1930, the industry changed rapidly with better spawn production, the development of synthetic manure, and improvements of mushroom growing houses- hence the production of healthier crops. Organizations such as the Mushroom Growers' Cooperative Association were developed to assist and protect growers. In attempt to find better marketing techniques for mushrooms, the Farm Credit Administration became involved. Pennsylvania State University also became a major factor in the growth of the U.S. mushroom industry helping improve productivity dramatically in the 70's and 80's allowing growers to produce more and more mushrooms per square foot of growing area.

Development of AMI

One organization was developed to coordinate the actions of independent growers and act on behalf of the mushroom industry as a whole. The American Mushroom Institute was brought to life by the Chester County, Pennsylvania growers. Unfortunately, the first meeting for the development of the AMI was held December 4, 1941, only three days before the Japanese attack on Pearl Harbor. With America's involvement in World War II, this new mushroom growers' organization was put on hold. After the war was over and things began settling down for the nation, the American Mushroom Institute was finally officially organized with over 275 growers signed up to join. On January 14, 1955, AMI was legally incorporated as a non-profit organization.

Their goal was to promote the consumption of all cultivated mushrooms through research, advertising, publicity, merchandising, consumer education and government relations as well as to assist the industry in developing better growing and handling methods. Every broadcast medium was employed to promote mushrooms. Radio, television, magazines and newspapers told of different ways to eat them.

Even produce stores and supermarket chains were displaying mushroom merchandising posters. The American public was learning that mushrooms weren't something just used to garnish steaks. The AMI promoted recipes that used mushrooms in casseroles, appetizers, salads and other combinations. These were the first organized marketing efforts of the American Mushroom Institute.

THE NATIONAL MUSHROOM GROWERS' ASSOCIATION

In 1985, the National Mushroom Growers' Association was established in Illinois to promote the sale of fresh mushrooms on a national basis. They developed a newspaper and magazine promotion programme. In spite of its small budget, the programme was very successful in receiving coverage from national women's magazines and newspapers.

THE MUSHROOM COUNCIL

In 1990, the Mushroom Promotion, Research and Consumer Information Act was passed by Congress to strengthen the mushroom industry's position in the marketplace, maintain and expand existing markets and uses for mushrooms, and develop new markets and uses for mushrooms. In 1993, the Mushroom Council was established to carry out the direction of this act. The Council started out with a meager budget and a lot of inspiration about promoting mushrooms.

They began doing research to closely define the mushroom user which became the foundation for all of their communication efforts. Once the ground work was laid, a successful promotions programme began to shape.

Immediate targets for consumer communication were food editors of newspapers and magazines, TV and radio personalities, chefs and cookbook writers. Mushroom recipes went out to hundreds of venues each year — thus increasing consumer awareness and demands for literature on mushrooms. In 1996 the Mushroom Council made the pages of more than ten national women's magazines including Family Circle, Women's Day and Good Housekeeping.

Today, the Mushroom Council plays a very important role in the national promotion of fresh mushrooms through consumer public relations, foodservice communications and retail communications.

Many different venues are used in promoting fresh mushrooms to consumers such as working with professional chefs in developing and promoting new recipes, working with produce department managers to maintain the highest quality mushroom product for customers and sending out thousands of brochures each year to consumers hungry for new mushroom ideas. Thanks to the Mushroom Council, mushrooms have their own month to be honored and eaten. September is National Mushroom Month.

Today mushrooms are commercially produced in virtually every state. Pennsylvania, however, still accounts for 61% of total U.S. production, which in 2006/07 reached 827 million pounds. From the caves of Paris to the dinner tables of millions of Americans, fresh mushrooms have come out of the dark and into a spotlight that's intensity is ever increasing.

KINDS OF MUSHROOM CULTIVATION

There are three different groups of mushrooms. Selecting the right type of mushrooms to be cultivated must be based on climatic conditions and market demand. Mushrooms offer a wide range of proteins, vitamins and minerals necessary for the body and are becoming more popular and in demand.

Producing PDA Medium

How to well prepare spawn production is necessary for proper spawn multiplication. This part can be extended in further projects, in the case where a disabled person wishes to expand his knowledge and start spawn production. Only those trainees that are especially interested in this part will have specific activities and hands on training. In general, this part will be only theoretical.

Selecting Tissue Culture

A young, fresh and very healthy mushroom is used to prepare a tissue culture. This procedure is very delicate and requires extensive understanding and an extremely clean environment. It may not be suitable for beginners in mushroom cultivation.

Multiplying Spawn on Sorghum Seeds

This is also a highly specialized part of mushroom production and will attract only a few trainees due to its complexity. Therefore, only basic theory will be given, mostly in the classroom.

Trainees should, however, know how to select and buy good quality spawn from various suppliers. They should also know all steps involved in mushroom cultivation to allow future expansion of their mushroom farm.

Producing Substrate Bags

Extensive practice will be required by trainees to make sure that they can produce spawn bags by themselves or be able to verify the quality of bags of spawn bag producers. This is hands-on training and will be, with the subsequent steps, the focus of training.

Pasteurizing Bags

Pasteurization is necessary to completely sterilize substrate bags. If bags are not properly pasteurized due to insufficient residence time in the pasteurization chamber or because temperature is insufficient, bags will be contaminated resulting in poor growth of mushrooms or complete spoilage of bags.

Inoculating Bags with Sorghum Seeds

Inoculation must be done with extreme caution. It is an extremely delicate step that will ensure higher yield with disease free substrate bags. Work must be done near a flame from an alcohol lamp during inoculation.

Incubating Bags

During incubation, moisture, light, temperature and ventilation must be monitored constantly. Incubation time will differ according to the type of mushroom and climatic conditions.

Opening Bags

Following incubation, mushroom bags must be opened according to the type of mushrooms.

Maintaining and Monitoring

Maintenance of the mushroom house is crucial for higher yields. When kept clean, there are less insects and pest, less diseases. Bags must be checked individually and kept clean.

Cultivating Straw Mushrooms

Straw mushrooms are very popular in South East Asia and are cultivated using a straw bed. Because of their popularity and market demand, it is interesting to learn how to cultivate this type of mushroom.

Packaging

When selling on the fresh food market or from the farm directly very little packaging is required. Most people use plastic or paper bags.

Marketing

Marketing remains the key to a successful enterprise. Care must be taken to always review the competition and to offer clients reliability of supply and quality of mushrooms.

Processing

Processing of mushrooms is limited only by a person's imagination. There are already numerous methods and recipes, which can offer value, added products. Nevertheless, in rural areas, the market may be small because of financial limitations.

Waste Management and Recycling

Waste must be handled properly in each step of the mushroom cultivation process. Recycling and utilization of waste is not only a good way of preserving our environment but also of saving money.

Troubleshooting

It is necessary to know the most common problems found in mushroom production, their symptoms and their remedies. Although this section will never replace the advice of an expert, it should help solve basic problems and help identify problems before they occur.

Preparing the Mushroom House

Mushroom houses can be built for as little as 500 Baht (US$ 12) made of readily available yet appropriate materials such as rice straw, grass, dried leaves, used rice bags and tree branches.

Starting the Business

As an entrepreneur in mushroom production, it is necessary to have basic knowledge in management and bookkeeping. This will allow tracking of profit and losses.

Keeping Records

Keeping records is very important since it allows monitoring of all expenses incurred in mushroom production. It also allows to verify how much profit is generated in the business and identify how certain costs can be reduced in order to generate more profit.

THE WILD EDIBLE MUSHROOMS

The next two lectures will be concerned with the mushroom eating. The term "mushroom" is used here in a broad sense as used in popular mushroom guides and include members of the Basidiomycota that produce fruiting bodies and some members of the Ascomycota as well.

The latter, as you should recall, produce asci and ascospores during sexual reproduction while mushrooms and other members of the Basidiomycota produce basidia and basidiospores. In addition, not all members of the Basidiomycota are mushrooms with stalk, caps and gills. There are coral fungi, polypores, puffballs and boletes, just to name a few. Boletes are very similar to mushroom in appearance. The most obvious difference being that they have pores, as the polypores, instead of gills.

However, instead of having fruit bodies that are leathery to woody, boletes are fleshy like mushrooms and there are a number of highly desirable species, with respect to their edibility.

Obviously, there are species such as the *Pycnoporus sanguineus* and *Geastrum indica* that cannot be eaten because of the texture of their fruitbodies and the powdery masses of their spores, respectively, but they have traditionally been included in popular mushroom guide books since one of the goals of the authors of such books is also to show the reader the diversity that exists in mushrooms.

Although the topic of eating mushroom is inevitably tied to mushroom poisoning, we will cover this topic in a later lecture. This is a very fascinating topic because there are many people that are intrigued by eating wild mushrooms and will go out, daily, and forage for them in spite of the possibility that they may inadvertently eat a poisonous mushroom.

Despite this danger, the number of people, in this country, consuming wild mushrooms increases each year. However, while incidents of mushroom poisonings continue to occur each year, sometimes with fatal results, mushroom poisoning is still not a major problem in the United States. Even with an increase in the number of people going out to collect mushrooms, there is no evidence that the number of incidents of mushroom poisonings have increased in recent years.

The practice of eating mushroom probably began during the hunting and gathering period, in our prehistory. They were collected along with fruits and berries, as well as other plant material that could be consumed.

Also, like plants the gatherers learned which ones were

edible and which were poisonous and if there were other uses for mushrooms, *i.e.*, medicinal or religious uses. However, unlike plants, mushrooms must have been have been shrouded in mysteries since unlike the plants, there was not an obvious way in which they could be reproduced. Even much later, during the dark ages, mushrooms became more firmly embedded in the mythology of the supernatural. Many myths arose because of their seemingly supernatural characteristics and strange habitat. Their growth was rapid and they seem to suddenly appear overnight as if from nowhere.

Thus, their origin appeared to be magical. They sometimes formed circular patterns or "rings" as in *Chlorophyllum molybdites* where the grass is greener *inside* the ring. Some glow in the dark. Many have bizarre shapes, and are ephemeral. They became part of the lives of fairies, elves and witches. This concept is evident even today in common name of mushrooms, such as "The Fairy Ring Mushroom" for *Marasmius oreades* and "Witches Butter" or Fairy Butter for *Tremella mesenterica*.

Because so little was known about mushrooms, many misconceptions concerning the edibility of mushrooms have developed. Some of the more common ones are briefly discussed below:

- There is a fool-proof test for distinguishing edible from poisonous mushrooms. The most common ones that can be heard are that "a poisonous mushroom will turn silver black while it is being cooked", "if you can peel the cap of the mushroom it is safe to eat" and "observing which mushrooms foraging animals consume will tell you which species are safe to eat". While there are some generalizations that can be made within certain groups of mushrooms, there is no fool-proof test that can be used for all mushrooms. Those species of mushrooms that are edible are known to be edible because someone at one time had tried it and discovered it to be safe to eat.
- Most mushrooms are poisonous. Of the thousands of species known, perhaps 60 or so are poisonous, and of these only a handful will be fatal if consumed

(these numbers will vary depending on your source). However, it does not require a lot of mushroom to poison a lot of people. In Europe, of those that die mushroom poisoning, probably 90% die as a result of mistaking *Amanita phalloides* (Death Cap) for *Amanita calytroderma* (Coccora). The remaining species, however, are not necessarily good to eat. I am using edible here to means non-poisonous and not necessarily good to eat. Thus, an edible mushroom may have a strong bitter, peppery or some other unpleasant taste, be bland or have no taste at all.

- There are a large number of people that die from mushroom poisoning each year. "Large" is somewhat ambiguous here. If we are talking about the number of people that go out collecting for mushrooms each year, in this country, then the number of people that die as a result of mushroom poisoning is few relative to that number.
- Poisonous mushrooms must taste bad. Many mushrooms that are non-poisonous may have a very bad taste. The opposite can also be true. *Amanita phalloides* is said to have a quite pleasant taste, but is one of the most deadly species of poisonous mushrooms.
- You can be poisoned by touching a poisonous mushroom. As deadly as some toxins may be, touching the mushroom is harmless. The harmful toxins in mushrooms must be consumed in order to harm you.
- Collecting mushrooms for consumption is unsafe and even experts have died from picking the wrong mushrooms. This last misconception is the one that continues to be perpetuated by the news media every year. Probably every year, you can read a headline that goes something like "Expert Mushroom Hunter Dies From Eating Deadly Mushroom". However, upon closer examination of such a story it is often

the case that the person that died is far from being an expert. Even those who are avid collectors that have been foraging for wild mushrooms, for only a short period of time, are unlikely to die from mushroom poisoning, if they have even had a minimum of training in the do's and don'ts of mushroom collecting and if common sense is used. There are a number of species that are very good to eat that cannot be mistaken for other species. If collectors stick with those species, mushroom poisoning is highly unlikely. New species can be tried through interaction with other collectors who have eaten other species.

- Species determined to be edible are always safe to eat. Whenever a new species is tried for the first time, even if it is one that is highly regarded and is said to be being very tasty, it is best to be cautious. Try only a few bites and wait 24 hours before consuming more. There are a vast number of compounds that occur in wild mushrooms that may cause adverse reactions, when consumed by a few individuals, but are safe for the general public. There is also the possibility of an allergic response to a particular species. Other precautions that should be taken:
  - When preparing mushrooms for a meal, always inspect the mushrooms to determine if it is firm and fresh. Bacterial and fungal decomposition may be taking place in old mushrooms.
  - Avoid eating raw mushrooms. Many edible species have toxins that are heat sensitive and will be rendered harmless by cooking the mushroom. Also, the cell wall of mushrooms is composed of chitin, which the human digestive system cannot break down. must also be degraded by heat so that we can absorb nutrients within cells. If the cell walls remain intact, the nutrients in the mushrooms will simply pass through our digestive system. Cooking will break down the

cell wall and release its contents, which are digestible.

- Mushroom are of no nutritional value. Although mushrooms will never be one of the world s staples, it has been a food supplement in various cultures. Nutritionally speaking, mushrooms fall between the best vegetables and animal protein source. Their protein content may vary anywhere between 15-40% of *dry* weight (keep in mind that mushrooms are more than 90% water). However, all essential amino acids are present in mushrooms, as well as water-soluble vitamins and all the minerals that our bodies require are present. A generous serving of mushrooms (0.5 lb) of fresh mushrooms provides approximately 70 kcal.

TYPES OF EDIBLE MUSHROOMS

Mushrooms add something special to every meal and, when you are familiar with the different types of edible mushrooms, you can eat a different mushroom every night.

Exotic mushrooms add a distinct flavour to your cooking, but unless you are a mushroom expert, known as a mycophagist, you are safer getting your mushrooms from the store. Some types of poisonous mushrooms look just like some types of edible mushrooms. While wild mushrooms may look wild and taste wild, it is better to play it safe when choosing your mushrooms. There are three types of mushrooms available at most markets: common, exotic, and wild. The common mushroom, known as a button or champignon mushroom, is the most readily available.

CULTIVATED EXOTIC MUSHROOMS

Cultivated exotic mushrooms are grown in a controlled environment and are very safe to eat. They are sometimes more expensive than button mushrooms but, as an occasional treat, are worth the extra money and effort to find them.

Shiitake Mushrooms

Shiitake mushrooms are also known as Black Forest

mushrooms or Golden Oak mushrooms. They are mostly cultivated in Japan, China, and South Korea, but are also available from Australia and North America.

When fresh, the mushrooms colour ranges from light golden brown to dark brown. They have a wide cap with a firm fleshy texture, but the stems are very tough and are either chopped very fine for sautéing or saved for making stock. These mushrooms are also available in a dried form. The dried shiitake can be stored for a long time and can be revived just by soaking in water. The water that the dried shiitakes have been reconstituted in can then be used to make a delicious mushroom sauce. As far as exotic mushrooms go, the dried shiitake is a good way to add great flavour to your recipes while saving money.

Oyster Mushroom

The oyster mushroom, also known as Pleurotte, gets its name from the way it looks and not its flavour. Oyster mushrooms are light tan or cream coloured with a large, fan-like cap and a short stem. These tender mushrooms have a delicate flavour, so they are best prepared simply so the flavour isn't overpowered.

Enoki Mushrooms

These mushrooms are also known as Enokitake or Enokidake. They have a tiny white cap on a long slender stem. They grow in bunches from a single base, so you will be selecting clusters rather than single mushrooms. You just trim off the base and give the Enoki a quick rinse to prepare them. Enoki have a crisp texture and a fruity, sweet flavour and are very good raw in a salad. If you are using them in a cooked dish, add them last to keep the texture and flavour.

Cremini Mushrooms

Cremini mushrooms are fun and tasty. Cremini are the slightly more mature variation of the common button mushroom. Use these wherever you would use button mushrooms but expect a deeper, richer flavour.

Portobello Mushrooms

The most mature version of the Cremini mushroom these mushrooms can grow up to 6-inches wide, are great for grilling or stuffing, and can be used as a substitute for meat in some recipes.

WILD MUSHROOMS

Wild mushrooms bring more flavour to every recipes, but only use wild mushrooms that you find at the market. Eating wild mushrooms that you find in the actual wild can be dangerous. These four wild mushrooms are available fresh as well as dried. You may want to consider the dried variation because they keep longer, have a more intense flavour, and the water that you use to restore them can be used to make a mushroom sauce.

Morel Mushrooms

Morels can be found in several varieties including black, golden, and white. Morels look like a conical sponge and are completely hollow inside. They are available fresh in the spring or dried all year long. Use them in butter or cream-based sauces.

Bolete Mushrooms

Also known as Cep, or Porchino, this brown capped mushroom has a light coloured bulbous stem and a cream coloured flesh. The smooth meaty texture of this mushroom has a rich earthy flavour and is best sautéed with butter and garlic. Bolete are usually available in late summer and early fall.

Chanterelle Mushrooms

Chanterelle are also known as Girolle. They are yellow to orange in colour and look like an inverted umbrella. This mushroom has ridges rather than gills. Chanterelle have a rich woodsy flavour and aroma and are best when sautéed with butter and a little garlic. Chanterelle are available during the summer and fall.

Black Trumpet

These mushrooms are related to Chanterelles, but are black in colour with much thinner flesh.

TRUFFLES

Truffles are very rare and only found in southern France and Northern Italy. Black truffles can cost as much as $130 to $390 dollars per pound while white truffles can cost as much as $1350 to $2700 per pound.

Black truffles grow only on the roots of oak trees while white truffles can be found growing on the roots of oak, hazel, poplar, and beech trees. Specially trained hogs and dogs are used to find these delightful fungi.

In general, truffles are shaved onto a meal just before serving. A more cost effective way of getting the rich, earthy flavour of these mushrooms into your food is to look for truffle oil, which is usually olive or vegetable oil infused with truffles.

DIFFERENCE BETWEEN EDIBLE AND NON-EDIBLE MUSHROOMS

EDIBLE MUSHROOMS : POPULAR AND READILY

Most of us are familiar with the most popular and readily available edible mushrooms because we purchase them from the super market. You may not go out foraging for mushrooms, but many people do collect, identify and eat wild mushrooms, an activity that can prove to be deadly. Therefore, only a person who is extremely knowledgeable and has been trained in the identification of mushrooms should pick and consume wild mushrooms—due to the number of poisonous species.

Toxins

The difference between edible and non-edible mushrooms is the toxins that are present in the non-edible or poisonous mushrooms. The fungi produce these toxins naturally, and the toxins that are present in a poisonous mushroom cannot be removed or made non-toxic by any process, including freezing, cooking, canning or any other process—these toxins are inherent to the mushroom.

Four Categories of Toxins

Mushroom toxins can be divided into four specific categories. Protoplasmic toxins/poisons destroy cells, and eventually lead to organ failure. Neurotoxins are compounds that cause various neurological symptoms like excessive sweating, convulsions, hallucinations, coma, depression and a spastic colon. The third category, gastrointestinal irritants, produce nausea, vomiting, diarrhea and abdominal cramps. Disulfiram-like toxins only produce symptoms if alcohol is consumed (within a 72-hour window after consuming the mushroom); the person will experience an acute toxic syndrome, which is short-lived.

Edible Species

People can have different reactions to the foods they eat, and this holds true when consuming mushrooms. What is "edible" for some may not be "edible" for everyone. There are approximately 250 North American edible species of mushrooms. These include Agaricus arvensis or horse mushroom, Agaricus campestris or field mushroom, Boletus badius or bay bolete, Boletus edulis or penny bun, Calocybe gambosum or St. George's mushroom, and Coprinus comatus or shaggy ink cap, to name a few.

Poisonous Species

Of the 10,000 North American species of mushrooms, 250 are edible and approximately 250 are poisonous, leaving an extremely large number of species that we know little about (edible or non-edible). Poisonous mushrooms, if ingested, can cause death within three to six days, which is why it is extremely important to seek treatment immediately. Symptoms are breathing problems, dizziness, vomiting, diarrhea and dehydration. Some poisonous species are Amanita phalloides or death cap mushroom, Amanita virosa or the destroying angel, Amanita muscaria or the fly Agaric, and Cortinarius rubellus.

How to Avoid Poisoning

To avoid poisoning you must be extremely knowledgeable in mushroom identification when collecting mushrooms, as there is no simple cut-and-dry method, or list of identifiable characteristics between an edible mushroom and a poisonous mushroom. If you do collect mushrooms, never mix the edible mushrooms with those that are non-edible, and only eat the edible mushrooms that are not damaged and are in good condition. Always refrigerate your edible mushrooms, and remember the number one rule: if you are in doubt about whether a mushroom is edible or non-edible, discard it.

8

Plant Transformation

Plant transformation is the introduction of a foreign piece of DNA, confering a specific trait, into host plant tissue. The foreign gene (termed the "transgene") is incorporated into the host plant genome and stably inherited through future generations. The correct regulatory sequences are added to the gene of interest i.e. promoters and terminators, then the DNA is transferred to the plant cell culture using an appropriate vector. The gene is attached to a selectable marker which allows selection for the presence of the transgene. Genes conferring resistance to a specific antibiotic are often used to serve this purpose. Once the plant tissue has been transformed, the cells containing the transgene are selected and regeneration back into whole plants is carried out. This is possible as plant cells are totipotent, which means that they contain all the genetic information to control the development of that cell into a potentially fertile plant. Therefore, the gene is contained in every single plant cell, however, where it is switched on is determined by the promoter which is controlling the gene. Plant transformation can be carried out in a number of different ways depending on the species of plant in question. This is discussed in the sections below. Plant transformation was developed as an alternative to conventional breeding methods which are more laborious than this fairly simple (now routine) laboratory proceedure.

GENETIC TRANSFORMATION

Transformation is the introduction of DNA representing a cloned gene into a cell so that it expresses the protein encoded by the gene. Although the physical insertion of DNA into a cell's nucleus is straightforward, the expression of proteins encoded by that DNA that is not part of a chromosome is often only transient. Introduced DNA that is inserted into one of the chromosomes will be passed during mitosis to all subsequent daughter cells. It is this "stable" transformation that will allow one to introduce one copy of DNA into one cell, and then allow the one transformed cell to regenerate a complete organism, where each cell contains a copy of that introduced DNA. The manipulation of an organisms DNA by transformation allows unparalleled ability to determine the function of a gene from levels of cell function, to organismal physiology to ecological roles. It also provides a way to dissect the functional significance of parts of the gene or specific amino acid residues of the resulting protein. Transformation additionally allows the engineering of plants or animals to produce novel proteins or specifically remove expression of certain proteins.

There are a number of ways that cloned DNA can be physically introduced into a cell. DNA can be micro-injected into cells, or shot into the cell on the surface of microprojectiles, or enter through holes in the cell membrane induced by a strong electric current. Drosophila and C. elegans are usually transformed through microinjection. Plant transformation can take advantage of a plant pathogenic bacteria (Agrobacterium tumifaciens) that move DNA from a plasmid it carries into plant cells as part of its life cycle. The mechanisms of this movement will be discussed in class. However, it is possible to manipulate the plasmid such that a gene of interest is placed into the plasmid in Agrobacterium so that the bacteria will introduce this DNA into a plant cell.

To transform most plants using Agrobacterium, a single plant cell that has received the new DNA from the bacteria has to be regenerated into a whole plant. This process involves the culturing of the transformed cell to provide replication of that cell. Levels of plant hormones can be manipulated to cause this mass of cells to form roots and shoots of a regenerated plant.This process can take weeks and the details vary from plant to plant. For Arabidospsis, an alternate method has been developed- called dip infiltration. In this method, Agrobacterium carrying the modified plasmid is introduced into the whole plant by submerging the plant in a bacterial solution. Applying a vacuum can help force the bacterial solution into the inner air spaces between plant cells, but this was found to be not necessary. Agrobacterium will move the DNA from its plasmid into many of these cells in the plant. Some of these transformed cells will be used to make the flowers of the plant, including the pollen and ovules. With the self-fertilization possible in Arabidodpis, seeds produced from these flowers will have the introduced gene at a low rate.

The major technical problem of transformation, regardless of the method used, is the low frequency at which it occurs. Only a small fraction of cells where the DNA has entered the nucleus does the DNA get spliced into a chromosome. Thus, one needs a way of identifying those cells or plants that contain the introduce DNA. Usually, one gene included in the introduced DNA is a selectable marker gene - for example a gene that confers resistance against a chemical that kills normal plant cells (antibiotic inbroader sense). Kanamycin is one such antibiotic that kills plant cells. Including a kanamycin resistance gene along with a gene of interest in the Agrobacterium vector allows one to select transformed plants by growing them on kanamycin. Only transformed plants will survive since they express the introduced kanamycin resistance gene. For the Agrobacterium infiltration method, the seed from the infiltrated plants are plated on agar containing kanamycin – the low number of plants containing the introduced DNA will germinate and grow on these plates.

REGULATORY ENVIRONMENT AND PUBLIC PERCEPTIONS

In most countries, planned field releases and commercial development of transgenic plants are first scrutinized and approved by regulatory authorities established by the national government, to ensure that products are safe to the environment and consumers. This process can be important to obtain the maximum social benefit from transgenic plant lines. For example, in several countries, release of transgenic insect-resistant plant varieties has been linked to mandatory programmes of insect monitoring and industry responses to avoid premature loss of useful insect control genes because of a build-up of resistant insect populations.

Scrutiny by regulatory authorities is also an important mechanism to reassure the general public of the safety of a new technology that is not well understood by most people. However, if the process is conducted inefficiently by the regulatory authorities, it can severely slow research. For example, it is essential to characterize a substantial number of independent transformed plant lines in both physiological experiments and in selecting genetically improved cultivars. The availability of sufficient containment greenhouse space rapidly becomes limiting if the process of evaluation before approval of field releases is slow.

The conservative assumption underlying regulations in many countries is that all transgenic plants are potentially hazardous. Scientific theory and practical experience show that this is not the case. The hazards relate to the genes transferred or the phenotype produced, not to the gene transfer method used. There have been no reports of any harmful environmental effects or other hazardous unforeseen behaviour of transgenic plants in the thousands of field trials conducted internationally to date. As public experience and understanding of plant transformation increase, it is to be hoped that regulatory processes may be streamlined, with the focus on products rather than on processes of plant genetic modification.

These releases have coincided with increasing dissemination of information on transgenic plants in forms accessible to the general public. In each case, consumers have responded positively to quality or price advantages, and in several cases demand has outstripped supply in the first season. However, it is clear that continued work is important to provide the broad community with information to support considered responses to emerging products.

INTELLECTUAL PROPERTY

As technical limitations are overcome, it is possible that commercial limitations will become more serious barriers to exploitation of genetic transformation. New technologies developed in this area are effectively inventions and are therefore eligible for patent protection. For example, patents have already been issued on most established or promising plant genetic transformation strategies and on many isolated genes, promoters, and techniques for plant gene manipulation. The patent literature has become an important source of information in plant transformation research, albeit more difficult and expensive to search than the scientific literature. A patent provides the inventor or assignee with a period of exclusive ownership, or formally a right to exclude others from making, using, or selling the invention.

There is no statutory exclusion for infringment when patented products or methods are used for research purposes. The widespread misconception that disclosure in the patent document allows researchers to practice the invention in order to improve on it possibly arises because patent owners are generally reticent in instituting infringement proceedings until the level of damages that may accrue becomes commercially significant. There is no obligation to license and no constraint on royalty levels provided the patent holder makes active use of the intellectual property. Some patents make extremely broad claims, and patent holders are not required to develop all possible manifestations of an invention to retain broad ownership. Penalties for infringement of proprietary rights can be severe, so it is important to determine whether the tools or topics of proposed research are already in the public domain or subject to patent protection. This can be difficult to establish without periodic patent searching, or even legal challenges. The position may differ between countries.

For example, particle bombardment for gene transfer into plant cells has been patented in the United States but not in Australia. Apparatus for particle bombardment involving a macroprojectile and stop plate has been patented in Australia but not apparatus involving particle acceleration in a gas pulse. Patent coverage for many genes and promoters is similarly restricted. For example, the maize ubiquitin promoter is the subject of granted patents or applications in Europe, Japan, and the United States but apparently not in many other countries, including Australia. Under these circumstances, a transgenic plant variety produced and used commercially without infringing any patent rights in one country could infringe certain patent claims if used (even for research or other noncommercial purposes) in another country.

To complicate matters further, patent applications are not available publicly in some countries (notably the United States) until the patent is granted, which can be years after the application is filed. There are moves to harmonize international practice, *e.g.* by providing for ownership for 20 years from the date of application and publishing 18 months after application to eliminate the practice of "submarine" patent applications that only surface after a competitor has independently made the same invention. The issues involved are complicated, and some important differences in patent law between countries appear unlikely to be resolved in the near future. Patents are intended to encourage and reward useful invention and technical innovation, and the new technology enters the public domain after a period of 17 to 20 years. In the interim, commercial restrictions can appear quite ruthless as patent holders adopt commercialization strategies to capture the value of protected intellectual property. In an era of tight public sector research funding and high research and development costs, the benefits of corporate investment to develop transformation technologies outweigh the inconvenience of patent restrictions. Debate continues on mechanisms to balance the competing interests.

TRANSFORMATION EFFICIENCY

The methods for gene transfer into plant cells, particularly *Agrobacterium* and particle bombardment, are now sufficiently developed to allow transformation of essentially any plant species in which regenerable cells can be identified. Broadly applicable selection methods are well established. The key to transformation of recalcitrant species appears to be development of methods to expose many regenerable cells to nondestructive gene transfer treatments. What currently limits the practical transformation of many plant species is the combination of a low frequency of transformation and a high frequency of undesired genetic change or unpredictable transgene expression.

These problems necessitate expensive large-scale transformation and screening programmes to produce useful transformants. The first constraint may be addressed by research into tissue culture systems to enrich for regenerable cells accessible to gene transfer. Contract transformation services may implement economies of scale to afford robotic systems for routine large scale target preparation and gene transfer treatments. A clearer understanding of the events surrounding gene transfer by *Agrobacterium* is also required. Is transient expression a satisfactory test for *Agrobacterium*-mediated gene transfer into plant cells, or can another convenient test be developed to allow rapid detection and optimization of this key event? Does *Agrobacterium* select between cell types, and if so what features determine favored cells for gene transfer? Can these features be imparted to highly regenerable cell types? Direct gene transfer experiments indicate that if naked DNA is transferred into many actively dividing and regenerable cells, a proportion will be stably transformed. Is the same true for cells receiving typically lower doses of T-DNA, or are there additional physiological requirements for efficient T-DNA integration?

Is T-DNA integration targeted to potentially expressed regions of the genome, or to regions undergoing active transcription? Can the transcriptional status of target cells be manipulated to achieve a high frequency of integration into regions suitable for subsequent transgene expression, but a low frequency of insertional inactivation of genes influencing the phenotype of regenerated transformants? There are at least as many relevant questions surrounding direct gene transfer. Is stable transformation efficiency as sensitive as transient expression to decreased DNA concentration? Does DNA concentration affect mean copy number or cotransformation frequency in resulting stable transformants? Is integration targeted to potentially transcribed regions as appears to be the case for T-DNA from *Agrobacterium*? Can artificial T-DNA complexes be manufactured, and will they influence the efficiency or integration patterns available from direct gene transfer?

Useful vs Absolute Transformation Efficiency

In the longer term, a more important goal than increased transformation efficiency is the development of transformation methods and constructs tailored for predictable transgene expression, without collateral genetic damage. We may conclude that much of the current effort in plant transformation directed towards increased transformation frequencies is naive and misdirected. We need to distinguish between absolute and useful transformation frequencies. The limiting process in the application of plant transformation for more sophisticated studies of plant physiology or for cultivar improvement is generally not the production of transformants but the screening (or subsequent breeding) required to eliminate transformants with collateral genetic damage that would interfere with meaningful physiological analysis or commercial use. Depending on the ratio of effort required for these processes a large increase in absolute transformation efficiency may be futile if accompanied by even a small decrease in the proportion of useful transformants. Conversely, a large drop in absolute transformation frequency may be more than compensated by a smaller gain in the proportion of useful transformants. These ideas are familiar to most practicing plant breeders but have understandably not been foremost in the minds of most transformation scientists while they struggled to develop reliable and efficient systems for gene transfer into target plant species.

Collateral Genetic Damage

To achieve a high proportion of useful transformants, we

need to understand more clearly the factors contributing to undesired genetic change during the transformation process. To what extent is such change associated with the integration of single or multiple copies of foreign DNA, as distinct from the processes of tissue culture, selection, and plant regeneration? Is genetic change induced or selected during such processes, or is it commonly the effect of preexisting mutations in somatic cells that are simply detected when entire plants are regenerated from single (transformed) cells? If change is induced, which are the mutagenic stages in the protocols, and can they be avoided?

If mutations are preexisting, can the procedures be tailored to selectively prevent regeneration of mutated cells? Compared to adventitious shoot proliferation, is somatic embryogenesis disadvantageous because of longer duration in culture, or advantageous because the complexity of the embryogenic process acts as a filter to eliminate many cells with mutations? Does the approach of germline transformation of uncultured explants followed by crossing to obtain nonchimeric transgenic progeny reduce the frequency of undesired genetic change, or just mask such change in the background of genetic variation from sexual reproduction? The relative importance of these questions varies between plant species; vegetatively vs sexually propagated crops provide an extreme example. Unfortunately, the answers to many of these questions may also be genotype specific.

Ideal and Model Transformation Systems

As the emphasis on useful transformation frequency increases, we may see a trend towards minimization or elimination of tissue culture stages, targeted integration of single copy transgenes, and direct (leaf-disc PCR) screening for transformants with useful genes to eliminate the need for reporter sequences. As our understanding of the genetic basis of agronomic traits increases, it is likely that this goal will be extended to the introduction of greater lengths of DNA encoding multiple genes.

We will need to determine the capacity of available methods to introduce such lengths of DNA intact. Although some of these questions may be answered and approaches developed with model plants, the features that make the models attractive for some genetic studies (*e.g.* small genome, small plant size, rapid generation time for *Arabidopsis*) generally cannot be exploited in practical transformation systems for most economically important plants. We must be prepared to select the models according to the questions, and test the answers for applicability to the practical targets.

Transformation, Breeding, and Genetic Diversity

As with conventional breeding, it is highly undesirable for plant transformation to lead to excessive genetic uniformity in current varieties of any crop. Even a single gene in all varieties can create problems. For example, the United States maize crop in 1970 was devastated because of disease susceptibility accompanying a cytoplasmic male sterility trait used to simplify hybrid seed production. This is another reason to aim for the capacity to transform diverse genotypes within a species, to develop diverse genes for desired phenotypes, and to eliminate unnecessary sequences from the transformation process.

When Practical Means Commercial

Plant transformation is already sufficiently developed to allow the testing and even commercialization of plants with novel phenotypes under simple genetic control. For continuing practical benefits, it will be necessary to extend our understanding of the biological basis for efficient plant transformation and develop improved technologies for predictable transgene expression without collateral genetic damage, at a pace matching the exciting scientific advances in gene cloning and characterization.

This will require support from industry for the underlying research. As transformation projects are increasingly undertaken with the possibility of generating commercially useful products, transformation scientists in turn must increasingly integrate social, legal, and economic issues as well as technical issues from the earliest stages of project design.

PURPOSES OF PLANT TRANSFORMATION

An Experimental Tool for Plant Physiology

The capacity to introduce and express (or inactivate) specific genes in plants provides a powerful new experimental tool, allowing direct testing of some hypotheses in plant physiology that have been exceedingly difficult to resolve using other biochemical approaches.

Exciting examples include the molecular genetic analysis of cellular signals controlling sexual reproduction and plant-microbe interactions; the roles of specific enzymes in metabolic processes determining partitioning of photosynthates, and thus harvestable yield; and the roles of specific enzymes and hormones in plant developmental processes, including those affecting quality and storage life of marketed plant products.

A Practical Tool for Plant Improvement

Much of the support for plant transformation research (and more broadly for plant molecular biology) has been provided because of expectations that this approach could:

a. Generate plants with useful phenotypes unachievable by conventional plant breeding,
b. Correct faults in cultivars more efficiently than conventional breeding,
c. Allow the commercial value of improved plant lines to be captured by those investing in the research more fully than is possible under intellectual property laws governing conventionally bred plants.

The first of these expectations has been met, with production of the first commercial plant lines expressing foreign genes conferring resistance to viruses, insects, herbicides, or post-harvest deterioration, and accumulation of usefully modified storage products, including several cases where there was no source of the desired trait in the gene pool for conventional breeding. The future prospects in this respect are also exciting, with preliminary indications that novel genes can be introduced to generate plant lines useful for production of materials ranging from pharmaceuticals to biodegradable plastics.

The extent to which the other practical or commercial expectations of plant transformation can be met depends on the efficiency and predictability of production of lines with the desired phenotype, and without undesired side effects of the transformation process. As the sophistication of the physiological hypotheses to be tested by transformation increases, exactly the same factors become limiting. This occurs because of the practical difficulty of screening large numbers of plants for the desired expression pattern and the need to avoid misleading results from unrelated physiological effects of unintended genetic changes during the transformation process.

BIOLOGICAL REQUIREMENTS FOR TRANSFORMATION

The essential requirements in a gene transfer system for production of transgenic plants are:

a. Availability of a target tissue including cells competent for plant regeneration,
b. A method to introduce DNA into those regenerable cells,
c. A procedure to select and regenerate transformed plants at a satisfactory frequency.

One of the simplest available plant transformation systems involves infiltration of *Agrobacterium* cells into *Arabidopsis* plants before flowering, and direct selection for rare transformants in the resulting seedling populations. Unfortunately, small plant size, rapid generation time, and high seed yield per plant are prerequisites for this method. These features are not shared by any economically important plant species. Other approaches to transformation via plant gametes have not been successful in practice. Therefore, the totipotency of some somatic plant cells underlies most plant transformation systems.

The efficiency with which such cells can be prepared as targets for transformation is today the limiting factor in achievement of transformation in recalcitrant plant species. Using either *Agrobacterium* or particle bombardment, it is now possible to introduce DNA into virtually any regenerable plant cell type. Only a small proportion of target cells typically receive the DNA during these treatments, and only a small proportion of these cells survive the treatment and stably integrate introduced DNA.

It is therefore generally essential to efficiently detect or select for transformed cells among a large excess of untransformed cells, and to establish regeneration conditions allowing recovery of intact plants derived from single transformed cells.

Alternatively, transformed cells must contribute to the germline so that nonchimeric transformants can be obtained in the progeny from sexual reproduction.

DEFINITION AND VERIFICATION OF TRANSFORMATION

This review is concerned with the stable incorporation and expression of genes introduced into plants by means other than fusion of gametes or other cells. It focuses on transformation involving integration of introduced genes in the plant nuclear genome, although some issues are equally applicable to transformed plants in which introduced genes are expressed from an organelle genome, or a replicating viral vector.

Ingo Potrykus in 1991 offered a provocative but clarifying assessment of plant transformation technologies based on a rigid definition of proof of integrative transformation, requiring a combination of genetic, phenotypic, and physical data. Unfortunately the combination specified was not useful in practice for verification of transformation in some plants. For example, analysis of sexual offspring populations is problematic in trees that are slow to reproduce sexually, and in some vegetatively propagated crops such as sugarcane with complicated (polyploid, aneuploid) genetics, and many sexually sterile cultivars.

Similarly, a "tight" correlation between physical and phenotypic data is not a defining characteristic of gene transfer methods that result in integration of multiple and often rearranged copies of the transferred DNA, because many transformants have unexpressed copies of introduced sequences. Integrative transformation has nevertheless been unequivocally verified in such cases.

Most critical researchers would therefore accept a more generally applicable subset of criteria as rigorous proof of integrative transformation:

1. Southern DNA hybridization analysis of multiple independent transformants, using a probe(s) for the introduced gene(s) and restriction enzymes predicted to generate hybridizing fragments of different length at different integration sites. It is important to confirm that sizes of hybridizing fragments including flanking DNA at each integration site are reproducible within a transformed line, and that they differ between independently transformed lines. High molecular weight signals in uncut DNA, PCR-generated bands, or signals from a single putative transformed line are not acceptable substitutes, because it is more difficult to exclude the possibility of artifacts in such data.
2. Phenotypic data showing sustained expression of the introduced gene(s) exclusively in the cells of plant lines positive for the gene(s) by Southern analysis. Unambiguous phenotypic data require:
   a. Negative results from all untransformed controls (the tested control population size must be at least equivalent to that yielding 10 independent transformants from a parallel treated population),
   b. An assay revealing the product of transgene expression within plant cells as distinct from contaminating microbial cells, preferably from a transgene shown not to be expressed in bacterial cells. Intron-GUS or anthocyanin regulatory reporter systems are suitable for such assays, as are in situ analyses for gene products without simple visual assays. Survival of lines on "escape-free" selection is not sufficient, because of the possibility of cross-protection by secreted products of contaminating microbial cells, or

selection of mutants resistant to the selective agent. Enzyme assays on cell extracts are inadequate because of the possibility of contaminating transformed microbial cells. Of course, more detailed molecular, phenotypic, and genetic characteriza-tion is likely to be undertaken on transformed lines produced for practical purposes. In some cases, target gene silencing rather than transgene expression may provide an unambiguous phenotype. Data on co-transmission of introduced gene copies and the resulting phenotype in sexual offspring populations, where available, provide compelling confirmation of transformation, given suitable controls. Applicability in several independent laboratories is an important practical confirmation, because some techniques with published molecular evidence have never been repeatable.

STRATEGIES TO ACHIEVE OF PLANT TRANSFORMATION

It is instructive to consider species such as rice, which was once considered recalcitrant to transformation but can now be transformed via direct gene transfer into protoplasts, particle bombardment of immature embryos or cell cultures, or *Agrobacterium* treatment of embryogenic callus. In each case, success seems to have followed identification (or production through tissue culture) of explants with many regenerable cells, optimization of parameters for gene transfer into those cells, and tailoring selection and regeneration procedures to recover transgenic plants. The nearest transformed relatives of an untransformed species of interest are an obvious reference point in initial work to develop suitable tissue culture, gene transfer, and selection regimens.

TISSUE CULTURE STRATEGIES

Tissue culture is not a theoretical prerequisite for plant transformation, but it is employed in almost all current practical transformation systems to achieve a workable efficiency of gene transfer, selection, and regeneration of transformants. Detailed consideration of the options for and optimization of tissue culture systems useful for plant transformation is beyond the scope of this review, but the broad technology and detailed protocols are addressed in recent techniques manuals.

In tissue culture systems for plant transformation, what is most important is a large number of regenerable cells that are accessible to the gene transfer treatment, and that will retain the capacity for regeneration for the duration of the necessary target preparation, cell proliferation, and selection treatments. A high multiplication ratio from a micropropagation system does not necessarily indicate a large number of regenerable cells accessible to gene transfer. Gene transfer into potentially regenerable cells may not allow recovery of transgenic plants if the capacity for efficient regeneration is short-lived. There seems to be no reason to prefer embryogenic or organogenic plant regeneration. In the happy event that several tissue culture systems meeting the primary requirement above are available for a species of interest, the choice can be made based on features affecting convenience or efficiency, including ready availability of explants, and minimal time in tissue culture. Somaclonal variation, once considered a potentially useful source of genetic variation for plant improvement, is now more a bane of gene transfer programmes. In some circumstances, particularly the direct introduction of genes for desired commercial traits into elite vegetatively propagated cultivars, the need to avoid such random genetic change may become the overriding consideration in the choice of tissue culture and gene transfer systems.

The desire to minimize somaclonal variation is one motivation for eliminating or minimizing the tissue culture phase, by gene transfer into intact tissue explants and regeneration without substantial in vitro culture. In several cereals, it has been possible to dispense with tissue culture for target preparation, by gene transfer into immature zygotic embryos, although embryogenic callus culture is still required to recover transgenic plants. The goal of genetic transformation without tissue culture has been approached in soybean, cotton, bean, and peanut by particle bombardment into meristematic tissue of excised embryonic axes, shoot proliferation to yield some lines with transformation of germline cells, and screening for transformed sexual progeny.

The limiting factors remain the ability to mechanically prepare the explants, transfer genes into regenerable cells, and select or screen for transformants at an efficiency sufficient for practical use in cultivar improvement. For example, the reported germline transformation rate for bean (0.06% of excised and bombarded apical meristems, 0.03% of assayed shoots) would make the process too expensive for many laboratories.

There remains unexplained cultivar specificity for transformation via meristem bombardment within some plant species such as bean, impracticality of gene transfer into meristems of others such as rice, and uncertainty about applicability in vegetatively propagated species such as sugarcane. While tissue culture remains an essential component of practical transformation systems for most plant species, research aimed at minimizing somaclonal variation deserves a high priority. Curiously little of the published research on somaclonal variation has been directed at this goal.

INTEGRATING COMPONENTS OF TRANSFORMATION STRATEGIES

Other combinations exist, but the table illustrates that the choice of transformation strategy influences many secondary parameters such as time in tissue culture and number of plants processed per transformant, which often determine the practicality of the system. It is commonly generalized that *Agrobacterium* produces simpler integration patterns than direct gene transfer, but both approaches result in a similar range of integration events, including truncations, rearrangements, and various copy numbers and insertion sites. Furthermore, the frequency distributions of copy number and rearrangements vary with transformation parameters for both gene transfer methods.

More careful work is required to optimize methods for simple integration patterns before any reliable conclusions are drawn about the relative potential of the techniques to deliver such patterns at a satisfactory frequency. The apparent targeting of T-DNA integration into transcribed regions is useful for gene and promoter tagging, and for transgene insertion into regions favoring subsequent expression. However, the observation that over 90% of T-DNA insertions may disrupt transcriptional units, with 15–26% of transformants showing visible mutant phenotypes resulting from T-DNA insertions, sounds an alarm for direct production of improved cultivars in highly selected crops, where most phenotypic changes from random mutations are likely to be adverse.

For such work, integration should ideally be directed to transcribed regions without disruption of existing plant genes. To achieve this will require more research to bring gene targeting technology in plants closer to the level achieved in model animals. Whether DNA introduced into plant cells by direct gene transfer is also preferentially integrated into transcribed regions or active genes has not been adequately tested.

Gene Transfer Strategies

Suggested approaches to development or optimization of transformation protocols using particle bombardment or *Agrobacterium* have been published, based on practical experiences in laboratories working on recalcitrant crops. For particle bombardment, it is generally most efficient to first examine the available tissue culture systems, determine the modes of regeneration and the location of the cells involved, optimize tissue culture conditions to increase the number or accessibility of such cells if necessary, and then develop conditions for nonlethal transfer of DNA into large numbers of such cells per bombardment.

For *Agrobacterium,* it is considered more efficient to first establish the conditions for gene transfer and then work on conditions for regeneration of transformed cells. This contrast may be biologically well-founded, because of the greater complexity and lesser understanding of the biological interaction preceding the gene transfer event from *Agrobacterium*. Unfortunately, there is no guarantee that a transformable plant cell type will prove regenerable, even in the hands of the most successful tissue culturist. If preliminary transformation experiments using techniques successful in similar plant systems are not successful, my advice is to establish by histological studies the precise cellular origins and timing of events leading to plant regeneration within the explants to be used as targets for gene transfer.

This is likely to avoid much wasted time and frustration from optimizing gene transfer and regeneration within the same region of the explant, but potentially in different cells, so that transformed plants are unlikely to result. Work in sunflower is a fine example of the value of this relatively simple check to explain and potentially overcome difficulty in transformation of a recalcitrant species. Assays for transient expression of introduced reporter genes in plant cells can provide unequivocal evidence of gene transfer. A great deal of time can be wasted unless this analysis is focused on regenerable cells, which often comprise a small and inaccessible fraction of the target tissue. Exhaustive experiments to maximize transient expression are also futile if they involve conditions harmful to regeneration or molecular characteristics of transformed cells.

For example, particle bombardment conditions can now be arranged to give highly reproducible results in transient assays, by delivering a large number of copies of potentially transcribable DNA into the nuclei of target cells. However, a different form and concentration of DNA is likely to be optimal for efficient production of low copy number transformants. There is little information on forms of DNA or sequences that may increase the frequency of stable transformation. There is considerable batch-to-batch variation in the frequency of transient expression events following cocultivation with *Agrobacterium*. The correlation between transient expression and stable transformation has not been thoroughly tested.

Agrobacterium employs a highly evolved and still incompletely understood gene transfer and integration system that appears optimized for efficient nuclear targeting and integration of a protein-complexed singlestranded DNA introduced as a small number of copies per cell.

Therefore, stable transformation may occur at a high frequency in cells without detectable transient expression of the introduced DNA. Positive results from transient assays for *Agrobacterium*-mediated gene transfer into regenerable cells are encouraging, but until the parameters affecting such expression are better understood, it is unwise to abandon hope too quickly based on negative results from transient assays. It may be necessary to introduce a considerable number of genes into plants for some purposes. The limits of available gene transfer techniques have not yet been defined. At least 12 separate plasmids and up to 600 kb of DNA can be introduced at once by particle bombardment, but the number of expressed genes has not been tested. There are some indications that large plasmids (>10 kb) may be subject to greater fragmentation during particle bombardment. Transposon-derived vectors have been shown to deliver an increased proportion of intact, single-copy inserts of up to 10 kb following direct gene transfer into protoplasts. Recent evidence indicates that use of a binary bacterial artificial chromosome vector, with helper plasmids enhancing production of VirG and VirE proteins, can allow efficient *Agrobacterium*mediated transfer of at least 150 kb of foreign DNA into the plant nuclear genome. Furthermore, the transferred DNA appeared to be present as an intact single copy that was faithfully inherited in the progeny of several of the characterized transformants.

Vectors overexpressing *virG* are also a component of the thoroughly verified systems for *Agrobacterium*-mediated transformation of rice, maize, and cassava, and deserve wider testing in recalcitrant plants. Other key variables in *Agrobacterium*-mediated gene transfer include *Agrobacterium* and plant genotype, treatment with *vir* gene inducers such as acetosyringone, wounded cell extracts, feeder cells or sugars; pH, temperature, cell concentration, light conditions, and duration of cocultivation; explant type, quality, preculture, hormone treatment, wounding, or infiltration; and use of appropriate antibacterial agents, antioxidants, ethylene antagonists, and/or methylation inhibitors to reduce damage and/or gene silencing in treated plant cells. With so many variables, and little evidence of combinations that are broadly applicable across plant species, it is evident why transient expression assays are useful, if imperfect, as indicators of suitable conditions for gene transfer, before more expensive studies to optimize stable transformation.

Selection Strategies

For transformation systems that generate substantial numbers of nonchimeric primary transformants, genes conferring resistance to a selective chemical agent, genes conferring a phenotype allowing visual or physical screening, or even PCR screening to identify plants containing transferred genes can all be used to recover transformants. Transformation systems that generate chimeric primary transformants including transformed germline cells, as intermediates in the production of homogeneously transformed (R1) progeny plants, generally require screening rather than lethal selection to reveal primary transformants. Screening approaches are expensive unless the transformation efficiency is high, and generally impractical if the proportion of transformants among regenerated lines is below 10^{-2} to 10^{-3}. In our hands, the recovery of transformed plants was 10-fold lower from visual screening compared with antibiotic selection. This may occur because antibiotic selection provides a continuous advantage to transformed cells, which may otherwise be overgrown by the far greater numbers of proliferating nontransformed cells. Under these circumstances, antibiotic selection may allow a higher proportion of transformed cells to multiply and regenerate, in addition to facilitating the recognition of transformants.

An excellent review has been published on selectable marker genes, assayable reporter genes, and criteria for their use in plant transformation studies. Broadly applicable, simple, and robust selection regimens now exist for transgenic plants, requiring little experimentation with the timing and concentration of selective agents to match the target tissue and gene transfer system. However, it is still important to consider the physiology of antibiotic action and resistance mechanisms when choosing or modifying selection protocols. There are also reports of interactions between selective agent and subsequent regenerability, and interactions between antibiotic and gelling agents. Attention is increasingly being directed to introduction of multiple agronomically useful genes into plant lines, without having to pyramid selectable genes in the process.

9

Medicinal Plants

Medicinal plants are plants which have a recognized medical use. They range from plants which are used in the production of mainstream pharmaceutical products to plants used in herbal medicine preparations. Herbal medicine is one of the oldest forms of medical treatment in human history, and could be considered one of the forerunners of the modern pharmaceutical trade. Medicinal plants can be found growing in numerous settings all over the world.

Some medicinal plants are wild crafted, meaning that they are harvested in the wild by people who are skilled at plant identification. Sometimes plants cannot be cultivated, making wild crafting the only way to obtain them, and some people believe that wild plants have more medicinal properties. Wild crafting can also be done to gather medicinal plants for home use, with people seeking out plants to use in their own medicinal preparations.

Other medicinal plants may be cultivated. One of the advantages of cultivation is that it allows for greater control over growing conditions, which can result in a more predictable and consistent crop. Cultivation also allows for mass production, which makes plants more commercially viable, as they can be processed in large numbers and priced low enough that people will be able to afford them.

People who work with medicinal plants can process them in a variety of ways. Many plants contain pharmacologically active compounds which can be accessed by making teas, tisanes, and other preparations. Plants can also be blended with each other to achieve a desired outcome, or processed to make homeopathic medicines, along with medicines designed for topical application, such as oils and creams.

The history of studying and working with medicinal plants is quite long. Chemists are always interested in studying medicinal plants which have not been researched before, to identify which compounds in the plants are active, and to see how those compounds work. Usually, the goal is to develop a synthetic version of the compound which can be easily produced in a lab and packaged in pharmaceutical preparations. Chemists may also be interested in historic medical treatments, examining plants to see whether or not preparations used historically would have worked, and if they would have, how they would have worked.

Preparations made from medicinal plants are available for sale in many health food stores and through the offices of naturopaths, practitioners of Ayurveda and traditional Chinese medicine, and other alternative health care providers. Some preparations are widely used in the conventional medical community as well; preparations of aloe, for example, are commonly used to treat burns.

INDIAN MEDICINAL PLANT AND MEDICAL SYSTEMS

Indian medical systems, among them the ancient science of Ayurveda, have always been aware of the medicinal value of plants. To cite but for at least 2500 years before the West recognised the medicinal properties of the rauwolfia root that Indian medicine men had been using it to calm violently disturbed patients. They called it snakeroot and used it to treat, apart from 'moon madness' or lunacy, a whole range of afflictions, from snakebite to cholera. In the 1940's Indian scientists isolated the active substances from rauwolfia and discovered its added benefit as a remedy for high blood pressure.

For thousands of years, Indian plants have been attracting attention in foreign countries. Dioscorides mentions many, including datura smoke for treating asthma, nux vomica for paralysis and indigestion, croton as a purgative. Pliny complained of the heavy drain on Roman gold to buy costly Indian drugs (and spices). Some Indian plants or their extracts have already been adopted by modern medicine, including psyllium husk (isabgol) for bowel problems. Many other plants that have been used exclusively in folk medicine now have allopaths hunting for them. These include herbs like Cassia fistula which shows antibiotic activity. A keen search for contraceptives for men has led to research on likely plant material such as bamboo shoots, betel leaf and papaya seed.

The Madagascar periwinkle with its pink/white flowers is a hardy perennial that grows without fuss in countless Indian gardens. So persistent is the flowering that the shrub has come to be known as sadabahar, meaning 'ever bloom'. In the 1950's, the periwinkle yielded some alkaloids, particularly useful in the treatment of leukaemia. Great piles of crushed periwinkle leaves are now exported from India to the U.S. to be ground and processed into anti cancer drugs. It takes 12 tons of leaves to extract one ounce of the active ingredient, hence the bulk.

India has an impressive list of medicinal plants, almost all of them native to the soil. Towering above the rest is the neem (margosa). All parts of this ubiquitous tree are bitter and are used in medicine. A decoction of neem leaves helps fevers, particularly malarial fevers, liver problems such as hepatitis, boils and all kinds of skin diseases. Extract of neem is a powerful insecticide, poisonous to insects and parasites.

The amla (emblica officinalis) has been hailed as a nugget of Vit. C in heat stable form. One amla fruit is said to pack more Vit. C than a dozen oranges. It is great for treating respiratory complaints and for rejuvenation of both body and the hair. According to Charka, august physician of yore and father of ayurveda, a regular intake of amla or amla based preparations is a sure method of stalling the ageing process.

Amla joins with two other plants haritaki and bibhitaki to make the super combination known as triphala (three-fruit-combine). Whether used externally or internally, the benefits conferred by triphala are legion. The most significant being rejuvenation of the membrane of the intestinal tract.

The small thorny tree known as bel (Aegle marmelos) yields a fruit that is a panacea for digestive disorders. The bamboo has, on the inside of its stem a white, powder deposit known as tavashir which has marked decongestant properties, particularly useful as a local application in tonsillitis. The large, handsome evergreen camphor tree is the traditional (as opposed to synthetic) source of camphor. Used extensively in ritual worship, camphor is a favoured ingredient of liniments and medicinal oils because it liquefies obstinate body secretions and causes them to flow. Gugul (Commiphora mukul), a small tree which grows in arid regions, produces a resin with marked anti-inflammatory properties, making it perhaps the best medicine going for arthritis. It also helps scrape away fat from the body.

Asafoetida is the resin collected from the living rhizome and root of the small tree Ferula foetida. There are few remedies superior to asafoetida for relieving colic and abdominal distension. The fragrant sandalwood comes from a small tree (Santalum album). Used as paste or powder, it calms skin eruptions. Taken internally it cools the body and mind, while helping to improve the concentration. Tagara (Valeriana wallichii) has long been used as a sedative and anti-spasmodic. Being a natural tranquillizer, it is particularly useful in the treatment of hysteria and epilepsy.

Castor oil, universally disliked but dependable, is a product of the castor plant, also known as eranda (Ricinis communis). The plant grows wild in India. So does berberis (Berberis aristata), used to control jaundice and inflammations ranging from gastro-enteritis to conjunctivitis. A special boon for those suffering from piles. Berberis is a native of hilly areas.

The hibiscus shrub has great cooling properties. Crushed leaves of hibiscus, applied to the scalp in summer, prevent dandruff and lend lustre to the hair. Dried and powdered henna leaves, made into a paste, soothe rashes, particularly eczema. The paste applied before a regular shampoo makes the hair soft and silky. The dried and powdered rhizome of the turmeric plant is a powerful antiseptic for external wounds as well as intestinal infections. And be it said to its everlasting glory, a level teaspoon of turmeric in a glass of hot milk, taken at bedtime, can and does stave off an attack of flu. Laced with honey, this combination even helps a case of trauma. The grass known as cuscus (vetiver) purifies the blood and helps reduce fever, while soothing both vomiting and diarrhoea.

AYURVEDIC MEDICINAL PLANTS

Acorus calamus: Boch, Vacha, Vayambu -This perennial herb of marshy habitats is easy to cultivate through rhizome cuttings in tropical and sub-tropical zones. The tubers are traded as it is reputed as brain tonic, coolant and drug for colic. It has high demand in the market. Commercial production from 3rd year.

Andrographis Paniculate: Kalmegh, Chiraita teeta -This bitter annual herb has hepato protective propenties and is an anthelmentic and liver tonic. It is a blood purifier too. The whole plant is used. it is one of the high demand spcies propagated through seeds and ideal for open or partial shade localities in low altitudes. Crop ready in 4-6 months.

Aquilaria agallocha: Agar, Sasi, Indian eagle wood - This tropical deciduous tree is very valuable for its transformed wood which on distillation yield Agar oil which has high export value. Cultivation is through seed raised seedlings. Suitable for both open and partial shade. Artificial induction of agar in live trees is possible. Takes 8-20 years for agar development.

Dioscorea floribunda: Kham alu - This is a torpical climber with underground tubers and bulbils. The tubers yields diosgeninan alkalloid used in pharmaceuticals. Propagation is through pieces of tubers and bulbils. Farming of this species is profitable. Inter cropping is also possible. Production from first year.

Oroxylum indicum: Bhatghilla, Jigat - This deciduous tree is naturally seen in the secondary forests in the tropics. It is in high demand now a days for its bark used for tanning and as medicine for fever and many other ailments and as tonic.

Propagation is through seeds. Bark ready, by 10 years, can be harvested sustainably through scientific methods

Piper longum: Pipli, Piper brachystachyum, Pmullesua, P. peepuloides-Round Pipli - Climbers or Undershrubs. An important medicinal plants of Ayurveda. Fruits are collected and traded, for which excellent scope of marketing exist. Ieal for under planting and for partially shaded areas. Multiplication through suckers, stem cuttings and seeds. Harvest expected from 2nd to 4th year.

Rauvolfia serpentine: Sarpagandha - This perennial undershrub can be cultivated in the low altitudes in open as well as shady areas. The roots are reputed fro the treatment of blood pressure. Roots ready to harvest form second years onwards. Propagation through seeds and stem cuttings

Tinaspora cordifolia: Amrit lata, Guduchi - This is a tropical climber which is used as a tonic and vitaliser. The stem is used for drug manufacture and traded. Ideal for multitier plantation. It has high demand. Propagated through stem cuttings.

Whithania somnifera: Aswagandha - A herbaceous perennial plant, reputed as Indian Ginseng and used for vitality and vigour. Can be cultivated in open and shady areas which are well drained and dry. The roots have great marketing potential. Propagation through seeds.

Aconitum ferox, Aconitum hetero-phyllum: Atish, Aconite - Perennial herbs of alpine and sub alpine habitats. Usually in open places. Roots used for medicine. Very good market prospects for the roots and tubers, Multiplication through seeds and tubers.

Coptis teeta: Mishmi teeta - This is a temperate herb found only in Arunachal Pradesh. It can be cultivated as under planting. Propagation is through seeds. The roots are sold for treatment of variety of diseases

Gymnadaenia archidis: Panch hath, Salam pancha - This annual herbaceous orchid produce high value medicinal tubers which are general tonic. Ideal is open places in alpine localities Propagation through tubers

Illicium griffuhii: Lissi: This is a high altitude tree valued for its fruits. The fruits are used as spice and medicine.

Multiplication is through seeds and branch cuttings. Ideal for mixed plantations. Has good market potential

Panax sikkimensis, Panax spp.: Ginseng - Perennial herbs with tubers, Grows in temperate and sub temperate zones. Ideal for cultivation as under planting. The tubers are highly priced and has high demand. This is a rejuvenating general tonic. Propagation through seeds and tubers. Harvest by 4-8 years.

Picrorrhiza kurroa: Kutki - This is a stemless perennial herb of alpine habitats. It is in high demand for a variety of herbal medicines. Can be grown in open localities and grasslands. Propagation is through seeds and suckers. Much rate in nature. Rhizome ready by 4th year.

Rubia cordifolia: Manjista - This is a perennial climber with four leaves of each node. It yields orange/red dye. It is a high demand species in the medicinal plant market. Ideal for sub-tropical and temperatezones. Prefers shady localities but possible to grow in open too. Propagation through seeds. Crop ready for harvest by 3rd year

Taxus baccata: Yew - It is a temperate conifer tree. The leaves yields costly taxol. Ideal for cultivation in high altitudes as mixed planting and propagation is through seeds. Easier to multiply through stem cuttings. Has very high demand in market

SAFED MOOSLI

India is bestowed with a wealth of medicinal plants, most of which have been used in Ayurveda. Safed moosli (Chlorophytum borivilianum L., Liliaceae) holds an important position in Indian herbal medicine. The roots are widely used as a natural "sex tonic" and is an integral part of more than 100 herbal drug formulations. Although Indian forests are rich in safed moosli demand is increasing rapidly in Indian and international drug markets. Foreign demand has been estimated as 300-700 tonnes annually, a quantity that Indian forests cannot sustain. This has created a pressure on Indian forests and if steps for timely conservation are not taken, the Indian forests will lose this valuable plant. At present the availability of Chlorophytum is decreasing and obnoxious weeds like Parthenium hysterophons and Lantana are taking its place.

Dried roots of Chlorophytum contain 42% carbohydrate, 80–9% protein, 3–4% fiber and 2–17% saponin. Research studies on Chlorophytum conducted in India and elsewhere indicate that saponins are responsible for medicinal properties. Saponins are thought to be highest in roots of forest origin.

More than 175 species of Chlorophytum have been reported in the world. Chloophytum comosum is widely used as ornamental plant where it is commonly known as spider ivy, spider plant, aeroplane plant, or walking anthericum. Thirteen species of Chlorophytum have been been reported in India. All these species differ in appearance, native species are sold as sufed moosli in the Indian drug market. Chlorophytum boriviliahum produces the highest yield and highest saponin content. Other native Indian Chlorophytum species include C. arundinaceum, C. tuberosu, C. laxum, and C. breviscapum

In nature, Moosli propagates vegetatively through its fleshy roots., rarely by seed. The black angular seed is similar to onion seed in appearance. Seed have poor germination and low viability. Seed rates of 3 quintals/hectare is considered optimum for growers.

Chlorophytum is found in soils rich in organic matter. It requires bright sunlight for good growth. Many tribal communities of India use the fresh leaves of Safed Moosli as potherb.) but the roots are the useful part of the plant for medicinal purposes. Once the root is harvested reseeding rarely occurs.

Innovative Indian farmers have initiated commercial cultivation of safed moosli. The crop is a popular rainy season (kharif crop) in India and a commercial root harvest can be obtained in 3–4 months. Spacing 30 × 15 cm is optimum. The crop seems adapted to a wide range of conditions. Few insect pests have been reported. Saponin content may be affected by fungicides and synthetic phyrethroides. Many moosli farms have started selection of cultivars.

There is now a heavy demand of organically grown safed

moosli with high saponin content in national and international drug market. In India moosli-based products are coming regularly to the market. The area under this crop is increasing rapidly in India.

MULTIPLE BENEFITS OF MEDICINAL PLANTS

MPs offer a wide range of subsistence, cultural and monetary benefits to people in the world. They provide affordable means of primary health care to poor and marginalized people, especially in impoverished rural areas. In some countries like China, Nepal and India, they are an important revenue generating resources providing critical income to economically marginalized and indigenous people. But most important, in a condition of sustainable harvesting and optimal usage, the medicinal plants could prove to be a model resource that can benefit both the environment and livelihoods in a balanced manner. The real challenge is how to strike this critical balance?

Given the fact that there are multiple benefits of MPs including:

1. Improved access to primary healthcare,
2. Enhanced livelihood security,
3. Potentially sustainable use of the biodiversity, and
4. Improved benefit sharing with local communities, the promotion of sustainable management of medicinal plants can help the biodiversity rich countries to meet the international obligations such as the Convention on Biological Diversity (CBD).

In the broader sense, medicinal plants can also contribute to address the chronic problem of global poverty and hunger. The realization of mega global targets such as those set by the Millennium Development Goals (MDG), Poverty Reduction Strategy and Programmes (PRSP) etc. will require interventions which are grass roots-based, poor-centred and livelihood focused. Put differently medicinal plants can meet the basic needs of the poor rural people. pro-poor marketing and enterprise development activities in medicinal plants can help poor collectors and growers of medicinal plants to increase their household income, which is dwindling due to increased input costs and decreasing returns.

China is estimated to have 12,807 species of plants out of which 11,146 are classified as medicinal plants used in traditional Chinese medicine (TCM). It is estimated that up to 492 species are currently under cultivation and the remaining 10,654 species are harvested from wild habitats According to Wang etc. the total production from wild sources is 8.5 million tons and the cultivated medicinal plants production was estimated to be 0.3 million tons in. These produce not only contribute to the health of Chinese people but also add approximately 2 billion USD to the national economy annually. In the southwest mountainous province of Guizhou,

Medicinal, aromatic and dye plants (MADPs) also have potential to present as commodities with competitive advantages for the poor regions of Asia, Africa and Latin America. It is observed that some of the poorest regions of the world such as the western and eastern regions of Himalayas, Borneo and Sumatra regions in Asia; Congo basin in Africa and Amazon catchments in South America are also rich in biological diversity where medicinal plants and other NTFP species grow in abundance. If we can promote a balanced conservation and cultivation of MADPs, rural poverty can be alleviated, gender imbalances can be addressed and local economy improved.

More broadly, many medicinal plants are found in forest ecosystems, where they are used to meet the health care needs and livelihoods pursuits of indigenous and local communities. Forests have been targeted in Central America and the Caribbean as priority eco-regions for conservation MPs are increasingly being recognized as an important resources for sustainable development, particularly as sources of safe, effective, and accessible health care that integrates traditional

MEDICINAL PLANTS OF INDIA

India is the home of several important traditional systems of health care like Ayurveda, Siddha and Unani. All these systems depend heavily on herbal products. In addition, allopathic drugs are also derived from a wide range of plant products. Biotechnology has further helped to accelerate progress in bio-prospecting for molecules of value in the preparation of life-sustaining drugs.

Several millions of Indian households have been using through the ages nearly 8,000 species of medicinal plants for their health care needs. Over one and half million traditional healers use a wide range of medicinal plants for treating ailments of both humans and livestock across the length and breadth of the country. Over 800 medicinal plant species are currently in use by the Indian herbal industry. However, except for about 120 species, all others are collected from the wild. This collection often involves destructive harvesting when parts like roots, bark, wood, stem and the whole plant (herbs) are used.

Unregulated wild harvest, alongside habitat loss and degradation, is leading to resource depletion, which in turn is endangering the very survival of these species. No wonder many of the species listed in the Red Data Books of IUCN and the Botanical Survey of India are valued for their medicinal properties.

India's traditional and folklore medicine bequeathed from generation to generation is rich in domestic recipes for common ailments. Traditional medicine encompasses protection and restoration of health over millennia. differing in concept and protocol, are well developed systems such as acupuncture and ayurvedic treatments that have been widely used to conserve human health in China and India.

Developed countries in recent times are turning to traditional medicinal systems that involve the use of herbal drugs and remedies. About 1,400 herbal preparations are used widely, according to a survey in Member States of the European Union. Herbal preparations are popular and are of significance in primary healthcare in Belgium, France, Germany and the Netherlands. Such popularity of plant-derived products has been traced to their increasing acceptance and use in the cosmetic industry as well as to increase public costs in the daily maintenance of personal health and well-being. beauty-oriented therapeuticals are skin tissue regenerators, anti-wrinkling agents and anti-age creams. Most dermaceuticals are derived from algal extracts that are rich in minerals and the vitamin B group. Skincare products such as skin creams, skin tonics, etc. derived from medicinal plants are grouped together as dermaceuticals. Also, amongst the poor, cures and drugs derived from plants constitute the main source of healthcare products.

Despite the increasing use of medicinal plants, their future is being threatened by complacency concerning their conservation. Reserves of herbs and stocks of medicinal plants in developing countries are diminishing, and several important species are in danger of extinction as a result of growing trade demands for safer and cheaper healthcare products and new plant-based therapeutic markets to more expensive target-specific drugs and biopharmaceuticals. Such concerns have stimulated action in chronicling and conserving medicinal plants.

Issues concerning intellectual property rights, compensation for loss of economically valuable biodiversity resources, and the acquisition and safeguarding of traditional healthcare knowledge are attracting increasing attention. Bio-prospecting of new drugs from medicinal plants and the exploitation of unprotected traditional knowledge in starting up potentially new bio-industries are the focus of new health enterprises. Such concerns that call for adherence to and observation of cultural and intellectual property rights have been addressed and enshrined in the Biodiversity Act (2002). The first countries to seriously tackle these issues are China and India. Indeed, programmes dealing with medicinal plant conservation, cultivation, community involvement and sustainable development being initiated elsewhere could benefit immensely from the Chinese and Indian experiences.

A Paradise of Medicinal Plants

The Koraput region of Orissa is globally famous for its rich biodiversity and local land races. More than 1,780 varieties of local land races of rice were here in past. More than 1,200 medicinal plant species are available in this region. Some of the endemic medicinal plant species in this region are used for curing different diseases like gastrointestinal disorders, malarial fever, bone-fracture, anti-helminthic, anti-inflammatory, anti-fertility, asthma, pyorrhea and rheumatoid arthritis. This healing system is part of the Indian traditional medicinal system. Bio-prospecting of such precious germplasm is likely to lead to development of new drugs.

Tribal people have been in the practice of preserving a rich heritage of information on medicinal plants and their usage. These people have faith in their traditional system of healthcare and generally (if not always) practise it. They have their own traditional physicians who use these plants as their material medica. They have rich and outstanding traditional knowledge and wisdom regarding material for healing of commonly occurring ailments. They have both the know-how and do-how for preparing the medicine and its administration. Unfortunately, this information is yet to be collected systematically and comprehensively and maintained in databases in a manner they would help in protecting their knowledge.

The Koraput region is rich in genetic resources of medicinal rices and other medicinal plants. The tribal population is poor but their bio-resources endowment is rich. Very little research has been done so far in the area of conservation, sustainable and value-added use, and equitable sharing of benefits,the medicinal plant heritage of Koraput. Only scientific work can help to convert bio-resources into economic wealth on an ecologically sustainable basis, thereby leading to an era of bio-happiness.

The M.S. Swaminathan Research Foundation proposed to set up a Research and Development Centre in Koraput to undertake intensive and integrated study on medicinal rices and other medicinal and aromatic plants. It is hoped that such an initiative will help to overcome the prevailing dichotomy of the poverty of the people and the prosperity of nature.

M.S. Swaminathan Research Foundation has been

working in the Jeypore region for the last 12 years. Activities in the area include conservation of biodiversity, promotion of sustainable livelihoods through micro-level interventions, establishment of community managed gene, seed, grain and water banks, promotion of genetic literacy and documentation of local conservation traditions. The initiatives taken up by the MSSRF have enabled the local tribal communities of Jeypore region to receive the prestigious Equator Initiative Award for conservation of local genetic resources and traditions. More so, MSSRF's interventions have raised the level of confidence in the local communities by way of interaction and cooperation. Establishment of SHGs involved in water resources management, wasteland reclamation and marketing of specialty rices (e.g., Kalajeera) and products of minor millets are some of the initiatives exemplifying the success of the work of tribal families, with support from MSSRF designed to create an economic stake in conservation.

The vast medicinal plant resources in the region have so far been neglected. The MSSRF's proposal to work in this area has received excellent support from the State Government. The State Government has provided 6 hectares (i.e. 15 acres) of land to MSSRF for the establishment of the Biju Patnaik Medicinal Plants Garden and Conservation Centre at Jeypore. The Honourable Chief Minister of Orissa, Shri Naveen Patnaik, performed bhumipuja to memorialize the Centre's opening.

The centre's major aim is to establish an ex-situ genetic conservation of medicinal plants of the major tribes of the region. The predominant tribes are Paroja, Bonda, Kandha, Kutia Kandha, Dongaria Kandha, Koya, Saura, Langia Saura, Gadaba, Bhumia, Bhatra. It is proposed to assign 1 acre of land for each major tribe for cultivating the plants they use for their health care needs. This in turn will serve as a repository of various genetic stocks of the region and can be of immense utility for the present and future generations.

TRADITIONAL KNOWLEDGE OF MEDICINAL AND OTHER ECONOMIC PLANTS

A questionnaire was designed to document traditional

knowledge of medicinal and other economic plants. Field studies were conducted in 3 hamlets and information obtained from Hakim and local people who had knowledge of therapeutic value of plants. These professionals belonged to different ethnic groups. Discussion of the properties of the plants were conducted with them with the help of informants. The number of peoples with whom the information were collected varied from 3 to 5 depending upon availability. Majority of peoples illiterate and about 15% of respondent were Primary, Matric and college education. More than 10 informants interviewed were active, cooperative and aged varied from 45 to 65 years. The average number of house holds in the hamlet were 52 with a population of 570 heads, where people lived with their own way of life, believe and cultural heritage. The number of dependent per family heads were 10 but the average number of children were 6. Majority of the residents (60 to 90%) depend on farming.

Per capita land holding varied from 0.37 to 1.20 ha, which was not sufficient to fulfil the basic needs. They were doing other jobs in addition to farming. The annual income varied from 12,000 to 25,000 with an average of 18,500. Respondent benefitted from natural resources other than firewood like collection of medicinal plants, morel, grazing and grass cutting. They enhanced their income from the sale of non-timber forest products. Majority of the respondent reluctant to tell the exact quantity of medicinal plants and morel extracted in a season.

However, some of them (10%) told that 1 to 1.5 quintal (fresh wt.) of medicinal plants and morel were collected per family for sale and local uses in a season. The plant remedies usually employed in common ailments like cough, asthma, dyspepsia, skin diseases, typhoid, malaria, eye-trouble, body pain, cuts and wounds. Thus people saved handsome amount instead of purchasing costly allopathic medicines for the treatment of these diseases. The inhabitants only preferred to visit hospital/Doctors in serious cases. The information collected on traditional uses of medicinal and economic plants.

The use of plants is indicative of intimate dependence and relationship of the peoples of hilly areas with the vegetation in their vicinity. However, there is an ample traditional knowledge of medicinal plants which need to be fully documented for restoration of disappearing knowledge as cultural heritage can be used as a source of new medicine.

CONSERVATION AND CULTIVATION/PROPAGATION

Many medicinal plants like Paeonia emodi, Podophyllum hexandrum, Angelica glauca, Rheum emodi, Dactylorhiza hatagira, Geranium wallichianum, Polygonum amplexicaule, Skimmia laureola, Valeriana jatamansi, Viola serpens etc. and morels are collected every year by locals and no attempt is made for their conservation or to protect them against grazing pressure. If this practice continued, there is possibilities of complete exhaustion of a particular herb in near future. Therefore, it is necessary to establish demonstration plot in the farmer's field to promote cultivation of medicinal plants to uplift socio-economic condition of communities. Financial and technical assistance may be provided to the farmers of small holdings through PARDYP project for cultivation of fast selling drug species having constant demand in the market. These species will generate additional income to the communities.

i. Preliminary rapid survey conducted in selected forest localities indicated that a number of valuable medicinal and economic plants became scarce due to ruthless extraction of their natural population and biotic interferences. It is imperative that a detailed survey of all commercially important medicinal and economic plants need to be carried out in Hilkot watershed area and suburbs in the next growth season to (i) assess their available potential in natural habitat, (ii) identify localities which abound in rich diversity of plants and (iii) preparation of a list of endangered plant species. This survey is essential to formulate a judicious plan of sustainable utilization, so that no species of medicinal or economic value of the area become endangered in future.
ii. The local populace needs guidance in identification,

collection, conservation and cultivation of profitable drug plants with the help of Demonstration plot proposed to be established in the farmer's field. This training programme can be provided by trained staff of PFI to create awareness and enhance professional capability of the community activists to maintain purity and quality of herbal drugs.

iii. Marketing survey of important herbal drug markets should be conducted to determine the supply and demand position and to identify the annual requirements of various plant-based manufacturing units. If this information is available, links with marketing channel between community organization and end-users will be established. Thus collectors and growers will be in a better position to get maximum benefit from the sale of herbal drugs.

iv. Nurseries/Drug farm of rare and profitable drug and economic plants should be developed by PARDY Project in collaboration with PFI for transfer of packages of cultivation practices along with seeds and planting stock to community for pilot scale cultivation. It should also prove beneficial to the entire community if female members are encouraged to become involved in the cultivation of medicinal plants as herbal gardening. Thus in-situ cultivation will boost up the mass production of fast selling drug species and their sustenance in natural habitats.

v. Phyto-chemical analysis should be carried out with the help of HEJ Research Institute of Chemistry, Karachi to find out active principles present in medicinal plants which have a potential for export or as concentrates. In case of positive result, market should be identified with the help of exporters. Any financial benefits which accrue from such activities would substantially benefit local communities.

vi. Project nursery established at Hilkot is in sufficient to meets the local requirement of planting stock. It should be extended and key species of conifers like

Abies pindrow, Cedrus deodara, Picea smithiana Pinus wallichiana and Taxus baccata may be raised alongwith broadleaved species viz: Aesculus indica, Ailanthus altissima, Amorpha fruiticosa, Alnus nitida, Celtis australis, Elaeganus hortensis, Ficus palmata, Ficus carica, Fraxinus excelsior, F. xanthoxyloides, Gleditschia tricanthos, Juglans regia, Morus serrata, Platanus orientalis, Populus ciliata, Populus deltoides, Quercus dilatata, Q.ilex, Robinia pseudoacacia, Sapindus mukorosii, Ulmus laevigata and Zizyphus vulgaris. These species may be utilized for rehabilitation of eroded land and conservation of plants to restore species diversity.

vi. Planting of Eucalyptus and Chir seedlings in moist temperate forests give negative impression to the visitors as these species are not suited to the climatic conditions.

AREAS OF TRADITIONAL SYSTEM OF MEDICINE

In Indian traditional system of medicine, knowledge about the drugs is largely centered on plants. At present, about 90% collection of medicinal plants is from wild sources and 70% of the plant collections involve destructive harvesting. Due to this, many useful plant species are becoming endangered or threatened. The rules and regulations put forth by the Indian government in protecting these raw materials for herbal drugs. It focuses on what type of legislative framework has been provided for specifically safeguarding the national interests and whether their constant evolution can be expected to be of benefit or detriment to Indian herbal sector.

India is one of the richest countries in the world as regards genetic resource of medicinal and aromatic plants. It constitutes 11% of total known world flora though its total land mass occupies only 2.0% of the globe. India has 15 agro-climatic zones, 47, 000 different plant species. Medicinal plants, as a group, comprise approximately 15, 000 species and account for about 32% of all the higher flowering plant species of India.

Out of these the Indian systems of medicine have

identified 1, 500 medicinal plants, of which 500 species are generally used in the preparation of drugs. While in modern system of medicine, the world over, 105 plants provide the basic raw material out of which only 40 plants are exploited in India. The medicinal plants contribute 80% of the raw materials used in the preparation of drugs.

With majority of population subscribing to herbal drugs there is a boom in indigenous medicinal sector. At present, about 90% collection of medicinal plants is from the wild sources and 70% of the plant collections involve destructive harvesting. Due to this, many useful plant species are becoming endangered or threatened.

The government is presently emphasizing on two basic essentials *i.e.* firstly on conservation, secondly on cultivation so as to increase the production of raw materials without destroying the natural habitat. Rather than encouraging collection from the wild habitat, promotion of cultivation of high demand and low availability rare plants is being advocated and lastly with rekindling in the demand for traditional medicines globally there is a huge potential in this sector & India has to take big steps to capitalize it and that too without compromising on the quality of the product.

CONSERVATION

The first and the most crucial aspect in present scenario of traditional medicine system is to conserve our already depleted resources. It's not that by restricting harvesting from natural habitats we are conserving our resources. "Conservation" in itself is a broad field which includes preservation, maintenance, sustainable utilization, restoration, and enhancement of the natural environment. We have to save the plant species by keeping their gene pool intact and maintained with all the wild qualities retained.

According to WHO report, as many as 80% of the world's people depend on traditional medicine for their primary health care needs and the greater part of traditional therapy involves the use of plants, plant extracts or their active principles. With the widespread increase in the demand of phytomedicines, there is a recent surge in extensive harvesting and collection of plant species. This great surge in use of medicinal plants as a source for drugs has been based on the fact that they are natural, with no side effects on their intake and they will be available on sustainable basis. But this is not true. With demand increasing and supply of raw material diminishing, there are no concerted efforts in checking the overexploitation of plants. So that in near future medicinal plants will become either rare or extinct.

In the light of this situation, WHO, IUCN, and WWF, convened an International Consultation on the conservation of medicinal plants in March 1988 "The Chiang Mai Declaration – Saving Lives by Saving Plants"– which affirmed the importance of medicinal plants and called on the United Nations, its agencies and Member States, as well as other international organizations, to take action for the conservation of medicinal plants. Later on February 16-19, 1998 an International Conference on Medicinal Plants for Survival entitled, "Medicinal Plants: A Global Heritage" was held in Bangalore which was a sequel to Chiang-Mai Declaration held a decade ago. The Bangalore conference affirmed that medicinal plants can save lives, livelihoods and cultures, provided that the plants themselves are saved.

The raw materials for these traditional systems are largely native plant species growing in the forests (about 95%). So in order to maintain a sustainable supply of the raw materials from the forests, overharvesting has to be stopped and conservation of forests has to be done. But there are no separate policies or regulations for conserving medicinal plants in India. Their conservation is generally covered under existing laws pertaining to forestry. Government of India has promulgated various acts for conservation of forests:

a) Forest (Conservation) Act, 1980 with amendments made in 1988, was an act to provide for the conservation of forests and for matters connected therewith. It extended to the whole of India except the State of Jammu and Kashmir and came into force on the 25th day of October, 1980. It put a restriction on the dereservation of forests or on the use of forest land for non-forest purposes which included the cultivation of tea, coffee, spices, rubber, palms, oil-bearing plants, horticultural crops or medicinal plants.

b) The Central Government through the Ministry of Environment and Forests under its National Forest Policy, 1988 the forest and wild life acts provides a regulatory framework for conservation and protection of forests and wildlife which include medicinal plants. Tribal People and Forests, it states that special attention should be paid for protection, regeneration and optimum collection of minor forest produce along with institutional arrangements for the marketing of such produce.

c) The National Bio-diversity Act, 2002 regulates access to forest resources including medicinal plants. Regulation of Access to Biological Diversity, under the heading "Prior intimation to State Biodiversity Board for obtaining biological resource for certain purposes" it states that :

"No person, who is a citizen of India or a body corporate, association or organization which is registered in India, shall obtain any biological resource for commercial utilization, or bio-survey and bio-utilization for commercial utilization except after giving prior intimation to the State Biodiversity Board concerned: "Provided that the provisions of this section shall not apply to the local people and communities of the area, including growers and cultivators of biodiversity, and *vaids* and *hakims*, who have been practicing indigenous medicine."

d) There are also guidelines notified to conserve specific medicinal plants listed under either Indian red data book, Convention on International Trade in Endangered Species of wild fauna and flora (CITES) and the negative list of exports notified by Government of India.

e) There are also schemes (in situ conservation) for supporting projects on conservation of some specific medicinal plants by setting up Medicinal Plants Conservation Areas (MPCAs) which are primarily located in forest areas

f) The medicinal plants present in the protected areas like national parks and sanctuaries are also accorded protection under the Wild Life (Protection Act), 1972.

g) The Botanical Survey of India carries out surveys and also conserves rare and threatened medicinal plants in its gardens.

h) The scheduled tribes and other traditional forest dwellers (recognition of forest rights) act, 2006.

Corollary to Forests Right Act, 2006

The FRA, 2006 and its effect on medicinal flora is debatable. Reactions of various academicians & environmentalists to the tribal act have been varied. Many of them applaud while others are opposed to it. The major opposition to the bill is largely the concern on the preservation of wild life. What about the medicinal flora in the forests? It seems that nobody thought on those lines. Moreover the escalating demands and diminishing supply have resulted in exorbitant pricing of medicinal herbs. In consequence it has attracted many into this trade of collection from the forests thereby depleting the herbal wealth. And this act in a way will give free access to the flora. Some sections of the act pertaining to this aspect are:

- Which states forest rights of forest dwelling scheduled tribes and traditional forest dwellers: *i.e.*
    - Section 3(1)(c) right of ownership, access to collect, use and dispose of minor forest produce which has been traditionally collected within or outside village boundaries. Where minor forest produce includes all non-timber forest produce of plant origin including bamboo, brush wood, stumps, cane, tusser, cocoons, honey, wax, lac, tendu, medicinal plants and herbs, roots, tubers and the like.
    - Section 3(1)(d) Other community rights of uses

or entitlements such as fish and other products of water bodies, grazing (both settled or transhumant) and traditional seasonal resource access of nomadic or pastoralist communities.

* Section 3(1)(k) Right of access to biodiversity and community right to intellectual property and traditional knowledge related to biodiversity and cultural diversity.

- One more dimension to this bill is that the basic unit for implementing the act is the Gram Sabha which has the authority for vesting forest rights.
  * Section 6(1) that the Gram Sabha will be the authority to initiate the process for determining the nature and extent of individual or community forest rights or both, that may be given to forest dwelling schedule tribes and other forest dwellers within the local limits of its jurisdiction under this act by receiving claims, consolidating and verifying them and preparing a map delineating the area of each recommended claim in such a manner as may be prescribed for exercise of such rights….

The Example of Uttrakhand

In Uttarakhand the organization "Jila Sahkari Bheraj Sangh "operational in every district of the state has the responsibility for collection of raw medicinal plants parts from wild areas. It is collecting herbal plants through unskilled and unqualified labors which are quite incompetent for the job as they lack proper knowledge of method of collection resulting in destructive harvesting of many economically important and highly demanded medicinal plants. If this practice is not curbed soon then the day is not far when the entire medicinal flora will come under endangered category. Therefore it is professed that a relook on the bill is required.

Cultivation

Cultivation of medicinal plants is also of critical importance to offset the uncontrolled collection of large quantities leading to destruction of many forest medicinal plants. It is the only method of choice for large term management and ex situ conservation of medicinal plants. The cultivation can be done through herbal gardens, nurseries, cultivation in fields, tissue culture etc. But to cultivate quality material certain regulations have to be followed otherwise situations like banning of Indian herbal medicines by Canada government (on the basis of the study report published by JAMA accusing Indian ayurvedic drugs of containing high levels of toxic metal contents) would arise recurrently. Steps need to be taken before the damage has been done.

BIOENGINEERING OF MEDICINAL PLANTS

Pharmaceutical importance/therapeutic value of medicinal plants is due to specific constituents/comibination of secondary metabolites present in them. Changes in the proportion of secondary metabolites are often required for the improvement of therapeutic values of medicinal plants. For example, increase in the artemisinin content of Artemisia annua in proportion to its immediate precursors and other terpenes is required to make the production of antimalarials from this plant more economically.

The biosynthetic pathways for the biologically active chemical compounds in medicinal plants are usually complex and high branches. Genetic manipulations can help increase/ decrease the contents of specific compounds in medicinal plants. Detailed understanding of these pathways will be a prerequisite for the identification, cloning and genetic engineering of the concerned structural and regulatory genes. These genetic techniques will also help develop designer medicinal plants. For example it will be possible to produce medicinal plants that will help raise the immunity towards infectious diseases in the use of such plants.

IN VITRO PROPAGATION TECHNIQUES

The biotechnological tools are important to select, multiply and conserve the critical genotypes of medicinal plants by adopting techniques such as micropropagation, creation of somacional varations and genetic transformations. Biotechnological tools can also be harnessed for production of secondary metabolites using plants as bioreactors.

In vitro propagation involves cell culture systems of a range of ex-plant tissues and mostly micropropagation is achieved from organised tissues by multiplication of meristems and auxillary buds. In many cases it provides an opportunity to maintain type-to type plant species and the propagation system can produce a large number of plants from a single clone. Plant regeneration from shoot and stem meristems has yielded encouraging results in medicinal plants like Catharanthus roseus, Cinchona ledgeriana and Digitalis spp. The production of tropane alkaloids by hairy root culture has been resorted in several medicinal plants like Atropa, Datura and Hyoscyamus. Plant cell suspension culture is the selection of variant cell lines for the genetic improvement of plants.

High secondary product yields in plant cell cultures of medicinal plants like Catharanthus roseus, Coleus blumei, Coptis japonica and Panax ginseng have been reported. Cryopreservation has been used successfully to store a range of tissue types, including meristems, anthers/pollens, embryos, calli and even protoplasts. Cryopreservation is already reported for many medicinal plants like Rauvolfia serpentina, Datura spp., Atropa, Hyoscyamus spp. etc.

Protoplast fusion or somatic hybridization has been used to bypass the sexual process. The objective is to transfer important genes which can not be transferred through sexual means due to the operation of incompatibility systems. Somatic hybrids between Atropa belladona and Datura innoxia were reported which showed higher amounts of tropane alkaloids. Biotransformation of psychotrine cephaeline to emetine production from cell cultures of Ipecac needs to be shown economically viable when compared with synthetic process of production of emetine.

Plant cell culture is of importance of improvement of medicinal plants. Complete plants have been regenerated from callus cultures, excised anthers and isolated protoplasts of many medicinal and aromatic plants. Many of the regenerated plants showed somaclonal variation and selections were made for high active principle yielding cell lines. Protoplast fusion has been plant is regenerated, micropropragation techniques can be used to multiply and clone the desired species. Gene transfer is possible from wild and related species to desired cultivars through wide hybridization including embryo rescue systems.

Thus, to sum up, various components of the application of tissue culture technology would be:

- Micropropagation
- Conservation through cryopreservation
- Bioproduction of value added secondary metabolites
- Biotransformation of bioactive molecules
- Genetic upgradation for improvement
- Somatic hybridization
- Somaclonal variations
- Transgenic plants

The only limiting factor in commercialization of large number of medicinal plants has been the cost of cultivation. As for other annual/biennial crops per acre requirment of planting material is very large, cost of propagule is of major concern. Tissue culture can thus be adopted for species which are:

- Difficult to regenerate by conventional methods and the only way to save them from extinction is to propagate them by tissue culture;
- Species where population has decreased due to over exploitation and thus initial bulking of the stock can be taken up by tissue culture
- Species which show lot of variability in terms of the active principles with medicinal properties. Tissue culture of selected clones will help in sustainable harvest and fetching better prices both in the domestic and international market.
- Trees with medicinal properties or elites can be identified based on their potential of yielding higher amount of active principle.

Tissue culture protocols have been developed for several plants but there are many more species which are over exploited and need conservation through in vitro techniques. Also there are large number of species for which limiting factor in expanding the area under the cultivation is the scarcity of planting material.

CHOOSING PRIORITIES

It is necessary to priotise the thrust areas to obtain the output of research efforts and other resources. Several factors help in determining the priorities. These include the distribution of flora, national or regional disease pattern, availability of modern health care etc. In addition we have to keep in mind the global priorities in developing new drugs so as to get a good financial return.

The disease pattern and the priorities have national characteristics but there are several diseases which are common to tropical areas and in fact to most developing countries. These include protozoal and helminthic infections like malaria, filaria, onchocerciasis etc. Many of these diseases do not exist in developed countries and large pharmaceutical houses, therefore, do not give high priority to develop new drugs for such conditions. There is a gross mismatch between the health needs of the developing countries and the interests of the pharmaceutical industry. These should, therefore, receive priority in national/regional plans. The above examples are only illustrative but we have to evolve our own list of priority for communicable diseases.

Primary health care usually requires comparatively milder medication and the acceptability of herbal medicines for such conditions is also much more. The main considerations should be adequate availability or possible cultivation on required scale, lack of toxicity and ease of formulation.

The global thrust areas for drugs from natural sources include disease conditions whose incidence is increasing and where the modern drugs are either unavailable or unsatisfactory. Some examples of such maladies may be summarised as follows:

- Tropical diseases; antimalarial, antifilarials and antileishmaniasis
- Chronic conditions: anti-arthritic agents, anti-rheumatic agents
- Immunomodulators, immunostimulants, adaptogens
- Hepatoprotectors
- Rapid wounds and ulcer healing agents
- Central stimulating or sedating agents
- Alzheimers disease: prospective agents
- Memory enhancers
- Analgesics
- Sedatives

In considering the validation of the claims of ethnomedical therapies and derived preparations for introduction into the health-care systems, following deserve consideration:

1. The inadequacy of animal models to serve as adequate systems to assess biological activities that can be extrapolated to the human situation. This is particularly so in some of the disease conditions for which no satisfactory modern therapy exists.
2. The minimizing of toxicity tests needed to introduce the drug into a health care system. This is particularly necessary when the drug has been in long human use, toxic manifestations could be assessed by studying its long term effect on patients already undergoing treatment in the traditional milieu and the mode of industrial processing does not significantly vary from the ethnomedical methods. Product comparisons by modern instrumental parameters can also be made as between processed product and ethnomedical preparation.
3. Clinical trials conducted under the supervision of competent authorities (e.g WHO) must be a necessary prerequisite.
4. Stimulation of traditional processing methods, as well as adherence to ethnomedical regiments will be most helpful in not missing the activitiy present in

an ethnomedical preparation. This will also stimulate examination of ethnomedical theories of disease with a view to interpretation of these, if at all possible, within modern concepts. (The idea particularly refers to long standing and well documented systems such as Ayurveda, Unani and the Chinese systems).

5. The Selection of the appropriate dosage form and mode of administration should be recently based on economic parameters as well as shelf-life potential in the situations prevailing in the developing world.
6. There is some concrete evidence that pure compound need not necessarily be the best drugs. But on economic ground as well as on the therapeutic grounds it will serve all interests well if the most appropriate processing methodology of a plant or combination of plants is examined in this light (This would also give rise to interesting researches on the synergistic and/or detoxificant effects of other constituents in the medicinal plants or non medicinal plants that are found often added to polyprescriptions used in traditional systems).

It is desirable to have a "need based" approach to research on medicinal plants including screening of plants for biological activity. Research efforts could thus be directed for a number of above mentioned diseases for which suitable drugs are not available in the modern system of medicine and where herbal drugs have a possibility of offering new drugs.

MEDICINAL PLANTS AS A PART OF CULTURE

It is evident that the Indian people have a tremendous passion for medicinal plants and use them for a wide range of health related applications from a common cold to memory improvement and treatment of poisonous snake bites to a cure for muscular distrophy and the enhancement of body's general immunity. In the oral traditions local communities in every ecosystem from the trans Himalayas down to the coastal plains have discovered the medical uses of thousands of plants found locally in their ecosystem. India has one of the richest plant medical culture in the world. It is a culture that is of tremendous contemporary relevance because it can on one hand ensure health security to millions of people and on the other hand it can provide new and safe herbal drugs to the entire world. There are estimated to be around 25000 effective plant based formulations are available in the indigenous medical texts.formulations used in folk medicine and known to rural communities all over India and around 10000 designed.

Macro analysis of the distribution of medicinal plants show that they are distributed across diverse habitats and landscape elements. Around 70 per cent of India's medicinal plants are found in tropical areas mostly in the various forest types spread across the Western and Eastern ghats, the Vindhyas, Chotta Nagpur plateau, Aravalis and Himalayas. Although less than 30 per cent of the medicinal plants are found in the temperate and alpine areas and higher altitudes they include species of high medicinal value. Macro studies show that a larger percentage of the known medicinal plant occur in the dry and moist deciduous vegetation as compared to the evergreen or temperate habitats.

Analysis of habits of medicinal plants indicate that they are distributed across various habitats. One third are trees and an equal portion shrubs and the remaining one third herbs, grasses and climbers. A very small proportion of the medicinal plants are lower plants like lichens, ferns algae, etc. Majority of the medicinal plant are higher flowering plants.

DISTRIBUTION OF MEDICINAL PLANTS BY HABITS

Of the 386 families and 2200 genera in which medicinal plants are recorded, the families Asteraceae. Euphorbiacae. Laminaceae, Fabaceae, Rubiaceae., Poaceae, Acanthaceae, Rosaceae and Apiaceae share the larger proportion of medicinal plant species with the highest number of species (419) falling under Asteraceae.

About 90 per cent of medicinal plant used by the industries are collected from the wild. While over 800 species are used in production by industry, less than 20 species of plants are under commercial cultivation. Over 70 per cent of the plant collections involve destructive harvesting because of the use of parts like roots, bark, wood, stem and the whole plant in case of herbs. This poses a definite threat to the genetic stocks and to the diversity of medicinal plants if biodiversity is not sustainably used.

CULTIVATION PRACTICES OF MEDICINAL PLANTS

Given the demands of the market for a continuous and uniform supply of raw materials, and the increasing depletion of the forest resource base, expanding the number of medicinal plants in cultivation appears to be an important strategy for research and development. However, according to one estimate, of more than 400 plant species used for production of medicines by Indian Industry, less than 20 are currently under the cultivation in the country.

The potential returns to the farmer from cultivation of medicinal plants is reported to be quite high. A 1995 study suggested that the cultivation of certain high altitude Himalayan herbs could yield products priced anywhere between Rs. 7,150 to 55,000 per hectare although it is not clear at which point in the marketing chain these prices are paid. What is clear however is that although estimates of returns vary widely, medicinal plants can be valuable crops. Rao and Saxena reported average annual (per hectare) income of Rs. 120,000 through mixed cropping of high altitude medicinal herbs. High altitude medicinal tend to command higher prices but those of lower altitudes are still significant. Data for some low-altitude crops from the Amarkantak region of Madhya Pradesh show economic returns for four profitable species. Cultivation is clearly a sustainable alternative to collection of medicinal plants from the wild.

Most of the produce of cultivated medicinal and aromatic plants is exported as crude drugs e.g. Psyllium, senna leaves, opium poppy and Asgand. Unfortunately, however, due to emphasis being placed on important cash crops, as well as the fact that the majority of the cultivated species are not indigenous to India, most cultivation efforts are not alleviating the pressure being exerted on the natural resource base.

Nevertheless, a number of techniques have been developed to increase the quality and yield of many of the cultivated species. It is estimated that Indian public sector research institutions have developed standardized practices for the propagation and agronomy of a total of about 40 species.

Much of the research progress to date has resulted from the decision of the Indian Council for Agricultural Research (ICAR) to establish an All-India Coordinated Research Project on Medicinal and Aromatic Plants(AICRPMAP), in 1972, under the auspices of the National Bureau of Plant Genetic Resources (NBPGR). Efforts have mainly focused on the development of agro-technology techniques, including propagation methods for medicinal and aromatic plants. Aromatic plants have however tended to receive more attention, perhaps because their market values are in general more widely known.

ICAR works through a network of research stations, including the National Research Centre for Medicinal and Aromatic Plants located in Anand, Gujarat, which specializes in domestication, and has created structural links between the NBPGR and its Plant Breeding Division in order to develop improved varieties of some of the medicinal plant species used in allopathic preparations.

Another major national public research organisation, the Council for Scientific and Industrial Research (CSIR), has also played a significant role with regard to cultivation of medicinal plants, through its creation of (CIMAP), the Central Institute of Medicinal and Aromatic Plants, in Lucknow. CIMAP is now an eminent institution in India focusing on agro-technology as well as basic studies; improvement and enhancement of the resource base, and chemistry and related research regarding product development from plants.

In connection with the two major research efforts described above, the Central Government initiated a five year programme (1992-1997) implemented by the Ministry of

Agriculture to accelerate research and development of medicinal plants. With the support of 16 state agricultural universities, state horticulture and agriculture departments, regional research laboratories and the International Crop Research Institute for the Semi-Arid Tropics (ICRISAT), the GOI is establishing herbal gardens, nursery centres and demonstration seed production centres nation-wide.

Ministry of Health & Family Welfare (Department of ISM&H) started a "central scheme for development and cultivation of medicinal plants" in the year 1990-91 to encourage development of agrotechnique for important species through Govt/semi-government organisations having expertise and infrastructure for this work. The scheme is expected to initiate studies on harvesting, drying, and storage of medicinal plants.

Private companies have also started to invest in the cultivation of medicinal plants, since they face difficulties with regard to increasing supply gaps as well as in some cases adulterated materials from the wild. One such company, the Arya Vaidya Sala, in Kottakal, Kerala, in addition to maintaining two large herbal gardens, has also undertaken research on the propagation of 10 species, the demand for which currently outstrips supply, or may soon do so.

FLOWER USED AS MEDICINE

ALO VERA

Common name: Aloe vera, Medicinal aloe, Burn plant, Gheekumari (Hindi), Khorpad (Marathi), Kathalai (Tamil), Chotthu kathalai (Malayalam)

Botanical name: Aloe vera/barbadensis

Family: Liliaceae (lily family)

Aloe, a popular houseplant, has a long history as a multipurpose folk remedy. Commonly known as Aloe vera, the plant can be snapped off and placed on cuts and burns for immediate relief. Aloe vera is a clump forming succulent whose fleshy gray-green leaves are arranged in a vase shaped rosette atop a very short stem. The leaves are up to 18 in long and 2 in wide at the base, slightly grooved on top, and terminating in a sharp point. The leaves have small grayish teeth on the margins. The main rosette gets up to about 2 ft high, and the plant continually produces little offset rosettes. In winter and spring, medicinal aloe bears small tubular yellow flowers on branched stalks up to 3 ft tall. The real Aloe vera has yellow flowers, but many of the clones available have orange flowers. Although Aloe Vera is a member of the Lily family, it is very-cactus like in its characteristics.

Medicinal uses: Aloe Vera contains over 20 minerals, all of which are essential to the human body. The human body requires 22 amino acids for good health — eight of which are called "essential" because the body cannot fabricate them. Aloe Vera contains all of these eight essential amino acids, and 11 of the 14 "secondary" amino acids. Aloe Vera has Vitamins A, B_1, B_2, B_6, B_{12}, C and E. In India, Aloe vera is believed to help in sustaining youth, due to its positive effects on the skin. Hence it is called *ghee kunvar* or *ghee kumaari*.

ARANDI

Common name: Castor bean, Castor oil plant, Wonder tree, Arandi (Hindi), Kege (Manipuri), Amanakku (Tamil), Vilakkennai Kottaimuttu (Tamil), Oudla (Kannada) Veranda (Bengali), Era-gach (Assamese), Chittamankku (Malayalam)

Botanical name: Ricinus communis

Family: Euphorbiaceae (castor family)

The castor bean plant, an erect, tropical shrub or small tree, grows up to 30 feet tall. As an annual in the cooler zones, it grows up to 15' tall. It is a very fast growing plant. The joints of the hollow stem, stalks and leaves are reddish to purple. The 6 - 11 lobed, palmate leaves with uneven serrated edge, are also red or coloured and often have a blue-gray bloom. There is also a green variety. The flat seeds are in a seedpod that explodes when ripen. All the top of the stem and stalks are the inflorescence with the male - and female flowers. The female flowers are the fuzzy red structures at the top of the flower spike with the male flowers positioned on the lower half, and have conspicuous yellow anthers The oblong fruit turns brown when ripe. In each seed pod (a capsule) there are three seeds. The seeds of castor bean or castor oil plant, are very poisonous to people, animals and insects; just one milligram of ricin (one of the main toxic proteins in the plant) can kill an adult. The castor oil is extracted from the beans, which is used for medicinal purposes. Commercially prepared castor oil contains none of the toxin.

Medicinal uses: In Manipur, leaves are warmed, crushed and applied to annus as a remedy for bleeding piles. Seed oil is purgative. Leaf-paste is used as poultice on sores, gout or rheumatic swellings. Decoction of root is given in lumbago. For lactation, leaves of the plant are heated and applied to a woman's breasts to improve secretion of milk.

ASIAN SPIDER FLOWER

Common name: Asian spider flower, Yellow spider flower, Cleome, Tickweed, Bagra (Hindi), Hulhul (Urdu), Naivela (Malayalam) Naikkaduku (Tamil), Nayibela (Kannada), Pilitalvani (Gujarati), Kukkavaminta (Telugu), Pivalatilavana (Marathi)

Botanical name: Cleome viscosa/icosandra

Family: Capparaceae (caper family)

Usually tall annual herb, up to a meter high, more or less hairy with glandular and eglandular hairs. Leaves 3-5-foliolate, petiolate; leaflets obovate, elliptic-oblong, very variable in size, often 2-4 cm long, 1.5-2.5 cm broad, middle one largest; petiole up to 5 cm long. Racemes elongated, up to 30 cm long, with corym¬bose flowers at the top and elongated mature fruits below, bracteate. Flowers 10-15 mm across, whitish or yellowish; pedicels 6-20 mm long; bracts foliaceous. Sepals oblong-lanceolate, 3-4 mm long, 1-2 mm wide, glandular-pubescent. Petals 8-15 mm long, 2-4 mm broad, oblong-obovate. Stamens 10-12 (rarely more, up to 20), not exceeding the petals; gynophore absent. Fruit 30-75 mm long, 3-5 mm broad, linear-oblong, erect, obliquely striated, tapering at both ends, glandular-pubescent, slender; style 2-5 mm long; seeds many, 1-1.4 mm in diam., glabrous with longitudinal striations and transverse ridges, dark brown.

Medicinal uses: The leaves are diaphoretic, rubefacient and vesicant. They are used as an external application to wounds and ulcers. The juice of the leaves has been used to relieve earache. The seeds are anthelmintic, carminative, rubefacient and vesicant. The seed contains 0.1per cent viscosic acid and 0.04per cent viscosin.

BARRIGNTONIA

Common name: Barrigntonia, Freshwater Mangrove plant, Samundarphal (Hindi), Nir perzha (Malayalam) Nijhira (oriya), Dhatripala (Kannada), Sathaphala (Marathi), Kurpa (Telugu), samudra pazham (Tamil)

Botanical name: Barringtonia acutangula

Family: Lecythidaceae (Lecythis family)

This is an evergreen tree of moderate size, called by Sanskrit writers Hijja or Hijjala. The fruit is spoken of as Samudra-phala and Dhtriphala or "Nurse's fruit," and is one of the best known domestic remedies. Also called Stream Barringtonia or Itchy Tree (after a catepillar with irritant hairs that sometimes colonises the undersides of the leaves) Barringtonia acutangula is a tree 5-8m high with rough fissured dark grey bark, red flowers are produced on pendulous racemes about 20cm long. Four sided fruits are produced periodically throughout the year. Partly deciduous in extended dry periods. This species grows on the banks of freshwater rivers, the edges of freshwater swamps and lagoons and on seasonally flooded lowland plains, commonly on heavy soils. Found in Madagascar and tropical Asia, amongst other places. Propagation is by seed. Tolerant of heavy clay soils with poor drainage, it can grow in a range of soils. Frost sensitive. Full sun to part shade.

Medicinal uses: This tree has long been used for medicine, timber and as a fish poison. In traditional medicine, when children suffer from a cold in the chest, the seed is rubbed down on a stone with water and applied over the sternum, and if there is much dyspnoea a few grains with or without the juice of fresh ginger are administered internally and seldom fail to induce vomiting and the expulsion of mucus from the air passages. More recently it has become the focus of research for pain-killing compounds. Anecdotal reports of the bark being used to quickly relieve pain by Aboriginals has led to the discovery of compounds with pharmaceutical promise for pain relief.

BLACK NIGHTSHADE

Common name: Black nightshade, Black-berry night shade, Nightshade, Poisonberry, Manatakkali (Tamil), Mokoi (Hindi), Mulaku-thakkali (Malayalam), Kasaka (Telugu), Laghukavali (Marathi), Makoya (Urdu)

Botanical name: Solanum nigrum

Family: Solanaceae (potato family)

Black nightshade is a plant, an annual weed that grows up to 60cm tall, is branched and usually erected, growing wild in wastelands and crop fields. Alternate leaves are ovate deep green with an indented margin and acuminate at the tip. Flowers are white with yellow coloured centre. The berries are green at early stage and turn to orange or black when ripened.

Medicinal uses: Black nightshade is used for skin diseases, rheumatism, and gout. Juice of the herb is given in chronic enlargement of the liver. It can cure ear, and eye diseases. It is sometimes prescribed to "remove the effect of old age."

CHASTE TREE

Common name: Chaste tree, Nirgundi (Hindi), Samalu (Bengali), Nocchi (Tamil), Nochi (Kannada), Vavili (Telugu), Vennocchi (Malayalam)

Botanical name: Vitex negundo

Family: Verbenaceae (verbena family)

Chaste tree can grow up to five meters tall. It can be described as a cross between a shrub and a tree with a single woody stem (trunk) Chaste tree's distinctive feature are the pointed leaves with 3-5 leaflets. Small, lilac or violet flowers on new growth from June to September. Flowers are the smallest of the commonly grown Vitex species. The leaves are used as a mosquito repellent. leaves are burnt in a heap which proves very useful to get rid of Mosquitoes.

Medicinal uses: It is an effective herbal medicine with proven therapeutic value. Chaste tree has been clinically tested to be effective in the treatment of colds, flu, asthma and pharyngitis. Studies have shown that it can prevent the body's production of leukotrienes which are released during an asthma attack. Chaste tree contains Chrysoplenol D, a substance with anti-histamine properties and muscle relaxant. The leaves, flowers, seeds and root of Chaste tree can all be used as herbal medicine. A decoction is made by boiling the parts of the plant and taken orally. Today, Chaste tree is available in capsule form and syrup for cough.

CHIR PINE

Common name: Chir pine, Himalayan longleaf pine, Chir (Hindi), Wuchan (Manipuri)

Botanical name: Pinus roxburghii

Family: Pinaceae (pine family)

Among the principal pines found in India, chir pine is the most important. Native to the Himalayas, it is good as a street tree too. This is one of the least exacting of the Himalayan trees growing sometimes on bare rocks where only a few species are capable of existing. It is a resinous tree capable of yielding resin continuously provided rill method of tapping is adopted. Erect, round-headed evergreen tree with one or more trunks. Grows at moderate rate to 30 ft., with spread of 20 ft at maturity. The bark is red-brown, thick and deeply fissured at the base of the trunk, thinner and flaky in the upper crown. The leaves are needle-like, in fascicles of three, very slender, 20-35 cm long, and distinctly yellowish green. The flowers are monoecious (individual flowers are either male or female, but both sexes can be found on the same plant) and are pollinated by wind. The cones are ovoid conic, 12-24 cm long and 5-8 cm broad at the base when closed, green at first, ripening glossy chestnut-brown when 24 months old. They open slowly over the next year or so.

Medicinal uses: The turpentine obtained from the resin of all pine trees is antiseptic, diuretic, rubefacient and vermifuge. It is a valuable remedy used internally in the treatment of kidney and bladder complaints and is used both internally and as a rub and steam bath in the treatment of rheumatic affections. It is also very beneficial to the respiratory system and so is useful in treating diseases of the mucous membranes and respiratory complaints such as coughs, colds, influenza and TB. Externally it is a very beneficial treatment for a variety of skin complaints, wounds, sores, burns, boils etc and is used in the form of liniment plasters, poultices, herbal steam baths and inhalers. The wood is diaphoretic and stimulant. It is useful in treating burning of the body, cough, fainting and ulcers.

COMMON CRAPE MYRTLE

Common name: Crape myrtle, Saoni (Hindi), Dhayti (Marathi), Chinagoranta (Telugu) Pavalakkurinji (Tamil)

Botanical name: Lagerstroemia indica

Family: Lythraceae (loosestrife family)

Crape myrtle is the smaller version of *Lagerstroemia speciosa,* commonly known as Pride of India or Queen crape myrtle. The deciduous crape myrtle is among the longest blooming trees in existence with flowering periods lasting from 60-120 days. Crapes come in heights as short as 18 in (46 cm) and as tall as 40 ft (12 m) Leaves are alternate and smooth, but leaf size depends on variety. Flowers are borne in summer in big showy clusters and come in white and many shades of pink, purple, lavender and red.

Medicinal uses: Seeds are narcotic. In Manipur, flowers and leaves are used as purgatives. Bark is stimulant and febrifuge (fever removing) Roots are astringent and used as gargle.

DWARF RHODODENDRON

Common name: Dwarf Rhododendron, Talis (Hindi), Talisri (Hindi)

Botanical name: Rhododendron anthopogon

Family: Apiaceae (rhododendron family)

This is probably one of the smallest of rhododendrons. Grows to no more that 2-3 ft high. The white or yellow flowers, tinged with pink, grow in small compact clusters of 4-6 and each flower is 2 cm across. The dark green oval leaves are strongly aromatic and densely scaly underneath. The leaves are mixed with Juniper and used as incense in Buddhist monastries as well as in Hindu religious ceremonies.

Medicinal uses: In Nepal, Dwarf Rhododendron is used in making an essential oil. Anthopogon oil, as it is usually referred to in Nepal, is obtained by steam distillation of the aerial part of this shrub. It is a fluid liquid of pale yellow colour and sweet-herbal, faintly balsamic aroma. Rhododendron can be used in gouty rheumatic conditions. The essential oil is a stimulant and affects fibrous tissue, bones and nervous system.

EAST-INDIAN SCREW TREE

Common name: East-Indian screw tree, Nut-leaved screw tree, Maror phali (Hindi), Murud sheng (Marathi), Mriga Shringa (Sanskrit), Yedmuri (Kannada), Valambiri (Telugu), Vadampiri (Tamil), Antamora (Bengali)

Botanical name: Helicteres isora

Family: Sterculiaceae (Cacao family)

A sub-deciduous shrub or small tree with grey coloured bark. Leaves simple, serrate margin, scabrous above and pubescent beneath. Flowers solitary or in sparse clusters, with red petals turning pale blue when old. Fruits greenish brown, beaked, cylindrical, spirally twisted on ripening. The twisted shape of the fruit is what lends most of it names like screw tree and maror phali.

Medicinal uses: The roots and stem barks are considered to be expectorant, demulcent, astringent and antiglactagogue. Bark is used in diarrhoea, dysentery, scbies, biliousness and is useful in gripping of the bowels. Root juice is used in antidiarrhoeal and antidysenteric formulations. Fried pods are given to children to kill intestinal worms.

FIRE FLAME BUSH

Common name: Fire Flame Bush, Dhawai (Hindi), Jargi seringi (Telugu), Dhobo (oriya), Dowari (Marathi), Godari (Telugu) Tatiripuspi (Malayalam), Velakkai (Tamil)

Botanical name: Woodfordia fruticosa/floribunda

Family: Lythraceae (loosestrife family)

Dhawai phool (Dhawai Flower) is one of the well known non-wood forest produces of Chhattisgarh having regular demand in national and international drug markets. Although all parts of this herb possess valuable medicinal properties but there is heavy demand of flowers only. It is collected and marketed for both industrial and medicinal purposes. The flowers yield yellow and red dye. It also produces gum which is used as substitute to gum-tragacanth. Barks and leaves are used for tanning. The traders at Dhamtari city, well known market of herbs in Chhattisgarh, informed that there is more demand of Dhawai for industrial purposes as compared to medicinal purposes. The Lythraceae are mostly tropical herbs or occasionally shrubs or trees comprising about 30 genera and 600 species. The leaves are simple, usually opposite or whorled; stipules are minute or absent. The flowers are bisexual, strongly perigynous, actinomorphic or sometimes zygomorphic, commonly 4-,6-, or 8-merous. The sepals appear as lobes of the perigynous zone, the petals are distinct and usually crumpled. The stamens commonly are twice the number of petals, and are usually in two whorls, one with the filaments longer than the other.

Medicinal uses: This is a drug largely used in native medicine. This enters into the composition of many preparations, decoctions, churnas and ghritas for various diseases, but chiefly dysentery and diarrhoea by reason of its being highly astringent.

GAMHAR

Common name: Gamhar (Hindi), Madhumati (Sanskrit), Peddgumudutekku (Telugu), Kumalaamaram (Tamil), Kumbil (Malayalam), Sivan (Marathi), Sirni (Konkani), Shivani (Kannada)

Botanical name: Gmelina arborea

Family: Verbenaceae (verbena family)

Gamhar is a beautiful fast growing deciduous tree occurring naturally throughout greater part of India up to 1500 m. It is a fast growing tree, which though grows on different localities and prefers moist fertile valleys with 750-4500 mm rainfall. It does not thrive on ill drained soils and remains stunted on dry, sandy or poor soils; drought also reduces it to a shrubby form. The tree attains moderate to large height up to 30 m with girth of 1.2 to 4.5 m with a clear bole of 9-15 m. It is a treat to see the gamhar tree standing straight with clear bole having branches on top and thick foliage forming a conical crown on the top of the tall stem. Bark light grey coloured exfoliating in light coloured patches when old, blaze thick, a chlorophyll layer just under the outer bark, pale yellow white inside. Flowering takes place during February to April when the tree is more or less leafless whereas fruiting starts from May onwards up to June. Flowers occur in narrow branching clusters at the end of branches. The yellow flower, tinged with brown, is trumpet shaped, 3-4 cm long. The trumpets flare open into a gaping mouth with 5 distinct lobes.

Medicinal uses: The root and bark of Gmelina arborea are stomachic, galactagogue laxative and anthelmintic; improve appetite, useful in hallucination, piles, abdominal pains, burning sensations, fevers, 'tridosha' and urinary discharge. Leaf paste is applied to relieve headache and juice is used as wash for ulcers. Flowers are sweet, cooling, bitter, acrid and astringent. They are useful in leprosy and blood diseases. In Ayurveda it has been observed that Gamhar fruit is acrid, sour, bitter, sweet, cooling, diuretic tonic, aphrodisiac, alternative astringent to the bowels, promote growth of hairs, useful in 'vata', thirst, anaemia, leprosy, ulcers and vaginal discharge. The plant is recommended in combination with other drugs for the treatment of snake – bite and scorpion-sting. In snake – bite a decoction of the root and bark is given internally.

GIANT POTATO

Common name: Giant potato, Large Forest Ipomoea, Bhuyikohada (Hindi), Nelagummudu (Telugu), Palmudamgi (Tamil), Mutalakkilannu (Malayalam), Bhui-kohala (Marathi)

Botanical name: Ipomoea mauritiana

Family: Convolvulaceae (morning glory family)

Giant potato is a type of morning glory plant. Like the sweet potato, it belongs to the Ipomoea genera. It grows as a vine. The origin of Ipomoea mauritiana is unknown, but it may be in tropical America, where the nearest relatives occur. It is naturalised in many parts of the world. This vine has stems that can grow to 10 m. Leaf blade is circular in outline, 7-18 X 7-22 cm, usually palmately 5-7-divided to or beyond middle, rarely entire or shallowly lobed. Inflorescences few to many flowered. Flowers are pink or reddish purple, with a darker centre, funnelform, 5-6 cm across.

Medicinal uses: The leaves and roots are used externally to treat tuberculosis and for the treatment of external and breast infections. In Ayurveda, a decoction of the tuberous roots are used for the preparation of medicinal wine. The Ayurvedic name is Kiribadu Ala, and it is also an ingardient in Chyavanprash.

GUMMY GARDENIA

Common name: Gummy gardenia, Cambi gum tree, Kamarri (Hindi), Kad Bikke (Kannada), Sirukkambil (Tamil), Cittamali (Telugu), Dikamalli (Gujarati), Kambimaram (Malayalam), Nadihingu (Sanskrit), Dikemali (Marathi)

Botanical name: Gardenia gummifera

Family: Rubiaceae (coffee family)

Native to India, Gummy gardenia is a small tree which grows up to 3 meters. Gardenia is a genus of about 250 species of flowering plants. They are evergreen shrubs and small trees growing to 1-15 m tall. The leaves are opposite or in whorls of three or four, 5-50 cm long and 3-25 cm broad, dark green and glossy with a leathery texture. The flowers are solitary or in small clusters, white or pale yellow, with a tubular-based corolla with 5-12 lobes ('petals') from 5-12 cm diameter.

Medicinal uses: This species can be helpful in treating digestive problems, including dyspepsia and diarrhea; or used as an astringent and expectorant for nervous conditions and spasms.

HIMALAYA ONION

Common name: Himalaya Onion, Jimbur

Botanical name: Allium wallichii

Family: Alliaceae (onion family)

Himalaya Onion is a deciduous bulb that grows to 1.0 meters high by 0.5 meters wide. It grows in Himalyan foothills between 2300-6600 m. It sports hemispheric umbels of purple flowers. In Nepal, Himalaya onion is often used for cooking, especially for flavouring dal boiled legumes. Rather uniquely, jimbu leaves are usually employed in the dried state and fried in butter fat to develop their flavour.

Medicinal uses: The bulbs, boiled then fried in ghee, are eaten in the treatment of cholera and dysentery. The raw bulb is chewed to treat coughs and colds. It is said that eating the bulbs can ease the symptoms of altitude sickness. Members of this genus are in general very healthy additions to the diet. They contain sulphur compounds (which give them their onion flavour) and when added to the diet on a regular basis they help reduce blood cholesterol levels, act as a tonic to the digestive system and also tonify the circulatory system.

HOPHEAD

Common name: Hophead, Philippine Violet

Botanical name: Barleria lupulina

Family: Acanthaceae (ruellia family)

Hophead is a popular medicinal plant distributed in mountains of southern and western India. Shrubbery plant with single dark green leaves, red-brown branches, and flowers that bloom in upright spikes. It is an erect shrub with smooth, hairless stems and leaves. Leaves narrowly obovate, spine-tipped, 3.5-9 cm long, 0.8-1.2 cm wide. Flowers occur in a terminal spike with overlapping bracts which are broadly ovate, 15 mm long, green with purple upper half. Flower consists of a 3m long corolla tube, opening into 1 cm long petals. Longer stamen filaments 2 cm long; shorter stamens fertile. Style is 3 cm long and smooth.

Medicinal uses: Traditional and therapeutic use is anti-inflammatory for insect bites, herpes simplex use by its fresh leaves, and roots for anti-inflammatory centipede bites.

HORNED LOUSEWORT

Common name: Horned Lousewort, Lousewort

Botanical name: Pedicularis bicornuta

Family: Scrophulariaceae (dog flower family)

Horned Lousewort, the curious species, inhabits tough and sometimes inaccessible areas of the Himalayan cold deserts. The plants are tough and sturdy and the corolla of these flowers are closed in a ball-like fashion to cover the delicate vital parts such as stamens and stigma from the outside pressures. The flowers have interesting cultural use in certain Himalayan areas. The flowers are considered an integral offering to please Goddess Kali and get one's wishes fulfilled. Further, no religious ceremony is considered to be complete without the offering of these flowers in the first prayers. The women also make garlands from the flowers to greet each other on important religious occasions and to garland Goddess Kali during festivals. Horned lousewort is a robust, erect perennial which grows upto 60 cm, with dense clusters of large globular yellow flowers. Leaves are alternately arranged, and are pinnately lobed. Flowers are 2 cm across. The calyx (the tube consisting of sepals) is inflated and hairy. Flower tube is narrow and hairy. The upper lip of the flower is s-shaped or spirally curved with slender two-lobed beak.

Medicinal uses: The flowers are used in Tibetan medicine, they are said to have a bitter taste and a cooling potency. They are used in the treatment of vaginal and seminal discharges.

INDIAN BARBERRY

Common name: Indian barberry

Botanical name: Mahonia napaulensis

Family: Berberidaceae (barberry family)

Indian barberry is an evergreen shrub growing to 2.5m by 3m, with large, pinnately compound leaves. The leaves are about 18 in (46 cm) long with 9 to 13 stiff, sharply spiny, hollylike leaflets. The fragrant lemon-yellow flowers, appearing in late winter, are borne in erect racemes 3-6 in (7.6-15 cm) long. The fruit is a berry, first green, then turning bluish black with a grayish bloom. They are about a half inch long and hang in grapelike clusters. It is in leaf all year, in flower from March to April. Fruit is eaten raw or cooked. An acid flavour, but it is rather nice raw especially when added to muesli or porridge. Unfortunately, there is relatively little flesh and a lot of seeds. The fruit can also be dried and used as raisins.

Medicinal uses: The fruits are said to be diuretic and demulcent. They are used in the treatment of dysentery. Berberine, universally present in rhizomes of Mahonia species, has marked antibacterial effects and is used as a bitter tonic.

KALI MUSLI

Common name: Orchid palm grass, Kali musli (Hindi, Marathi), Tala-muli (Oriya), Nela tengu (Kannada), Nelppana (Malayalam), Nilappanaikkilanku (Tamil), Talamuli (Bengali)

Botanical name: Curculigo orchioides

Family: Liliaceae (lily family)

Kali Musli is a herbaceous tuberous perennial with a short or elongate root stock bearing several fleshy lateral roots; Leaves sessile or petiolate 15-45x1.3-2.5 cm, linear or linear lanceolate, tips sometimes rooting, scape very short, clavate. It has hardy leaves and can take shade: the leaves will just get a bit longer in the shade than in full sun shine. During flowering period it open a golden yellow flower at the leaf base every day. This can form a cute miniature plant pot in your room.

Medicinal uses: The rhizomes of the plants are used for the treatment of decline in strength, jaundice and asthma. According to Ayurveda, root is heating, aphrodisiac, alternative, appetizer, fattening and useful in treatment of piles, biliousness, fatigue, blood related disorders etc. According to Unani system of medicine, root is carminative, tonic, aphrodisiac, antipyretic and useful in bronchitis, ophthalmia, indigestion, vomiting, diarrhea, lumbago, gonorrhea, gleet, hydrophobia, joint pains etc.

KARVY

Common name: Karvy (Marathi), Khum (Manipuri)

Botanical name: Strobilanthes callosus

Karvy is a purplish-blue wild flower, which blooms once every eight years. The plant was first discovered by one Nees- a resident Britisher of Mumbai in the last century. The Karvy plant grows wild around Mumbai, Madhya Pradesh, Parts of Gujarat and in large areas of Konkan and North Kannara Ghats, Each year the plant comes alive with the advent of Monsoon,and once the rains are over, what is left behind is dry and dead-looking stems.This pattern repeats itself for seven years. In the eighth yar, the plant explodes into mass flowering. The Karvy plant has many uses as well. The leaves and the stems are also used for thatched roofs after the season is over.

Medicinal uses: The Karvy leaves are crushed and the juice is a sure cure for stomach ailments.

LITTLE IRONWEED

Common name: Little ironweed, Purple feabane, Sahadevi (Hindi), Sadodi (Marathi), Puvamkuruntal (Tamil), Sahadevi (Telugu), Kuksim (Bengali)

Botanical name: Vernonia cinerea

Family: Asteraceae (daisy family)

Little ironweed is an annual or short-lived perennial to 50cm with ovate leaves. The stems branch repeatedly at the top to hold aloft the small cylindrical, purple flower heads. Flowers throughout the year. Originally from Central America, now a pantropical weed, it is sometimes considered native to Western Australia. Found in upland crop areas, waste places and roadsides throughout India.

Medicinal uses: The seeds yield a fatty oil and are used as an anthelmintic and alexipharmic; they are said to be quite effective against roundworms and threadworms. They are also given for coughs, flatulence, intestinal colic and dysuria and for leucoderma, psoriasis and other chronic skin-diseases. The seeds are made into a paste with lime juice and used for destroying pediculi.

MADHAVI LATA

Common name: Hiptage, Helicopter Flower, Madhavi lata (Hindi), Madhabi (Manipuri), Madhvi (Kannada), Madubhlata (Bengali), Vasantakaala malligai (Tamil)

Botanical name: Hiptage benghalensis

Family: Malpighiaceae (Barbados cherry family)

Madhavi lata, native from India to the Philippines, is a vine like plant that is often cultivated in the tropics for its attractive and fragrant flowers. A woody climbing shrub with clusters of pink to white and yellow fragrant flowers and 3-winged, helicopter-like fruits. Flowers have very interesting shape and look like a decorative accessory, with fluffy-toothed edges. The fragrance is very strong and pleasant, resembles fruity perfume. Leaves are narrow and drooping. This plant can be trimmed as a bush, and can be crown in container, too. Used medicinally in India. Make sure to provide lots of light for profuse blooming.

Medicinal uses: The bark, leaves and flowers are aromatic, bitter, acrid, astringent, refrigerant, vulnerary, expectorant, cardiotonic, anti-inflammatory and insecticidal. They are useful in burning sensation, wounds, ulcers, cough, asthma

MYRICARIA

Common name: Myricaria, False tamarisk

Botanical name: Myricaria squamosa

Family: Tamaricaceae (Tamarix family)

A deciduous erect shrub that grows to 3.3 feet high by 1.65 feet wide. It grows geragriously by streams, and prefers many types of soil with a pH ranging from acid to alkaline and full sun with moderate moisture. The stem is reddish brown, leaves tiny, linear lanceolate, blue-green, densely clustered, stalkless. Flowers whitish pink, clustered in spike 3-5 cm long. Native to Himalayas from Afghanistan to central Nepal and eastern Tibet.

Medicinal uses: The entire plant is used in Tibetan medicine, where it is considered to have an astringent taste and a cooling potency. Antitussive and febrifuge, it localizes poison, ripens pimples and dries up serous fluids. It is used in the treatment of inflammation due to poisoning, the spreading of fever from various infections, pimples that do not ripen, coughing, accumulation of serous fluids in bone joints, and meat poisoning.

NONGMANGKHA

Common name: Nongmangkha (Manipuri), Banheka (Assamese)

Botanical name: Phlogacanthus thyrsiflorus

Family: Acanthaceae (ruellia family)

A gregarious shrub, common in the Manipur valley. This plant has long orange-red tubular flowers, appearing in upright spikes at the end of branches. Leaves are ovoid to lance-like, with smooth margins.

Medicinal uses: In Manipur, local people prefer it to *Malabar Nut (Justicia adhatoda)* It is useful for curing coughs, colds and asthma and is easy to administer. Flowers are antidote to pox, prevents skin diseases like sore, scabies etc.

PERENNIAL BUCKWHEAT

Common name: Perennial buckwheat, Tall Buckwheat

Botanical name: Fagopyrum dibotrys

Family: Polygonaceae

Perennial growing to 1m by 2m at a fast rate. It is frost tender. It is in flower in September. The flowers are monoecious (individual flowers are either male or female, but both sexes can be found on the same plant) and are pollinated by Bees and flies. We rate it 4 out of 5 for usefulness. The plant prefers light (sandy), medium (loamy) and heavy (clay) soils, requires well-drained soil and can grow in heavy clay and nutritionally poor soils. The plant prefers acid, neutral and basic (alkaline) soils. It can grow in semi-shade (light woodland) or no shade. It requires dry or moist soil.

Medicinal uses: The whole plant is anodyne, anthelmintic, antiphlogistic, carminative, depurative and febrifuge. It stimulates blood circulation. A decoction is used in the treatment of traumatic injuries, lumbago, menstrual irregularities, purulent infections, snake and insect bites.

PERSIAN LILAC

Common name: Chinaberry tree, Persian lilac, Pride of India, Bead tree, Lilac tree, Bakain (Hindi), Seizrak (Manipuri),

Bakan-nimb (Marathi), Bakarjam (Bengali), Kattu vembhu (Tamil)

Botanical name: Melia azedarach

Family: Meliaceae (mahogany family)

The Persian lilac tree is frequently confused with Neem. However, the structure of the leaves and the colour of the flowers, white in Neem and lilac in Persian lilac, are sufficient to distinguish between the two. A large evergreen tree native to India, growing wild in the sub-Himalayan region. In India, Muslims are credited with the spread of the tree. The bark is reddish brown, becoming fissured on mature trees. The deciduous leaves are bipinnate (twice feather-like) and 1-2 ft long. The individual leaflets, each about 2 in long and less than half as wide, are pointed at the tips and have toothed edges. In spring and early summer, Persian lilac produces masses of purplish, fragrant, star shaped flowers, each about 3/4 in in diameter, that arch or droop in 8 in panicles. They are followed by clusters of spherical, yellow fruits about 3/4 in in diameter that persist on the trees even after the leaves have fallen. All parts of Persian lilac tree are poisonous. Eating as few as 6 berries can result in death. Birds that eat too many seeds have been known to become paralyzed.

Medicinal uses: Bark and fruit extract is used to kill parasitic roundworms. In Manipur, leaves and flowers are used as poultice in nervous headache. Leaves, bark and fruit are insect repellant. Seed-oil is used in rheumatism. Wood-extract is used in asthma.

PORCUPINE FLOWER

Common name: Porcupine flower, barleria, Vajradanti (Hindi), Kundan (Tamil), Mullu goranti (Kannada), Kuttivetila (Malayalam), Pilikantashelio (Gujarati)

Botanical name: Barleria prionitis

Family: Acanthaceae (ruellia family)

Porcupine flower is an erect, prickly shrub, usually single-stemmed, growing to about 1.5 m tall. The stems and branches are stiff and smooth and light brown to light grey in colour.

The leaves are up to 100 mm long and 40 mm wide, and oval-shaped though narrow at both ends (ellipsoid) The base of the leaves is protected by three to five sharp, pale coloured spines, 10-20 mm long. The yellow-orange tubular flowers are found bunched tightly together at the top of the plant, but they also occur singly at the base of leaves. The flowers are 40 mm long and tubular, with several long protruding stamens. The seed capsule is oval-shaped and 13-20 mm long, with a sharp pointed beak. It contains two fairly large, flat seeds, typically 8 mm long by 5 mm wide, covered with matted hairs. Barleria has a central tap root, with lateral roots branching off in all directions.

Medicinal uses: It has numerous medicinal properties including treating fever, respiratory diseases, toothache, joint pains and a variety of other ailments; and it has several cosmetic uses. A mouthwash made from root tissue is used to relieve toothache and treat bleeding gums. The whole plant, leaves, and roots are used for a variety of purposes in traditional Indian medicine. For example, the leaves are used to promote healing of wounds and to relieve joint pains and toothache. Because of its antiseptic properties, extracts of the plant are incorporated into herbal cosmetics and hair products to promote skin and scalp health.

QUEEN CRAPE MYRTLE

Common name: Pride of India, Queen Crape Myrtle, Jarul (Hindi), Jarol (Manipuri), Kadali (Tamil), Taman (Marathi)

Botanical name: Lagerstroemia speciosa

Family: Lythraceae (loosestrife family)

This is the not-so-common pink variety of the more familiar purple flowered Queen Crape Myrtle. This tree is one of the most outstanding summer bloomers. Lagerstroemia speciosa is a larger form of the more commonly grown L. indica (Crape myrtle.) It is called Queen Crape Myrtle because it's the Queen of the Crape Myrtles, dominating with grand size and larger, crinkled flowers. The name Crape myrtle is given to these tree/shrubs because of the flowers which look as if made from delicate crape paper. Lagerstroemia speciosa is a large tree growing up to 50' but it can be kept smaller by trimming. It stands on an attractive, spotted bark that often peels. This bark is commercially used and is a valuable timber. The large leaves are also appealing as they turn red right before they drop in the winter. A postal stamp was issued by the Indian Postal Department to commemorate this flower.

Medicinal uses: Seeds are narcotic; bark and leaves are purgative; roots areastringent, stimulant and febrifuge (fever removing) In Manipur, the fruit is used as local application for apathe of the mouth. Decoction of dried leaves is used in diabetes.

RIVER BEAUTY

Common name: River Beauty, Dwarf Fireweed

Botanical name: Epilobium latifolium

Family: Onagraceae (evening primrose family)

A deciduous perennial that grows to 1.0 meters (3.3 feet) high by 0.5 meters (1.65 feet) wide and prefers many types of soil with a pH ranging from acid to alkaline and partial to full sun with moderate moisture. This plant withstands frost and has hermaphrodite flowers. Leaves narrow-elliptic, hairy beneath. Four petalled purplish pink flowers are 5 cm across, in leafy spike-like terminal clusters. Found in the Himalayas and the Uttaranchal hill stations. River gravels, margins of streams and damp slopes.

Medicinal uses: The entire plant is used in Tibetan medicine, it is said to have a bitter taste and a cooling potency. Analgesic, antidote, anti-inflammatory, antipruritic, antirheumatic and febrifuge, it is used in the treatment of fevers and inflammations, plus also itching pimples.

SAFFLOWER

Common name: Safflower, Dyers' saffron, False saffron, Kusum (Hindi), Kusumlei (Manipuri), Kusumba (Tamil), Gul rang (Urdu)

Botanical name: Carthamus tinctorius

Family: Asteraceae (daisy family)

Safflower is an annual plant native to the Mediterranean

countries and cultivated in Europe and the U.S. Its glabrous, branching stem grows from 1 to 3 feet high and bears alternate, sessile, oblong, or ovate-lanceolate leaves armed with small, spiny teeth. The orange-yellow flowers grow in flower heads about 1 to 11/2 inches across. This thistle is valued for its orange-yellow flowers in summer and for the oil contained in its seeds. The orange-red flowers of safflower sometimes serve as a substitute for saffron, since they give a (rather pale) colour to the food. They are frequently sold as "saffron" to tourists in Hungary or Northern Africa (and probably many other parts of the world) Their value as spice is nearly nil, but their staining capability justifies usage in the kitchen.

Medicinal uses: Taken hot, safflower tea produces strong perspiration and has thus been used for colds and related ailments. It has also been used at times for its soothing effect in cases of hysteria, such as that associated with chlorosis. Powdered seeds made into a poultice used to ally inflammation of the womb after child birth. Flowers of this herb is useful for jaundice.

SHISHAM

Common name: Indian rosewood, Shisham (Hindi), Sissu (Manipuri), Sitral (Bengali)

Botanical name: Dalbergia sissoo

Family: Fabaceae (bean family)

Shisham is a medium to large deciduous tree, native to India, with a light crown which reproduces by seeds and suckers. It can grow up to a maximum of 25 m in height and 2 to 3 m in diameter, but is usually smaller. Trunks are often crooked when grown in the open. Leaves are leathery, alternate, pinnately compound and about 15 cm long. Flowers are whitish to pink, fragrant, nearly sessile, up to 1.5 cm long and in dense clusters 5-10 cm in length. Pods are oblong, flat, thin, strap-like 4-8 cm long, 1 cm wide, and light brown. They contain 1-5 flat bean-shaped seeds 8-10 mm long. They have a long taproot and numerous surface roots which produce suckers. It is primarily found growing along river banks below 900 m elevation, but can range naturally up to 1300 m. Shisham is best known internationally as a premier timber species of the rosewood genus. However, Shisham is also an important fuel wood, shade, and shelter. With its multiple products, tolerance of light frosts and long dry seasons, this species deserves greater consideration for tree farming, reforestation and agro forestry applications. After teak, it is the most important cultivated timber tree in India, planted on roadsides, and as a shade tree for tea plantations.

Medicinal uses: Decoction of leaves is useful in gonorrhoea. Root is astringent. Wood is alterative, useful in leprosy, boils, eruptions and to allay vomiting.

SNOW LOTUS

Common name: Snow Lotus

Botanical name: Saussurea tridactyla

Family: Asteraceae (daisy family)

Snow Lotus was discovered by Bower at an elevation of 19,000 ft. In parts of Sikkim, where Himalayan conditions of climate prevail, we have a completely different class of flora. This where plants like the Snow lotus are found. The snow lotus is a high altitude plant (over 12,000 feet above sea level) with brilliant white flowers appearing over dark green leaves which grow through the rocks of mountain peaks. The flowers form in a dense head of small capitula, often completely surrounded in dense white to purple woolly hairs; the individual florets are also white to purple. The wool is densest in the high altitude species, and aid in thermoregulation of the flowers, minimising frost damage at night, and also preventing ultraviolet light damage from the intense high altitude sunlight. The term Snow Lotus is also used for related species S. involucrata and S. laniceps.

Medicinal uses: The whole plant is harvested in July and August to yield the herb that is used as a tonic for weakness, a therapy for menstrual disorders, and a remedy for arthritis. Due to the harsh environment of the snow lotus and the strong demand for its use in traditional herbalism, the snow lotus has become quite rare. Snow Lotus is native to the Himalayas.

STINKING CASSIA

Common name: Stinking cassia, Foetid cassia, Sicklepod, java bean, Tarota (Hindi), Thaunum namthibi (Manipuri), Senavu (Tamil), Sogata (Kannada), Chakunda (Bengali), Sakramardakam (Malayalam)

Botanical name: Senna obtusifolia, Cassia tora/obtusifolia

Family: Leguminosae (pea family)

A small erect glabrous shrub, about one meter tall, commonly found growing wild on roadsides. True to its name, foetid/stinking cassia has a disagreeable smell. It is widely spreading with numerous ascending, hairless branches. The compound leaves are arranged spirally and usually have three pairs of symmetrically egg-shaped leaflets up to 2 inches long. One to three yellow flowers appear on short axillary stems. The linear pods grow to 8 inches long, curve downward and contain many shiny, angular seeds. It occurs abundantly in open pastures, and is very common on roadsides and wasteland. In organic farms of India, Cassia tora is used as natural pesticide.

Medicinal uses: According to Ayurveda, the leaves and seeds are useful in leprosy, ringworm, flatulence, colic, dyspepsia, constipation, cough, bronchitis, cardiac disorders.

TOOTHACHE PLANT

Common name: Toothache Plant, Paracress, Akarkar (Hindi)

Botanical name: Spilanthes acmella

Family: Asteraceae (daisy family)

Toothache Plant" or "Paracress", Spilanthes acmella is a flowering herb in the Asteraceae family. Its leaves and flower heads contain an analgesic agent that may be used to numb toothaches. It is native to the tropics of Brazil, though it is grown as an ornamental (and occasionally as a medicinal) in various parts of the world. A small, erect plant, it grows quickly and sends up gold and red flower heads in the fall. The first frost reduces it to slime, but in warmer climates it is perennial. Eating Spilanthes is a memorable experience. The leaf has a smell similar to any green leafy vegetable. The taste, however, is somewhat reminiscent of Echinacea, but lacking the bitter and sometimes nauseating element of that medicinal. First, a strong, spicy warmth spreads outward across one's tongue, turning into a prickling sensation. With this the salivary glands leap into action, pumping out quantities of saliva. As the prickling spreads, it mellows into an acidic (slightly metallic) sharpness accompanied by tingling, and then numbness. The numbness fades after a time (two to twenty minutes, depending on the person and amount eaten), and the pungent aftertaste may linger for an hour or more.

Medicinal uses: The leaves and flower heads contain analgesic, antifungal, anthelminthic, and antibacterial agents, but some of the compounds are destroyed by desiccation or freezing.

TULSI

Common name: Holy basil, Tulsi (Hindi, Tamil, Telugu), Trittavu (Malayalam), Tulshi (Marathi)

Botanical name: Ocimum sanctum

Family: Labiateae

Tulsi (Ocimum sanctum) is a widely grown, sacred plant of India. Hindus grow Tulsi as a religious plant in their homes, temples and their farms. They use Tulsi leaves in routine worship. Tulsi, grown as a pot plant, is found in almost every traditional Hindu house. The natural habitat of Tulsi varies from sea level to an altitude of 2000 m. It is found growing naturally in moist soil nearly all over the globe. Tulsi is a branched, fragrant and erect herb having hair all over. It attains a height of about 75 to 90 cm when mature. Its leaves are nearly round and up to 5 cm long with the margin being entire or toothed. These are aromatic because of the presence of a kind of scented oil in them. A variety with green leaves is called Shri Tulsi and one with reddish leaves is called Krishna Tulsi. Tulsi flowers are small having purple to reddish colour, present in small compact clusters on cylindrical spikes. The fruits are small and the seeds yellow to reddish in colour.

Medicinal uses: Because of its medicinal virtues, Tulsi is used in Ayurvedic preparations for treating various ailments.

WILD INDIGO

Common name: Wild Indigo, Fish Poison, Tephrosia, {Sarphonk, Sharpunkha } (Hindi)

Botanical name: Tephrosia purpurea

Family: Fabaceae (pea family)

Native to East India, Wild Indigo grows as common wasteland weed. In many parts it is under cultivation as green manure crop. Its is a plant of the genus Tephrosia having pinnate leaves and white or purplish flowers and flat hairy pods. This plant contains a mild toxin called tephrosin which chemically stuns fish but does not effect mammals. The extract is obtained by crushing the whole plant by mortar and pestle, or rocks, and then scattering it in tide pools. In a few minutes, small fish would float up to the surface and could be caught by hand. The flesh from the fish is safe to eat. This system of fishing, good for older people and children, was called hola.

Medicinal uses: According to Ayurveda, plant is digestible, anthelmintic, alexiteric, antipyretic, alternative, cures diseases of liver, spleen, heart, blood, tumours, ulcers, leprosy, asthma, poisoning etc. According to Unani system of medicine, root is diuretic, allays thirst, enriches blood, cures diarrhea, useful in bronchitis, asthma, liver, spleen diseases, inflammations, boils and pimples; Leaves are tonic to intestines and a promising appetizer. Good in piles, syphilis and gonorrhoea.

10

Plant Ecology

Plant ecology is a branch of the scientific field of ecology which focuses specifically on plant populations. There are a number of applications for plant ecology, ranging from helping people develop low water gardens to studying endangered ecosystems to learn about how they can be protected. Researchers from this field tend to come from an interdisciplinary background which can feature training in a wide variety of scientific pursuits, including plant anatomy, general ecology, biology, and so forth.

The field of plant ecology includes the study of plants and their environment. Rather than just looking at plants in a vacuum, researchers consider how they interact with each other and their environment to create an interconnected system.

Plant ecology can include the study of entire ecosystems, such as the rainforest or plateau, or the study of specific areas of interest, like plant populations which manage to survive next to a polluted stream. Plant ecologists also look at animals, soil conditions, and other influences on a plant's environment.

Ecology is a complex and vast field of study which can encompass everything from understanding how natural environments function to how humans interact with the natural world, and how various behaviors can fundamentally alter the natural environment. In plant ecology, people can focus on topics like climate change and its effect on plants, plant evolution, how plants disseminate themselves in nature, symbiotic relationships between plant species, plant diseases, and so forth.

A great deal of field work is involved in plant ecology, as researchers like to see their subjects in nature so that they can learn in context.

A single sample of a plant can provide interesting information and data, but actually seeing that plant growing can provide a researcher with a great deal more data. For example, looking at a plant alone, a researcher might not understand why its leaves are shaped the way they are, but when the researcher sees the plant in nature, he or she might realize that the leaves conferred some sort of benefit on the plant or the surrounding environment, ranging from signaling the presence of the plant to pollinators to providing shelter for seedlings so that they can grow up.

Plants make up a vital part of the natural environment, and plant ecologists are well aware of this. In a healthy ecosystem, plants provide food and shelter for animals, secure the soil to prevent erosion, cast shade to create microclimates, conserve water to keep it in the ecosystem instead of allowing it to be lost, and participate in the breakdown and recycling of organic material to keep the ecosystem thriving. Plants are also of critical interest because they produce oxygen, and plants have been heavily implicated in the creation of the Earth's currently oxygen-rich atmosphere.

CLIMATE CONDITIONS OF ECOLOGY

To descriptive ecology we owe the recognition of a number of major vegetation types that are associated with particular climatic conditions, as for example the occurrence of the deciduous forests in areas where a favourable climate alternates with an unfavourable, due to low temperature or inadequate humidity. Another example is the association of evergreen coniferous forests with areas where the length of the growing season is restricted.

But now that the broader features of the relations of plant communities with climatic types have come to be recognized the unexplored areas of the world's surface, though likely to provide further examples and interesting variants, are unlikely to contribute materially to our real understanding of the causal factors of distribution unless investigated in considerable detail. Further progress demands a detailed analysis of climatic and other habitat conditions throughout the seasonal cycle and experimental studies of individual species to determine their tolerances and the critical phases in their development which climatic conditions may promote or inhibit and the temperature and humidity limits these demand.

Other features of the climatic complex that call for more detailed analysis are the responses of individual species to direct and indirect effects of wind action and the influence of radiation of different intensities and wave lengths. The comprehensive work edited by Professor Duggar constitutes a valuable summary of the position attained at that period, since when the amount of research, especially upon photoperiodism, to which we shall revert, has been both extensive and significant.

In the competition for radiant energy potential heights and spread are morphological features that determine the degree to which one kind of plant or individual can become a sunshade to another but clearly the time factor is here significant and in a population of seedlings, for example, those individuals that germinate first will have an advantage over those germinating later which emphasizes the survival value of what has been termed germination energy.

The more continuous the light screen provided by the foliage of a species the more effective will be its suppression of the plants in its shade though the mechanical vulnerability to wind imposes on leaf area the compromise presented by the compound character of most large leaves, although the rosette-leaves of many biennials which have the support of the soil or other vegetation beneath are immune from this type of injury and are often large and quite entire. We can, indeed, in many morphological features discern indications of this struggle for light.

The dominance of the tree habit in the climax phase

where habitat conditions can support forest is but an expression of the fact that in the struggle for light the tallest members tend to survive. The wane of the arboreal vegetation is probably an accompaniment of man's increasing interference with nature making ever-augmented inroads upon woody vegetation so that today, almost throughout the world, herbaceous communities are becoming more conspicuous.

It is, perhaps, due to the importance of the time factor that the more successful species are in general those that have the potentiality of large seed-output and the marked association of average seed size with the shadiness of the plant community that a species normally colonizes is a further emphasis on the importance of the light factor in competition at the juvenile phases of developments.

In the competition for nutrients the extent and rate of development of the root system to which we have already referred, is manifestly correlated with the success of the assimilating organs and the mode of spread of a species whether by seed or vegetatively will mainly determine the habitat conditions that it can invade.

From experiments with Barley growing in competition with *Holcus mollis* H. H. Mann and T. W. Barnes concluded that though the root space and supply of plant food was apparently ample for both they reduced the growth of each other and the dominant appeared to be determined by the *time of development* as well as by the density. One could multiply examples but it is clear that temporal factors play an appreciable part in the competition both for light and nutrients and emphasize the need for a much more detailed knowledge than we at present possess concerning the life histories of the chief species contributing to plant communities and the conditions that modify them.

An interesting example of the differential effect of species upon one another was exhibited by some experiments carried out with *Juncus effusus.* A. Lazenby found that the number of seeds of this Rush which germinated and the subsequent growth differed strikingly according to the other species of seeds sown with them. Thus when sown with Bent *(Agrostis tenuis)* and White Clover *(Trifolium repens)* only about one-tenth of the population of Rush plants was obtained as when the accompanying species were Ryegrass *(Lolium perenne)* and White Clover.

It is only natural that the visible, overground, parts of the plant should have received major attention from both morphologists and ecologists though it is perhaps remarkable, having regard to the early recognition of the importance of the root-system, from the nutritional as well as the mechanical aspect, that its nature, extent and mode of development should have so long been neglected. Such neglect is perhaps partially to be explained by the difficulty of exhuming the entire root system, in most soils, as a consequence of which their extent has often been underestimated.

The valuable researches of Weaver and his associates in America have served to call attention to this neglected field of study. From these the considerable labour involved in such studies can be appreciated but also the great diversity and significant distinctions that obtain. Sandy soils afford an especially favourable medium for such investigations since by blowing away the sand from a working face as it dries entire root systems can be excavated without risk of losing the finer ramifications and by appropriate means these can be supported in their original positions as they emerge from the matrix. The present writer's own studies on the root systems of plants characteristic of various phases of dune development have shown how varied these can be not merely between different species but also between different individuals of the same species when growing in conditions of diverse water supply and aeration.

Root studies have emphasized the distinction between those that exhibit a restricted but richly branched system, which exploit a relatively small volume of soil intensively, and those in which the root system is extensive but the large soil volume is much less completely interpenetrated.

USE OF SCIENTIFIC METHODS IN ECOLOGY

Systems analysis is an important techniqve of ecosystem research and environmental management. Watt has pointed out that ecological systems are characteristically dynamic and complex, usually involving interactions between many variables, and often displaying lag effects, cumulative effects, thresholds, and nonlinear causal relationships. Such complex phenomena cannot always be studied by traditional techniques of individual research and scholarship. Computer analysis and team research are often necessary.

Systems analysis is a logical scientific method which approaches complex phenomena in several stages of operation: (1) *systems measurement,* in which the objectives of the problems are outlined and accurate data are obtained on important variables which relate to these objectives; (2) *data analysis,* in which the relationships between variables are explored through appropriate statistical procedures, and those variables most important in regulating the system are determined, (3) *systems modelling,* in which functional or mathematical models are composed to provide a theor,etical basis for relating the variables, (4) *systems simulation,* in which variables are anipulated mathematically to evaluate the consequences of changes within the system, and (5) *systems optimization,* in which the best strategies for achieving the objectives are evaluated and selected.

This approach is basically similar to standard scientific procedure which involves description, classification, hypothesis formation, experimentation, and clinical tests or field trials. The particular characteristic of systems analysis, however, is that it can operate in very complex systems which require computerized data handling and do not lend themselves to direct experimentation. One can —a city, an ocean, or a range of mountains. Thus, mathematical modelling and computer simulation is sometimes the only feasible experimental approach in large-scale ecological research. Team research is also a usual component of systems analysis, for rarely can a single person possess all the skills necessary for the complete systems approach.

Systems analysis can be illustrated with the common problem of improving water quality in a badly polluted river. *Systems measurement* would first involve a statement of the objectives in water quality and river characteristics which are desired. These would be expressed in terms of physical characteristics (temperature, clarity, dissolved oxygen, nutrient levels, trace element concentrations, etc.), and biological characteristics (bacterial, algal, crustacean, insect, fish pop ulations, etc.) which are desired in the river. Systems measurement would then involve making a detailed inventory of existing conditions, so that accurate data would be obtained on the major physical and biotic features of the river in its present polluted condition. Systems measurement would finally involve the identification of the major influences on the stream. This would require knowledge of its watershed, weather patterns, land-use patterns, geologic formations, domestic inputs, industrial operations, and stream flow characteristics. Hence, the enormity of just stage one, systems measurement, becomes apparent. This stage in a relatively small river could easily take a team of 5 to 10 scientists several years to get baseline data and understand the prevailing situation in specific terms.

Stage two, *data analysis*, would involve computer and statistical analysis of relationships between variables. How do land-use patterns, industrial operations, and domestic inputs interact with topography, weather, and stream flow characteristics to influence the physical and biotic qualities of the'river? Some specific questions in this area would be: What are the sources of the nutrients? How do the nutrient levels influence the biotic communities? Are oxygen and temperature levels within satisfactory ranges If not, why not? Are toxic chemicals present in the stream. If so, what are their origins, their effects, and their fates? A great many questions of this type can be asked, and it is apparent that multivariate analyses, as well as other statistical procedures, must be utilized.

The third stage, *systems modelling,* would be undertaken when the investigators felt they had a lead on the origins and relationships of the important variables within the system. They could then propose a mathematical relationship between various factors influencing the prevailing conditions within the river. Data analyses might suggest, for example, that pesticide run-off from agricultural operations was poisoning the river and responsible for the absence of certain organisms. The analyses might also suggest that excessive nutrients from domestic sewage were creating high bacterial populations which reduced dissolved oxygen below satisfactory levels.

The fourth stage, *systems simulation,* would consist of computer runs with different variables modified. The model would then predict changes in other variables. For example, systems simulation would estimate and predict changes in the river if agricultural practices were altered, if sewage treatment plants were installed, or if industrial operations were curtailed. It becomes apparent that modern computer techniques are essential at several stages in systems analysis, especially in data analysis and in systems simulation. Ideally, an integrated computer technology program should be utilized throughout the entire systems research if possible, from data collection to systems optimization.

The fifth stage, *systems optimization,* would determine the best course of action to achieve the goals. This process would relate the biological and physical data with economic feasibility studies. Alternatives and options could then be examined in realistic terms. The stages of systems analysis which can be used in any ecologic problem.

Systems analysis is also essential in working in the opposite direction from that outlined above—in determining, for example, the effects of a new industrial operation or land-use modification on existing conditions in an ecosystem. What would be the effects, for example, of constructing five or six nuclear power plants on the shores of Chesapeake Bay, and using the waters of the bay for cooling the nuclear reactors? This became an economic and ecological issue in Maryland, Virginia and Delaware in 1970 and 1971, when construction permits were issued to the Baltimore Gas and Electric Company to proceed with the construction of the first large nuclear power plant on the Bay at Calvert Cliffs below Annapolis. In numerous state and federal hearings on this issue it became clear that systems measurement data were not adequate to predict the effect of heated effluents on plankton ecology, fish spawning and growth, animal migrations, aquatic vegetation, and many other aspects of estuarine ecology. Broad spectrum systems analyses are urgently needed for a number of environmental and social problems, as well as for natural resource management problems.

Mathematical modelling and systems analysis may not provide the final answer to environmental problems, but in many situations they provide the most helpful possibilities for relating the complex array of variables which exist in ecologic problems. They provide the only reasonably objective way of evaluating cost and benefit relationships of environmental modifications, providing that accurate and complete data can be obtained. There are many problems, of course, in relating economic and ecologic values. It is not always possible to assign numerical cost or benefit figures to some ecologic considerations.

It is also essential to remember that systems analysis initially depends upon computer technology and mathematical models are of little help if the basic ecologic data are incorrect or grossly incomplete. The field biologist still plays the essential first step in the most elaborate-ecosystem analysis. In some circumstances, just as in weather prediction, a naturalist or field ecologist who has never seen a computer might have knowledge and experience of more value than an incomplete or hastily composed systems analysis program using the most advanced computer technology. Aldo Leopold never used computers, yet he provided some of the most accurate insights which have ever been achieved into the ecology and management of America's environmental problems.

Watt has supplied detailed discussions and mathematical

presentations of systems analysis in ecological research. Van Dyne and Patten have compiled many important papers on systems analysis in relation to the study and management of ecosystems.

It is increasingly important tounderstand the dynamics of ecosystems, their patterns of succession and evolution, and their patterns of diversity and stability. E.P. Odum has written a major review of these topics and has shown that ecosystems may be characterized as pioneer, developmental and mature. Various stages within this continumm possess certainproperties of production, respiration, community structure, nutrient cycling, homeostasis, etc. For example, young developmental stages of an ecosystem tend to have greater gross production in relation to respiration, but lower species diversity and less stability than mature states. Thus, developmental stages tend to be favored in agricultural practice, but they are also more vulnerable to ecologic damage or catastrophe. We will explore these relationships in more detail throughout subsequent chapters after various components of the ecosystem are considered separately.

TERM OF PLANT ECOLOGY AND PLANT GEOGRAPHY

The term "geobotany" includes both plant ecology and plant geography. As far as possible it is desirable to refer to ecological "distribution" when describing the habitat conditions and limitations and to phytogeographical "range" when defining the geographical boundaries of taxa, plant communities, etc. It is, however, to be noted that by long usage "distribution" is frequently synonymous with "range." Phytochoria should be defined by their ranges though many other data are included in their descriptions.

The aims of plant geography may be briefly defined as:

1. To find out and to record the occurrences of plants, especially as species, in localities fixed geographically;
2. To determine the units into which the earth can be divided on the basis of similarity of ranges of taxa and to describe these units;

3. To name and classify these units as phytochoria;
4. To determine, as far as possible, the causes which have resulted in the ranges and in the make-up of the phytochoria.

We have noted that plant geography is based on taxonomy and is very closely associated with ecology. From some points of view it can be considered a branch of geography. When "causes" of ranges are under discussion it becomes obvious that it is the most synthetic branch of botany. Not only does the phytogeographer have then to take into account the morphological and physiological particulars of the plants themselves as individuals, as taxa, or as plant communities but he has to obtain data from geology, from archaeology, from history, from meteorology, from pedology, from zoology, and from his botanical colleagues who have specialized in the study of this or that aspect of plant life.

Plant geography as a subject in its own right is relatively modern. It is true that records of plant ranges, as then known, are given by many early authors but they are usually incidental to other studies.

Theophrastus, in his *Enquiry into Plants* heads Book IV with "Of the trees and plants special to particular districts and positions" and gives interesting information for many plants of the eastern Mediterranean Region. There is little in the works of the herbalists, or of pre-Linnean authors generally, that can be called plant geography in any proper sense, though there are many references to places whence plants came and some local studies of range and distribution.

Tournefort, in his *Relation d'un voyage du Levant*, 1717, described, somewhat vaguely, altitudinal zonation on Mt. Ararat in Armenia. Linnaeus recognized and described plant communities, mainly for Scandinavia. Albrecht von Haller of Bern for Switzerland and Jean-Louis-Giraud Soulavie for southern France published accounts that include phytogeographical material for the areas with which they were concerned. Carl Ludwig Willdenow, in his *Lehrbuch der Botanik* has a chapter on the history of plants of which he says *"Unter*

Geschichte der Pflanzen verstehen wir die Einflus des Klimas auf die Vegetation, die Veranderungen, welche die Gewachse wahrscheinlich erlitten haben, wie die Natur fur die Erhaltung derselben sorgt, die Wanderungen der Gewachse und endlich ihre Verbreitung uber den Erdball."

There is much in Willdenow's chapter relevant to plant geography, but more that is better considered as concerning plant ecology. It is generally held that Alexander von Humboldt was the "father" of plant geography. He published with A. Bonpland an *Essai sur la Geographie des Plantes accompagne d'un tableau physique des regions equinoxiales,* Paris, 1805. In 1817 there appeared his Book *De distributione geographica plantarum secundum coeli temperiem et altitudinem montium Prolegomena.* This is written in Latin and deals with the range and distribution of plants in relation to climate, with the major zones of torrid, temperate, and frigid. Both latitudinal and altitudinal zonation are considered and his coloured diagrams of the latter are famous.

Auguste Pyramus de Candolle, published in 1809, in the *Dictionnaire raisonne et universel d'Agriculture,* an account of "Geographie agricole et botanique," and in 1820, in the *Dictionnaire des sciences naturelles* XVIII his *"Essai elementaire de geographie botanique"* of 64 pages. In these works he deals especially with the relationship between land utilization, botany, and the external factors of the environment.

Joachim Friedrich Schouw, a Dane, published a general textbook of plant geography in Danish in 1822 and in German (*Grundziigen einer allgemeinen Pflanzengeographie*). In the first part of his book he deals with the ecological factors, warmth, moisture, light, etc., and in the second part with the occurrence, range, and distribution of single species, genera, families, and the whole plant kingdom. He first used the ending -etum for plant communities, such as Ericetum, Coryletum, Fagetum, and Quercetum. In the third part he gives a summary of the flora of the earth on the basis of zonations in longitude, latitude, and altitude.

An interesting work that is often overlooked is that of F. J. F. Meyen, *Grundriss der Pflanzengeographie, Berlin, 1836, of which an English translation by M. Johnston was published in 1846 by the Ray Society under the title Outlines of the Geography of Plants. This mainly follows the lines laid down by Humboldt and Schouw but is still well worth reading. It has an extensive "Supplement" dealing with the history of cultivated plants.*

Alphonse de Candolle, in 1855, published two volumes on plant geography. J. D. Hooker has a long essay-review on this work. Its historical importance is that it appeared shortly before the announcement of the theory of natural selection by Darwin and Wallace and the publication of Darwin *Origin of Species*. It is a clear account of the facts of geographical ranges and of ecological relationships as then known and understood but is based on the idea that the majority of species were created such as they now exist. J. D. Hooker was at this time in an "on-the-fence" position regarding the general theory of evolution and his comments on and criticisms of A. de Candolle are extremely illuminating to anyone who tries to understand the mental difficulties of those who were first meeting with the new evolutionary ideas that were so quickly to become biologically orthodox.

KNOWLEDGE OF PHYTOGEOGRAPHY

Many other names of botanists who contributed to the knowledge of phytogeography in the first half of the 19th century could be mentioned. One has to remember that from the time of Linnaeus to the time of Darwin there was a tremendous amount of geographical exploration that often included botanical research. It is true that this was very largely systematic and economic but without taxonomy there can be no development of plant geography. Collections poured in from all over the world and were described in "floras" and monographs. Gardens, botanic and horticultural, were enriched and systems of classification were gradually improved.

The work of botanists, whether in taxonomy or in phytogeography, was then essentially descriptive and classificatory. In plant geography, however, there had been some advances on this somewhat static position in that correlations were found between ranges and environmental factors. The theory of evolution was, however, not generally accepted till after the publication of Darwin *Origin of Species* in 1859. The influence of evolutionary theory in explaining the facts of plant geography very speedily became apparent in the writings of botanists.

It is also worth noting that Darwin considered biogeography as of very great importance in supporting his theory of evolution by natural selection. He devotes two chapters to "Geographical Distribution" in the Origin of Species. The development of plant geography was very great during the second half of the 19th century. The flora and vegetation of many countries were explored and described and many of the problems that arise in attempting to explain their origin were often clearly stated.

Only a few outstanding names can be mentioned and that of J. D. Hooker is foremost because of his work "in the field" and his extensive publications in this subject. Hooker, as Assistant Surgeon and Botanist, accompanied James Clark Ross in the *Erebus* and *Terror* expedition to "Antarctica" and collected and studied the flora in Madeira, Cape Verde Islands, St. Helena, Kerguelen Island, Tasmania, The Falklands, Hermite Island, New Zealand, and the Cape. His journey to the eastern Himalaya and botanizing in Sikkim and Assam occupied the whole of 1848 and much of 1849. In 1860, he visited Syria and Palestine, in 1871 Morocco, and in 1877 North America on botanical expeditions. A full account of the phytogeographical researches of Sir Joseph Dalton Hooker was published in 1953.

Partly contemporaneous with J. D. Hooker were the great German botanists — A. Grisebach, A. Engler and O. Drude with their text-books and other comprehensive works on plant geography. The important series of monographs by various authors edited by Engler and Drude under the general title *Die Vegetation der Erde* covered many countries of the world. Karsten und Schenck edited the volumes of *Vegetationsbilder* Jena, 1904 to 1944, 1, 26.

Since 1900 a number of general books on plant geography

have been published. The following are given in the bibliography and have been consulted in preparing the accounts of modern methods and results that follow: H. Solms-Laubach, Graebner, Hayek, Campbell, Wulff, Cain, Good, Croizat, and Dansereau.

Special mention must be made of the improvements in plant geography resulting from the rise of ecology and the more recent advances in physiological ecology. The great work of A. F. W. Schimper, *Pflanzengeographie auf physiologischer Grundlage,* Jena 1898, with its English translation *PlantGeography upon a physiological basis,* by W. R. Fisher, revised and edited by P. Groom and I. B. Balfour, Oxford 1903, had a tremendous influence in stimulating interest and research in the subject. Some of Schimper's conclusions, as those on xeromorphism, have been strongly criticized and have to be modified as a result of more evidence though it is interesting to note that more recently still it has been shown that some of the criticisms were too extreme.

A third edition of Schimper *Pflanzengeographie,* by F. C. von Faber, was published at Jena in 1935 in two volumes. A textbook by E. Warming was originally published in Danish, in 1895, under the title *Plantesamfund,* with German editions in 1896 and 1902. What is described as "practically a new work" by E. Warming assisted by M. Vahl, based on *Plantesamfund,* appeared in 1909 as *Oecology of Plants, an introduction to the study of plant-communities,* Oxford. There were later German editions of which the fourth by E. Warming and P. Graebner has the title *Lehrbuch der okologischen Pflanzengeographie,* Berlin 1930- 1933. While Warming's first book quoted above is ecological rather than

Phytogeographical, the last edition is wider in its outlook. E. Rubel's scheme for the delimitation and nomenclature of plant communities is also of phytogeographical importance. The full account was published as *Pflanzengesellschaften der Erde,* Bern-Berlin, 1930. Like the works of Schimper and Warming, it has an ecological basis.It is worth recording that the text-books on plant geography and closely related plant ecology mentioned above contain numerous bibliographical references.

The boundary between ecology and phytogeography is frequently passed in many of the papers published in ecological journals such as the *Journal of Ecology, Ecology, Oikos,* and *Vegetationsbilder*. The publication *Pflanzenareale,* with range maps and explanatory text, is more definitely phytogeographical but has apparently ceased publication.The use of palaeobotanical evidence in plant geography can be gauged from Wulff's 1932-1944 publications already noted and from Seward book *Plant-Life through the Ages,* Cambridge, 1931.

There are also the very important works of Reid and Chandler and Chaney, and the publications referred to in Cain Recently there has been the introduction of cytogenetical data into the realm of plant geography. There is no doubt that researches on the cytology and breeding phenomena of plant species will become of increasing importance in tracing the history of their ranges. At present the known facts are meagre relative to the number of species in even poor floras, while cytogenetic investigation of the rich floras of the tropics has been little more than commenced.

NATURAL RELATIONS OF BIO-ECOLOGY

SIGNIFICANCE OF BIO-ECOLOGY

The term bio-ecology has been proposed primarily for the sake of emphasis, but partly also for greater clarity and definiteness. Although the field is here regarded as coextensive with ecology, the meaning and content of that term still vary too widely in use to permit employing the two as exact synonyms at present. This conclusion gains force from the fact that the term ecology is itself not infrequently replaced by biology, sociology, geography, or geobotany, and that its synthetic nature is too often obscured by such subdivisions as autecology, synecology, insect ecology, and human ecology. To those who regard the cause-and-effect relation as the very essence of ecology, the study of man and of human society is obviously a division of the latter, but it is clear that man's importance to himself will for some time tend to maintain and even emphasize the existing specialization into sociology, economics, behaviorism, psychology, and other fields.

This is indicated in particular by the rise of behaviorism, which had its origin essentially in animal ecology, but has taken its own course with diminishing interest in ecological concepts and methods. The consequent loss of focus and of synthesis has been reflected in a generally hostile or indifferent attitude to an approach vital to the ecological study of man.

As matters stand, it appears that the word ecology will come to be applied to the fields that touch man immediately only as the feeling for synthesis grows. The natural procedure will be for its outlook and methods to be adopted gradually by the human sciences and for the use of the term to lag far behind, as is the fate of terms in general.

Moreover, students of ecology will continue to be trained primarily as botanists, zoologists, sociologists, or economists for some time to come—probably indeed as long as university departments are organized on the present basis. Hence, to emphasize the proper synthetic approach and to maintain the ideal constantly before specialized workers, the term bio-ecology appears to be well warranted.

It possesses the further great merit of being immediately understood, a quality certainly not exhibited at present by ecology with its various uses. This advantage will be correspondingly enhanced, as the field becomes on the one hand more analytic, on the other more synthetic. However, it must be admitted that, in respect to terminology especially, habit and point of view will continue to rule for many workers, in spite of the benefits to be procured from uniformity and consistency.

Scope and Significance

As indicated previously, bio-ecology is considered to be ecology in the widest sense, but with the recognition that the inclusion of human ecology will be delayed until the feeling for synthesis and experiment becomes more general. In consequence, the application of the term will for the present be largely restricted to the study of biotic communities or microcosms, in which man regularly assumes roles of varying importance.

Moreover, it is inevitable that the term ecology will continue to be applied to the study of plant or animal communities separately, as a matter of habit or training, or of predilection. Nevertheless, the fragmentation of animal communities on the basis of taxonomic groups is greatly to be deplored, since it destroys the last semblance of unity. Unfortunately, this is such a common practice as to be a matter of much concern to the future of both animal ecology and bio-ecology. This condition can hardly be remedied except by replacing the present highly specialized training with synthetic instruction to a considerable degree.

In view of the great diversity of interests and hence of approaches to this vast field, the word ecology will continue to have a number of rivals, in spite of its unique fitness. In accordance with the emphasis, these range from biology, biogeography, and geobotany to sociology, biocenology, and biocenotics, and the more specialized limnology, hydrobiology and oceanography.

This condition will exist as long as investigators are specialists; it is perhaps less to be deplored since each brings a different point of view to the larger field, and this is probably true likewise of the various efforts at a subdivision of the field. However, the very essence of ecology is the synthesis derived from the exhaustive analysis of the community and its habitat, and bio-ecology must rest upon this principle as its secure foundation. The advent of bio-ecology having been delayed by the separation of biology into botany and zoology, its rapid development should not now be hindered by renewed division and philosophical analysis.

Nature

Ecology is in large measure the science of community populations. It is concerned with natural communities primarily, and has developed a considerable fund of organized knowledge of plant communities and their dynamics, and a lesser body of similar knowledge on the animal side. Because of the synthesis inherent in it, ecology is also to be regarded as a point of view and a method of attack for various great biological problems. Not only does it concern itself more or less with the whole of biology, but also it must borrow largely from chemistry and physics, from climatology, geology, and soil science, and at the same time make basic contributions to the practical sciences of agronomy, horticulture, forestry, grazing, entomology, conservation, etc., to say nothing of education, economics, sociology, and politics. It cannot, and does not, venture to draw a line between the past and the present, and it has as significant a role to play in geological as in modern times.

More than a quarter of a century ago, the statement was made that ecology was to be considered the central and vital part of botany, and this is equally true for biology. It was further stated that plant ecology is physiology carried into the actual habitat, and in consequence its paramount theme is stimulus and response. It confines itself primarily and exhaustively with the cause-and-effect relation between the habitat on the one hand, and the organism and the community on the other.

All further relations arise out of this, and all other approaches are incomplete unless they lead back to it. With the inclusion of animals in the biotic formation (biome), this relation naturally becomes more complex, but it is none the less valid. Since physiology often finds visible expression in behaviour, coaction between the organisms assumes a role often more important than direct response to the habitat.

From this springs the view that development is the basic process of ecology, as applicable to the habitat and community as to the individual and species. It recognizes that life constitutes a dynamic system and that static studies are valuable only as they throw light on development or serve some practical purpose in this connection. Furthermore, it was postulated that development is a cyclic process and that the apparent points of rest in it are relative to cycles of different rank. At the very outset it was clearly perceived that a dynamic system renders measurement indispensable, and hence the past three decades have seen a consistent advance in this respect, especially in plant ecology and to some extent in hydrobiology.

Equally imperative is the thorough-going utilization of experiment, essential not only to finer analysis and more exact measurement, but also to increasingly objective viewpoints.

In connection with the preceding, it should be realized that progress in zoo-ecology has been much slower. The natural unity has been obscured by the separate treatment of taxonomic groups and by such faunistic concepts as that of life zone, which, in view of the widespread destruction of many species, has rendered synthetic interpretation very difficult. Moreover, although animals are obviously physiological in their response to climate, food, etc., much progress can be made in the field of interactions (coactions and reactions) without the use of physiological experiments.

Furthermore, the correlations involved are usually to be suggested by studies in the biotic community and then lead properly to physiological experiments that permit more definite control and exact analysis. In sharp contrast to plant physiology, animal physiology as taught and applied has little concern with physical factors, while general physiology deals with particular internal processes and physiological ecology with one or more species withdrawn from the community for some particular study. The consequence is the ignoring or splitting of the physiology of interactions, since this field finds its inspiration in the study of the biotic community itself.

A signal extension of ecological ideas is involved in the application of climax and succession, that is of development, to lake and ocean. This demands the definition and recognition of climaxes in large bodies of water, and hence of corresponding climates. As indicated later in the discussion, this is deemed a logical extension of these terms from land to land and water, and thence into lake and ocean. This further involves questions of dominance, of competition, reaction and coaction, of development and structure, all of which exhibit more or less characteristic differences in deep water.

Relations of Paleo-ecology

Development is a continuous process, and hence its division on the basis of time past and present can be justified only on the score of convenience. No radical division exists in geology, where the flow of time is registered chiefly by major and minor events. With biology and its human subdivisions, however, the technique and usually the evidence also differ so much in nature or form that the distinction appears much greater than it is. This fact has naturally not passed unnoticed by paleontologists, but it is the peculiar province of paleo-ecology to insist upon the basic essence of continuing development and to emphasize the fact that the present is but a passing stage of this.

From the standpoint of development, uniformity is inevitable and universal, but it is a uniformity of process and cycle more than of end results. This becomes all the more evident when it is realized that cycles of varying intensity and duration are so telescoped that lesser ones constantly recur within the next larger, producing a complex system in which the respective cycles are difficult to discover. Moreover, while cycles in deformation, climate, physiography, soil, climax, migration, and abundance bear an organic relation to one another, response takes place at varying rate and degree, and the mosaic of processes becomes correspondingly intricate.

The principles and methods of paleo-ecology have been outlined in more or less detail for vegetation, and these have been applied to the revaluation of fossil floras with such success as to indicate their fundamental nature. As with modern ecology, these must necessarily undergo certain extensions and modifications with the adoption of the biome as the community. Furthermore, while relatively slight changes are needed to fit the case of land climates and climaxes, those of deep water exhibit conditions at once so different and so uniform as to require much greater modification.

As has been emphasized elsewhere, it is an axiom that the key to the past is fashioned by the present, to use these terms in their everyday significance. On the other hand, the present is the sole heir to the past, and no adequate understanding of it is possible without tracing the continuity of developmental processes from the one to the other. In short, there is no more warrant, other than that of convenience and emphasis, for separating paleo-ecology than for dividing bio-ecology, and the best development of ecology demands the synthetic organization of the entire field, even though detailed analyses will continue to be made by specialists.

The Concept of Plant Community

The idea of the plant community in general extends backward for nearly two centuries, but the recognition of the biotic community is a recent matter. Post recognized that the organic world should be dealt with in its entirety, but seems to have had no definite idea of the community as a unit. How clearly Mobius perceived the existence of a biotic community can probably never be settled, in spite of his introduction of the term biocenose. He certainly saw something of a community relation in the oyster assemblage, but carried the concept no further, and his suggestion was practically lost to view for a generation or more.

A somewhat similar doubt arises in respect to Dahl's adoption of the word biocenose from Mobius, for it appears that Dahl employed the term mostly as a synonym of zoocenose. As indicated later in some detail, Clements, Shelford, France, and Vestal realized the significance of the biotic community more fully and more or less independently, but the distinction of the biome as the basic concept in climax and succession was first made in 1916.

Since this time, there has been a slow but gradual recognition of the importance of the concept, exemplified in particular on the animal side by Shelford and his students, on the plant side by Phillips. For the reasons already touched upon, it is not to be expected that this will become the universal approach, and this is probably not desirable, since some problems require intensive analysis, such as is best secured by working with plants or animals alone.

If it becomes generally recognized that the investigation of climax and succession must reckon with the biotic formation as the natural community unit, this will insure the proper perspective and methods. Although of a secondary character, the historical development of the ideas set forth in this volume is important in an understanding of the terms and concepts presented.

Mobius

Under the title, "An oyster bank is a biocenose or a social community," Mobius gave a detailed account of the animal life of an oyster bed as brought up by the dredge. He stated that very few plants grew upon the banks, namely, a single Zostera and some of the Florideae, while the desmids and diatoms of the plankton served as food for the oysters. Each oyster bed was regarded to a certain degree as a community of living beings, a collection of species and a massing of individuals, and since science possessed no term for such a grouping, he proposed the word biocenose.

Space and food were held to be necessary as the first requisites of every social community, even in the sea, and he clearly perceived that changes of physical factors, and disturbances by man as through overfishing, often greatly modified the social group. There is little evidence that Mobius regarded the biocenose as constituted by both animals and plants, though such an assumption has long persisted in connection with the use of the term.

The single mention of plants, the emphasis upon their role as food, and the comprehensive discussion of the species of animals all tend to confirm this conclusion. This is supported by Petersen's statement that "Mobius has called the animals living on an oyster bank a *biocenosis*," and he also employed the term as synonymous with animal community. As is shown in the next paragraph, Dahl likewise thought to employ the word in the sense of Mobius, but without rendering his own usage either very definite or consistent.

Dahl

In three successive editions of his guide for collecting and preserving animals, Dahl adopted Mobius's term, but clearly not in the sense of a biotic community, at least in most instances. This is further shown by the fact that he speaks only of zootopes or animal habitats, and in addition states that the biocenose is for the zoologist what the plant community is for the botanist.

Three types of biocenose were recognized, namely, phytobiocenose, zoobiocenose, and allobiocenose, composed respectively of the animals to be found on a particular plant or its parts, on an animal, or on inorganic or decaying organic bodies. The subdivisions of the first two and especially the phytobiocenose correspond to all the organs and parts of the host and obviously represent only the most minute animal assemblages. Among the allobiocenoses were included autonomous communities, but usually without indication of their biotic nature.

Clements

In "Research Methods in Ecology", it was stated that plant and animal communities frequently coincide. Since animals were regarded as typically motile, their dependence upon the habitat was considered to be less evident. Vegetation as the source of protection and food plays a more obvious if not a more important part. It was stated that the animal ecology of a terrestrial region could be properly investigated only after the habitats and the plant communities have been organized as the basis for studying development and structure.

In a study of the life history of the lodgepole pine burn forest, animals were found to play a controlling part in succession. The frequent regeneration in burns, by contrast with the absence of seedlings elsewhere, led to the conclusion that a major effect of fire was to destroy or drive out the seed-eating animals, and permit the establishment of the pure stand of pine (consocies) as a characteristic subclimax.

In a monographic discussion of succession, the biotic formation was regarded as an organic unit comprising all the species of plants and animals at home in a particular habitat. Plants were considered to exert the dominant influence, although it was recognized that this role might sometimes be taken by the animals.

The biotic community is fundamentally controlled by the habitat and exhibits both development and structure. In its development the biome reacts upon the habitat and thus produces a succession. In discussing the scope and significance of paleo-ecology, it was stated that recognition of animals as a part of the community promised to open a new outlook in synthetic ecology.

Adams, Ruthven

In sketching the plan for a survey of Porcupine Mountains and Isle Royale, Michigan, Adams based this upon the relations of the biota to environment, adopting Stejneger's definition of the biota as "the total of animal or plant life of a region." While there was no definite recognition of the biotic community, the emphasis upon the habitat and upon processes in terms of succession, and the use of plant communities as a groundwork, mark the treatment as distinctly synthetic.

The actual survey was carried out by Ruthven upon this broad basis and led to the conclusion that the hardwood forest represents the climax of the region, its habitat increasing at the expense of other societies so that the associated biota tend to become general for the area. Later, a more extensive investigation of Isle Royale was made by Adams and his co-workers, utilizing the same methods.

Even greater attention was paid to succession, though this was treated separately with respect to the four animal groups, viz., invertebrates, beetles, birds, and mammals. The biological survey of a sand-dune region in Michigan followed the same general plan. In a bibliographical treatise Adams presented the conclusion that such projects should deal with the balance within the entire biotic community.

It was stated that for any comprehensive study it is necessary to determine the biotic base or optimum toward which conditions tend and at which equilibrium occurs. Some uncertainty exists, however, as to the author's use of the term biotic, since he speaks of all this as providing the best method of studying the animals of a region. Moreover, in the ecological investigation of prairie and forest invertebrates, the animals were treated as separate and the plant associations considered as furnishing the environment for them.

Shelford

In a preliminary survey, Shelford traced the relation of Cicindela to the succession of plant communities. The distribution of eight species of tiger beetles was in close correspondence with the zoned habitats and communities, and the conclusion was reached that a similar harmony existed with respect to the fauna in general.

In a series of five articles on ecological succession, the same author elaborated the developmental relation between plant and animal communities. These were stated to be very generally in agreement. Disagreement was said to be temporary, and to accompany rapid successional changes. Succession was stated to be due to an increment of changes in conditions produced by the plants and animals living at a given point.

In the treatment of the animal communities of eastern North America, this theme of the interaction of the two groups of organisms was further developed. Several of the communities were designated by means of a prevalent or characteristic animal and one or more plant dominants, though in general plant communities were treated as constituting the habitat for animal ones.

Thus were distinguished a white tiger beetle or cottonwood association, an ant lion or black oak, a *Hyaliodes* or black oak-red oak, a green tiger beetle or white oak-red oak-hickory, and a wood frog or beech-maple association. Succession was emphasized as the chief principle underlying the relations of communities. Plants were recognized as the dominant sessile forms of the land, while animals were considered to be the chief members of the successions in streams, and the primary nature of the climax was stressed.

Shelford further endeavored to correlate the behaviour of the animal constituents with the life forms of the plants. The terminology was based upon the idea of the uniformity of the physiological responses of the important animals in the community. However, this physiological basis for community classification was found to be impracticable because of the lack of response data, and the plan was abandoned as not, yet susceptible of clear expression.

Enderlein

Enderlein followed Dahl in employing the term biocenose for a wide range of communities, and further adopted the latter's grouping on the basis of habitats. However, he departed from Dahl's usage by distinguishing areas of more or less unrelated biocenoses as *biosynecies* or biosynecic districts, a departure criticized by Dahl in the same year as unwarranted. Enderlein regarded the occurrence of a species in a single biocenose or its extension over two or more as marking a significant distinction, designating the one as *homocene,* the other as *heterocene.*

The same concept was extended to the biosynecie, for which corresponding terms, *stenotope* and *eurytope,* were proposed. Upon this basis, four groups of species were recognized in accordance with their occurrence in one or more of both types of community: for example, *stenotope-homocene,* found in but one biocenose and one biosynecie; *stenotope-heterocene,* present in a single biosynecie but in two or more biocenoses.

These distinctions seem not to have been applied by the author himself in his studies of the insects of moor and dune in west Prussia, though stenotope and eurytope have been utilized in a small degree, while the distinction between biocenose and biosynecie appears to have dropped from view. In fact, the extensive account of the distribution of insects is based upon taxonomic groups and not upon communities, though the composition of the plant cover is discussed as a background.

France

France has advanced the concept of the *edaphon,* as the counterpart of the plankton, comprising under this term the community of the permanent animal and plant organisms of the soil (geobionts). This consists of the most varied types, but ones mutually tolerant and thus able to hold their own; they are distinguished by a number of adaptations and an entirely distinct and peculiar mode of life.

The habitat of the edaphon is characterized by a more or less complete absence of light, periodic limitation of moisture by drought or frost, and an excess of nitrogen. The groups of organisms regarded as belonging to the edaphon are as follows:

1. Bacteria;
2. Fungi;
3. Algae;
4. Protozo;
5. Rotatoria;
6. Worms;
7. Arachnids.

The inclusion of mycorhiza and earthworms was said to require further consideration, while the subterrene mammals, insect larvae, and rooted plants were ruled out of the communal life.

Vestal

In connection with the successional study of a sand prairie in Illinois, Vestal has tested the assumption that plant and animal associations are coextensive and to a large degree interdependent, the animals being entirely dependent upon the plants and the latter partly so upon the animals. In such case, the limits of the animal community are those of the plant association, and both may be spoken of as a single biotic community, composed of plant and ani mal assemblages.

This relation once established, certain problems in animal ecology would be much simplified, for whereas the animal assemblage is at first obscure, that of the plants is evident, its characteristic physiognomy serving as an index to the animals of the community. It was concluded that the evidence drawn from the study of the sand prairie, though very incomplete, was in accord with the theory and justified the treatment of the plant and animal associations together.

This theme was further developed in an analysis of the internal relations of terrestrial associations, as a result of which it was concluded that plants and animals agree in similar response to the common environment and in types of geographic distribution.

It begins to appear that plant and animal assemblages are coextensive parts of a biotic association, which as a whole constitutes the real terrestrial community of living organisms. Plant and animal assemblages are mutually interdependent, but the plants are dominant in established associations. Such assemblages are composed of ecologically similar groups correlated with the same physical factors or with each other.

Gams

Gams considers that no logical ground exists for excluding animals from communities of organisms, and hence he incorporates these in the vegetation. To him, "vegetation research" is synonymous with his new term "biocenology" and with "biocenotics" of the zoo-ecologists, both of which he regards as closely related to ecology, though not identical with it.

His discussion, however, is confined largely to plants, the most important exception being his outline of the life forms of the combined plant and animal kingdoms. This is based upon the assumption that the criteria available take rank in the following order:

1. Motility
2. Substratum
3. Habitat
4. Nutrition.

This is thought to be supported by the general acceptance of plankton as a biotic community. The three major divisions of his system are as follows:

1. Adnate or attached form, *Ephaptomenon;*
2. Radicate or rooted form, *Rhizumenon;*
3. Errant or free form, *Planomenon.*

The first group is divided into aquatic, amphibious, aerial, and innate, further subdivisions being autotroph and heterotroph, saprobe, parasitic, and phagont.

Gams emphasizes the fact that, while biocenose has been employed by a number of zoo-ecologists, viz., Dahl, Enderlein, Babler, Shelford, Hesse, Doflein, and Thienemann, this has been in connection with animal communities of very unequal rank. He further suggests that phytocenose may be utilized for the plant population of a habitat and zoocenose for the animals, but this suggestion is scarcely in harmony with the concept of the biotic community.

Bibliography

Ali, Rahat : *An Introduction to Herbal Medicine in Ethnobotany,* Vista International Pub House, Delhi, 2012.

Charasia Et. All: *Advances in Agriculture Environment and Health,* Satish Serial Pub., Delhi, 2009.

Chaturvedi, G.S. : *Abiotic Stresses and Plant Productivity,* Aavishkar Pub, Delhi, 2010.

Choudhary, Ravinder : *Agriculture Growth in India,* Educational Pub., Delhi, 2011.

Das, Susheela M. : *A Textbook of Plant Physiology : Theory and Objectives,* Wisdom Press, Delhi, 2011.

Daubenmire, R. F.: *Plants and Environment*: New York, Wiley, 1947.

Dutt, Ashwini : *Economic Botany,* Adhyayan Pub., Delhi, 2008.

Gupta, P.K. : *A Handbook of Soil Fertilizer and Manure,* Agrobios, Delhi, 2011.

Hanumantha Rao : *Agriculture, Food Security, Poverty and Environment: Essays on Post-reform India,* Oxford University Press, Delhi, 2006.

Jackson, E. : *Crop Management and Soil Conservation,* Biotech Books, Delhi, 2011.

Jain, Vinod Kumar : *Biofertilisers for Sustainable Agriculture,* Oxford Book Company, Delhi, 2009 .

Kannaiyan, S. : *Bioresources Technology for Sustainable Agriculture,* Associated Pub., Delhi, 1999.

Kumar, Arvind : *Concepts of Tropical Agriculture,* Daya, Delhi, 2006.

Kumar, Asoke : *Agriculture and Waste Management for Sustainable Future,* New India Publishing Agency, Delhi, 2011.

Kumar, U. : *Methods in Plant Tissue Culture,* Agrobios, Delhi, 2011.

Mishra, Mridula : *Agriculture and Food Economics*, Serials Pub., Delhi, 2010.

Mukerji, K. G. and C. Manoharachary: *Current Concepts in Botany*, I K International, Delhi, 2006.

Pandian, I.D. : *Introduction to Modern Botany*, A.K. Pub., Delhi, 2008.

Parashar, I.B. : *Achievements and Prospects in Mycology and Plant Pathology*, International, Delhi, 1997.

Pareek, L.K. : *Trends in Plant Tissue Culture and Biotechnology*, Agrobios, Delhi, 2005.

Pradhan, Madhusmita : *Basics of Botany*, Anmol, Delhi, 2008.

Pullaiah, T. : *Plant Tissue Culture : Emerging Trends*, Regency Pub., Delhi, 2011.

Reddy, Mallikarjuna and Aparna Rao: *Applied Horticulture*, Pacific Books International, Delhi, 2010.

Roy, Shikha : *Plant Tissue Culture and Applied Plant Biotechnology*, Aavishkar Publishers, Delhi, 2011.

Sambasiva, Rao, B. : *Agriculture in India: Policy and Performance*, Serials Pub., Delhi, 2003.

Sathyanarayana, B. N. : *Plant Tissue Culture : Practices and New Experimental Protocols*, I K International, Delhi, 2007.

Sharaf, Sandhya : *Greenhouse Management of Horticulture Crops*, Oxford Book Company, Delhi, 2012.

Sharma, Rajni : *Plant Tissue Culture*, Campus, Delhi, 2000.

Shukla, R.S. and P.S. Chandel: *A Textbook of Plant Ecology : Including Ethnobotany and Soil Science*, S. Chand Publisher, Delhi, 2009.

Singh, Gaurav : *Development of Agriculture Biotechnology : Research and Analysis*, A.K. Publications, Delhi, 2011.

Singh, H.P. ; J.P. Singh and S.S. Lal: *Challenges of Climate Change - Indian Horticulture*, Westville Publishing House, Delhi, 2010.

Singh, R.K. : *Advances and Development in Botany*, ALP Books, Delhi, 2010.

Trivedi, Pravin Chandra : *Applied Botany*, Aavishkar Pub., Delhi, 2005.

Umrani, Ramesh : *Basics of Economic Botany*, Anmol, Delhi, 2009

Vashishtha, B.B. : *Advances in Arid Horticulture*, International Book Dist, Delhi, 2004.

Index